¡EXACTO!

¡Exacto! is an accessible guide to Spanish grammar.

Using an appealing visual layout, the essentials of Spanish grammar are presented in tables and charts allowing learners to navigate the information easily and view explanations, examples of usage and any exceptions to the rule at a glance.

Key features:

- Grids and tables ensure key information is available for quick reference and review
- Graded to allow students to home in on the material most suited to their current level
- Coverage of Spanish as a world language, with examples from different varieties of Peninsular Spanish and American Spanish
- Grammar and workbook in one, with exercises within each unit to practise and consolidate learning
- A glossary of grammatical terminology ensures all explanations within the book are clear and accessible
- An answer key making it ideal for self-study.

Suitable for class use and independent study, this new edition of *¡Exacto!* is the ideal grammar reference and practice resource for all learners of Spanish, from beginners to advanced students.

Ane Ortega was a lecturer in Spanish at The Open University, UK, and is currently a lecturer in Language Education at the Begoñako Andra Mari Teacher Training University College of Bilbao, Spain.

Tita Beaven is a senior lecturer in Spanish at The Open University.

Cecilia Garrido was for many years a senior lecturer in Spanish at The Open University. She retired from the University in 2015.

Sean Scrivener is an editor attached to the School of Languages and Applied Linguistics at The Open University.

Routledge Concise Grammars series

https://www.routledge.com/Routledge-Concise-Grammars/book-series/766

¡Exacto! A Practical Guide to Spanish Grammar, Third Edition

Ane Ortega, Tita Beaven, Cecilia Garrido, Sean Scrivener

Yufa! A Practical Guide to Mandarin Chinese Grammar, Second Edition

Wen-Hua Teng

Da! A Practical Guide to Russian Grammar

Tatiana Filosofova and Marion Spöring

Soluzioni: A Practical Grammar of Contemporary Italian, Third Edition

Denise De Rôme

¡EXACTO!

A Practical Guide to
Spanish Grammar

Third Edition

**Ane Ortega, Tita Beaven,
Cecilia Garrido and Sean Scrivener**

Spanish List Advisor: Javier Muñoz-Basols

Routledge
Taylor & Francis Group
LONDON AND NEW YORK

Third edition published 2018
by Routledge
2 Park Square, Milton Park, Abingdon, Oxon, OX14 4RN

and by Routledge
711 Third Avenue, New York, NY 10017

Routledge is an imprint of the Taylor & Francis Group, an informa business

First edition published by Hodder Education 2009
Second edition published by Routledge 2013

British Library Cataloguing-in-Publication Data
A catalogue record for this book is available from the British Library

Library of Congress Cataloging-in-Publication Data
Names: Ortega, Ane, author. | Beaven, Tita, author. | Garrido, Cecilia, author. |
    Scrivener, Sean, author.
Title: ¡Exacto! : a practical guide to Spanish grammar / Ane Ortega, Tita Beaven,
    Cecilia Garrido and Sean Scrivener.
Description: Third edition. | Milton Park, Abingdon, Oxon : New York, NY : Routledge, [2018] |
    Previous editions published in London : Hodder Education, 2009; 2nd ed. | Includes
    bibliographical references and index.
Identifiers: LCCN 2017045945 | ISBN 9780415785082 (hardback : alk. paper) |
    ISBN 9780415785068 (pbk. : alk. paper) | ISBN 9781315228334 (ebook)
Subjects: LCSH: Spanish language—Grammar. | Spanish language—Grammar—Problems,
    exercises, etc. | Spanish language—Textbooks for foreign speakers—English.
Classification: LCC PC4112 O73 2018 | DDC 468.2/421—dc23
LC record available at https://lccn.loc.gov/2017045945

ISBN: 978-0-415-78508-2 (hbk)
ISBN: 978-0-415-78506-8 (pbk)
ISBN: 978-1-315-22833-4 (ebk)

Typeset in Minion
by Apex CoVantage, LLC

Contents

How to use this book

Bienvenidos a ¡Exacto! This section will give you useful information on how to make the most of the grammar book. Read it carefully before you start to use it.

¡Exacto! is a user-friendly Spanish grammar book which concentrates on the essentials but also covers more complex areas of the Spanish language. It uses an appealing visual layout in tabular form and explains grammar in a clear and concise way.

Features of *¡Exacto!*

- A glossary of grammatical terms, explained in a user-friendly way and with examples.
- Visually-appealing grammar explanations with easy-to-read tables and plenty of examples.
- Exercises to practise and consolidate the grammar content of each unit, and a key with answers.
- Real-life examples, including extracts from journalistic and literary sources to help you see grammar in action.
- Coverage of points of special difficulty for the English-speaking learner, indicated by the icon ◉.
- Cross-referencing to related points of grammar, sign-posted by the icon ☞.
- Coverage of Spanish as a world language, with examples from different varieties of Peninsular Spanish and American Spanish. Information about relevant regional varieties is indicated by the icon 🌍.
- Indications of levels of difficulty, both in the grammar explanations and in the exercises, to help you choose what is relevant for you.
- Verb tables, with regular and irregular forms, in a separate appendix for quick reference.
- A grammatical index to help you locate all your queries on Spanish grammar.

Who is *¡Exacto!* for?

¡Exacto! assumes little formal knowledge of Spanish grammar. It covers the basics comprehensively but takes you further to the most challenging areas of Spanish grammar, with extensive coverage of Spanish verb and sentence structure. Whether you need to brush up the basics or need a tool to help you with the challenges of intermediate/upper-intermediate/advanced levels, *¡Exacto!* is for you.

This book does not take any knowledge for granted, either of the Spanish language or of grammatical terminology. To assist you with the grammatical labels, each term is introduced where it is used, and is explained in depth in the glossary at the beginning of the book.

Levels

To help you find what is most relevant for your level of Spanish, the content and exercises in *¡Exacto!* have been graded according to three levels. Watch out for the icons | Level 1 | | Level 2 | | Level 3 | both in the unit or sub-headings and on each *ejercicio*. Here is a description of each level:

| Level 1 |

Level 1 covers the basics of Spanish grammar, from beginners to lower-intermediate level, GCSE, up to level B1 of the Council of Europe and the Open University level one Spanish courses. You will find the basic concepts under this icon, the main rules of the workings of Spanish with only minimum exceptions, simple and frequent vocabulary, standard register, and everything you need for the basic communicative functions. Practice includes simple drills and exercises to help you consolidate the basics.

| Level 2 |

Level 2 consolidates the basic grammar and starts expanding your knowledge of the Spanish language to include exceptions to the main rules, nuances of meanings and usage in all word categories, especially in the verb, and more complex structures such as appropriate uses of subordination. It bridges the gap towards intermediate levels, including AS/A levels, up to level B2 of the Council of Europe and the Open University level two Spanish courses. Examples and exercises include more extended use of vocabulary, although they are still related to common topics, and the functions and communicative situations found in the intermediate levels.

| Level 3 |

Level 3 covers less common vocabulary, often of the semi-specialised type, and areas of complex language use, including work on subordination, manipulation of tenses and handling of language at text level. You will need to look carefully at the sections indicated with this icon if you are at an advanced level, doing an A level or undergraduate course, courses equivalent to the C1 and C2 levels of the Council of Europe, or up to the Open University level three Spanish courses. Exercises include use

of authentic texts of increased difficulty, such as literary extracts, and the register is expanded to include formal and informal/colloquial language, with more emphasis on idiomatic use.

We hope you find *¡Exacto!* clear and easy to use. *¡Buena suerte!*

The authors

Glossary

Adjective (qualifying) – *Adjetivo calificativo*
A word that describes or adds information about a noun, e.g. *Un viaje* **maravilloso** (a **wonderful** trip), una **buena** *persona* (a **good** person).

Adverb – *Adverbio*
A word that describes a verb, an adjective, or another adverb in terms of manner, degree, time or place, e.g. in *Se vive* **bien aquí** (One lives **well here**), *bien* and *aquí* are adverbs describing how and where one lives.

Adverbial clause – *Oración subordinada circunstancial/adverbial*
Type of **subordinate clause** which takes the place of an adverb, i.e. which describes a verb in the way an adverb would, e.g. *Vendré* **cuando me lo pidas** (I'll come **when you ask me to**). Adverbial clauses can express cause, concession, condition, comparison, purpose, manner, place or time.

Adverbial phrase – *Locución adverbial*
Group of words which behaves like an adverb. For instance, **aquí mismo** (right here) or **poco a poco** (little by little).

Affirmative – *Afirmativo*
Quality or characteristic of a verb or sentence which carries a positive meaning (e.g. *Me gusta bailar* as opposed to the negative *No me gusta cantar*).

Affixes – *Afijos*
A beginning or an ending which is attached to a word or stem. Attached to the beginning they are called **prefixes – prefijos**, e.g. *voluntario* → **in**voluntario (voluntary → **in**voluntary); attached to the end of the word they are called **suffixes – sufijos**, e.g. *trabajar* → *trabaja**dor*** (work → work**er**) Do not confuse suffixes with gender, number and verb endings.

Agreement – *Concordancia*
Grammatical phenomenon where some elements have to take on (agree with) some grammatical features of the element that governs them. Elements in a noun phrase must agree in **number** and **gender** with the noun, e.g. in *las montañas soleadas* (the sunny mountains) the article *las* and the adjective *soleadas* agree in **gender** (feminine) and **number** (plural) with the core of the phrase, the noun *montañas*. Verbs in tenses also agree in **number** and **person** with their subject, e.g. in *Los ruiseñores cantaban* (The nightingales were singing) the verb *cantaban* agrees in person and number with the subject *los ruiseñores* (third person plural).

American Spanish – *Español de Hispanoamérica*
Varieties of Spanish spoken in Spanish America.

Antecedent – *Antecedente*
In a **relative clause**, the antecedent is the noun which the relative clause qualifies or describes. For instance, in ***El perro*** que ladró *era el mío* (**The dog** that barked was mine), *el perro* is the antecedent of the relative clause *que ladró*.

Apocopation – *Apócope* Phenomenon where some words – mainly adjectives – lose their endings when they precede other words, e.g. *grande* becomes *gran* in *una gran casa* (a great house).

Article – *Articulo* Word which indicates whether the noun it precedes refers to a specific element (person, animal, thing, etc.), for which the **definite articles** *el, la, los, las* (English 'the') are used, or an unspecified element, for which the **indefinite articles** *un, una, unos, unas* (English 'a', 'some', 'any') are used.

Auxiliary verb – *Verbo auxiliar* Verb which 'helps' the main verb to make up a tense. In the continuous tenses (e.g. *estoy comiendo* – I am eating), *estoy* (from *estar*) is an auxiliary, and in the compound tenses (e.g. *he comido* – I have eaten), *he* (from *haber*) is an auxiliary.

Clause – *Oración* Group of words forming a coherent unit around a verb. The term is used to refer to each of the 'sentences' which make up a complex sentence, in which a main clause and **subordinate clauses** can be found. See also **complex sentence, noun clause, relative clause** and **adverbial clause**.

Command – *Orden* An order, e.g. *¡Ven aquí inmediatamente!* (Come here immediately!). See also **Imperative**.

Comparative – *Comparativo* Element which compares a quality of a person, animal, thing, etc. with the same quality in another, e.g. *Ruth es **menos** decidida **que** Marta* (Ruth is **less** decisive **than** Marta).

Complex sentence – *Oración compuesta* Sentence made up of various clauses, at least one being a main clause governing one or more **subordinate clauses.** The main clause is the central axis of the complex sentence and has meaning by itself; subordinate clauses are dependent on the main clause and do not make complete sense on their own, e.g. in the sentence <u>*Cuando llegues*</u> llámame *<u>para que te recoja</u>* (<u>When you arrive</u> **call me** <u>so I can pick you up</u>), *llámame* is the main clause and the other two are subordinate clauses.

Compound tense – *Tiempo compuesto* Tense made up of a main verb and one or two auxiliaries, e.g. all **perfect tenses** (*hemos venido, había traído, habría estado comiendo*, etc.).

Conjugation (of verbs) – *Conjugación verbal* Each of the six forms (one for each person) that a **tense** has, e.g. the conjugation of *amar* in the future indicative is: *amaré, amarás, amará, amaremos, amaréis, amarán*.

Conjunction – *Conjunción* Also **connector**. A word or phrase which links together words, phrases and clauses. There are two types: **co–ordinating conjunctions**, which join elements of equal value (e.g. *Juan llegó tarde **y** yo también*) (Juan arrived late **and** so did I) and **subordinating conjunctions**, which join subordinate clauses (e.g. *No lo hizo **porque** no quiso*) (She didn't do it **because** she didn't want to). In *¡Exacto!* the term **'connector'** has been used to refer to all link words.

Connector – *Conector* Also **conjunction** and **link word.** Any word or phrase that links together different clauses. In *¡Exacto!* 'connector' has been used as a general term.

Construction – *Construcción/Estructura* A general term for any grammatical structure, e.g. *ir a* + infinitive, *tener que* + infinitive, etc.

Co-ordinating conjunction – *Conjunción coordinada* See **Conjunction**.

Copulative verb – *Verbo copulativo*	The verbs *ser, estar* and *parecer* are known as *verbos copulativos* ('copulative verbs' or 'linking verbs' in English) when they lack a lexical meaning and their only function is to link two elements on equal terms in the sentence. In the examples *Marta es mi hermana* (Marta **is** my sister) and *Marta parece muy simpática* (Marta **seems** very friendly), *es* and *parece* link the subject *Marta* with the attributes 'my sister' and 'very friendly'.
Demonstrative – *Demostrativo*	Word which qualifies a noun, indicating its proximity in relation to the speaker (English 'this', 'that', 'these' and 'those'). Demonstratives can be **adjectives**, e.g. *Esta casa es preciosa* (*This house* is beautiful), or **pronouns**, e.g. *Estos me gustan más que aquellos* (I like **these** better than **those**).
Diaeresis – *Diéresis*	A pair of dots that appears above the vowel 'u' after 'g' to indicate that the 'u' should be sounded, e.g. *lengüeta*. (See Unit 1 Accentuation.)
Diacritic accent – *Tilde diacrítica*	An accent that is used to distinguish a word that would otherwise look and sound the same as another word with a different meaning, e.g. *dé* (give), to distinguish it from *de* (of, from). (See Unit 1 Accentuation.)
Diphthong – *Diptongo*	A combination of two vowel sounds that are pronounced as part of the same syllable, e.g. *dia-rio, hue-vo*. (See Unit 1 Accentuation.)
Direct object – *Objeto directo*	See **Object**.
Direct speech – *Discurso directo/Estilo directo*	See **Indirect speech**.
Enclitic – *Enclítico*	Element bound to a preceding host, such as the English 'n't' in 'could**n't**'. In Spanish, personal **pronouns** are often found in enclitic positions, for example in **pronominal verbs** and in the **imperative**, e.g. *Tengo que lavarme el pelo* (I have to wash my hair), *¡Dámelo!* (Give it to me!).
Endings – *Desinencias/ Terminaciones*	Variations in form that words undergo as required by their grammatical roles. Typically these are **gender** and **number** endings in nouns, adjectives and articles (*casas, hermosas, los*) and number, person and tense endings in verbs (*vivimos, llegaban*). Not to be confused with **suffixes**.
Feminine – *Femenino*	See **Gender**.
Finite verb	Verb which is able to undergo a change in form to show tense, mood and person. It can be the main (conjugated) verb in a sentence or clause, and it may take any auxiliary verb in order to amplify its meaning. Non-finite verb forms are words like **infinitives** and **participles** which cannot combine with a subject to form a clause or sentence in their own right.
Gender – *Género*	Grammatical category which defines a word as **masculine** or **feminine**. For instance, in *la casa encantada* (the enchanted house) the noun *casa* is feminine and the article *la* and the adjective *encantada* are also feminine. Where the gender is neither masculine nor feminine it is said to be **neuter**.

Gerund – *Gerundio*	Also known as the present participle. An impersonal form of the verb which is used (a) with an **auxiliary** to form the continuous tenses (e.g *estoy **comiendo***) and (b) in **subordinate** clauses, where its subject agrees with the verb in the main clause, e.g. *Juan, **sintiéndose** muy enfermo, pidió ver a sus hijas* (Juan, **feeling** very ill, asked to see his daughters).
Grammatical category – *Categori'a gramatical*	Any constituent part of a language's overall grammar system which can be analysed and described, such as **gender**, **number**, **person**, **tense**, **mood**, **voice**, etc.
Hiatus – *Hiato*	The pronunciation of vowels as separate syllables when together, e.g. *te-atro, ba-úl, ca-í.* (See Unit 1 Accentuation.)
Imperative – *Imperativo*	Form of the verb which expresses an order. It can be affirmative, e.g. *¡**Dame** eso!* (**Give** me that!), or negative, e.g. **No hables** *con nadie* (**Don't talk** to anyone).
Impersonal form of the verb – *Forma no personal/ impersonal del verbo*	A verb form which is not conjugated and is therefore invariable In Spanish, as in English, there are three: the **infinitive** (e.g. *soñar* – to dream), the **gerund** (e.g. *soñando* – dreaming) and the **past participle** (e.g. *soñado* – dreamt). (Note that past participles do vary in form when they are used as adjectives, *e.g. la línea está ocupad**a*** – the line is engaged.)
Impersonal sentences – *Frases impersonales*	Sentences whose **subject** is unknown, irrelevant, generic or indeterminate, e.g. *Se dice que llegará a ser presidente* (It is said that he will get to be president), *Uno no sabe qué hacer en estas circunstancias* (One does not know what to do in these circumstances).
Indefinites – *Indefinidos*	Words that refer to persons, animals, things, etc., which are not specific or clearly defined, e.g. *alguien* (somebody), *algo* (something), *alguna* (some).
Indicative – *Indicativo*	The **mood**, or category of verb tenses, which expresses fact or certainty.
Indirect object – *Objeto indirecto*	See **Object**.
Indirect speech – *Discurso indirecto/Estilo indirecto*	Form of expression for reporting what somebody has said but without using his or her exact words. When the literal words are used we talk about **direct speech**. Compare: *Pedro dijo: "Vendré mañana a las 8"* (Pedro said: 'I'll come tomorrow at 8 o'clock') (direct speech) and *Pedro dijo que vendría al día siguiente a las 8* (Pedro said he would come the following day at 8 o'clock) (indirect speech).
Infinitive – *Infinitivo*	The 'name' of the verb and the form that verbs have in the dictionary. In Spanish infinitives are characterised by the three endings *-ar*, *-er*, *-ir* (e.g. amar, comer, vivir). The infinitive is an **impersonal form of the verb**.
Interrogatives – *Interrogativos*	Also known as question words and 'wh-' words. Words that introduce a question: *qué, quién(es), cómo, cuándo, dónde, cuánto (-a, -os, -as)*, as in the English 'what', 'who', 'which', 'how', 'when', 'where', etc.

Interrogative sentence – *Frase/oración interrogativa*	Sentence which asks a question, e.g. *¿Lloverá mañana?* (Will it rain tomorrow?).
Intransitive verb – *Verbo intransitivo*	Type of verb which does not require a direct object. This is because the action described by the verb does not affect a person, object or thing directly, as in the case of verbs of motion, e.g. *Baila* estupendamente (**He dances** beautifully) and *Mañana* **me levantaré** *a las 7* (Tomorrow **I'll get up** at 7). See also **Transitive verbs.**
Irregular verb – *Verbo irregular*	Verb which does not follow the regular conjugation or form. Some verbs are always irregular, such as *ser*, while others are irregular only in some tenses, such as *jugar* (in some persons of the present indicative and subjunctive and in the imperative). See also **Regular verb.**
Link word – *conector*	A loose and general term referring to any element which joins other elements together, such as conjunctions and relative pronouns. See also **Connector**, **Conjunction** and **Preposition**.
Main clause – *Oración principal*	See **Complex sentence**.
Masculine – *Masculino*	See **Gender**.
Modal verb – *Verbo modal*	Special type of verb or verbal construction which combines with another verb to give it greater scope for the expression of nuance or mood, e.g. *tener que* conveys the idea of necessity in relation to the verb it complements (e.g. *Tengo que trabajar el sábado* – I have to work on Saturday). Modal verbs in Spanish include: *poder*, *saber*, *deber, deber de, tener que*, *haber*, *soler* and *acostumbrar (a)*.
Mood – *Modo*	Category of verb tenses which expresses the attitude or perception of the speaker; for instance, it can show whether s/he perceives something as a fact or an uncertainty. There are three moods in Spanish: **indicative**, **subjunctive** and **imperative**.
Negative – *Negativo*	Quality or characteristic of a verb or sentence which does not carry a positive meaning, e.g. *No tengo hambre* (I am not hungry). In relation to a word, one whose meaning is not affirmative, such as *nunca* (never), *ninguno* (no one/none), *nadie* (nobody), etc.
Neuter – *Neutro*	See **Gender**. Where the gender is neither masculine nor feminine it is said to be **neuter**. In some languages nouns can be neuter; in Spanish, abstract concepts tend to be expressed more using the neuter form of pronouns, e.g. *¿Qué es* **lo** *que más te gusta de Juana?* (What is it that you like most about Juana?).
Nominalisation – *Nominalización/ Sustantivación*	Process by which a part of speech other than a noun behaves like a noun or a noun phrase, for instance, **el mío** (mine), **el que** *más odio* (**the one** I hate most), *El comer demasiado no es bueno* (**Eating** too much is not good).
Noun – *Sustantivo*	Type of word used to refer to a person, animal, thing, place, event or concept, e.g. *tía* (aunt), *caballo* (horse), *campeonato* (championship), *libertad* (freedom).

Noun clause – *Oración sustantiva/completiva*	A type of subordinate clause which takes the place of a **noun phrase**, e.g. *Quiero* **un vestido nuevo** (I want **a new dress**) (noun phrase); *Quiero* **que me compres un vestido nuevo** (I want **you to buy me a new dress**) (noun clause).
Noun phrase – *Sintagma nominal*	A word or group of words (without a verb) which behaves like a noun and performs its functions (as subject, object, etc.). Examples are pronouns, nominalized infinitives and clusters of words around a noun, as in the following examples:
	Ella *compró* ***el coche nuevo*** (**She** bought **the new car**) and ***El saber*** *no ocupa* ***lugar*** (**Knowledge** is never wasted, literally knowledge doesn't take up **space**).
Number – *Número*	Grammatical category which defines a word as singular or plural. Number applies to noun phrases (*el bosque encantado*/***los*** *bosque****s*** *encantado****s***) (the enchanted wood/ the enchanted wood**s**) and to verbs (*viene/viene****n***).
Object (of a verb) – *Objeto*	In sentences with a **transitive verb**, the object of a verb is a noun, a noun phrase or a clause which is considered to be affected by the verb, either directly or indirectly. When the action of the verb affects the object directly, that object is said to be a **direct object**; the noun (noun phrase or clause) answers the question 'what?' or 'to whom?' in relation to the verb. For instance, the sentence *Julián quiere* ***más vacaciones*** (Julián wants **more holidays**) answers the question *¿Qué quiere Julián?* (What does Julián want?). Similarly, when the action affects the object indirectly, it is said to be an **indirect object**. The noun (noun phrase or clause) answers the questions 'to whom or what?' or 'for whom or what?' For instance, *Julián* ***le*** *ha prometido un viaje a Port Aventura* ***a su hijo*** (Julián has promised **his son** a trip to Port Aventura) answers the question *¿A quién ha prometido Julián un viaje a Port Aventura?* (To whom has Julián promised a trip to Port Aventura?).
Part of speech – *Parte de la oración*	Category of word (according to traditional classification). The parts of speech are: **adjective**, **article**, **noun**, **pronoun**, **adverb**, **verb**, **conjunction** and **preposition**.
Passive voice – *Voz pasiva*	See **Voice**.
Past participle – *Participio*	An **impersonal form of the verb** which is used (a) to form the compound tenses with the auxiliary haber (e.g. *he comido* – I have eaten), (b) to form the passive voice with the auxiliary *ser* (e.g. *será* **retrasado** – it will be **postponed**) and (c) as an adjective (*estoy* **preocupada** – I am **worried**).
Peninsular Spanish – *Español peninsular*	A general term for the varieties of Spanish spoken in mainland Spain.
Perfect tenses – *Tiempos compuestos*	See also **Compound tenses**. Tenses made up of the auxiliary *haber* (have) + past participle. All perfect tenses have inherent in them the notion of 'finished action' and often of 'beforeness' (e.g *Ya ha terminado el tratamiento* – He has already finished his treatment).

Person – *Persona*	Grammatical category of verbs which indicates the person (*yo*, *tú*, etc.) performing the action. In Spanish the person is indicated in the ending of the conjugated verb, e.g. *como (yo)*, com**es** (tú), com**en** (ellos/ellas/ustedes).
Plural – *Plural*	See **Number**.
Possessive – *Posesivo*	Word that indicates a relationship of possession or ownership. Possessives can be **adjectives** (e.g. <u>*Su jardín*</u> *es precioso* – **Her** <u>garden</u> is beautiful) or **pronouns** (e.g. *No es **mío**, es **tuyo*** – It's not **mine**, it's **yours**).
Prefixes – *Prefijos*	See **Affixes**.
Preposition – *Preposición*	An invariable word which links together two other words or groups of words (often noun phrases) in order to indicate a relationship of time, space, personal attitude, possession, etc., e.g. *El coche* <u>*de mi madre*</u> (<u>*My mother's*</u> car), *Iré* **<u>con</u>** <u>*Julián*</u> (I'll go **with** <u>Julián</u>).
Prepositional phrase – *Frase preposicional*	See **Preposition**.
Present participle – *Gerundio*	See **Gerund**.
Pronominal verb – *Verbo pronominal*	Verb which is always accompanied by a pronoun of the class *me, te, se, nos, os, se.* They are recognised in the dictionary because the infinitive has an enclitic or bound *se* (e.g. *caerse* – to fall). Two well-known types of pronominal verbs are **reflexive verbs** (e.g. afeitarse – to shave (oneself)) and **reciprocal verbs** (amarse *(unos a otros)* – to love (each other)).
Pronoun – *Pronombre*	A word which takes the place of a noun, e.g. in *Juana nos engañó. Ella sabía la verdad* (Juana deceived us. She knew the truth), *ella* is used instead of *Juana* to avoid repeating the name, which is already understood. There are different types: **personal** (e.g. **Me** *dio su dirección* – He gave me his address), **interrogative** (e.g. *¿****Quién** eres?* – **Who** are you?], **demonstrative** (e.g. Este *es Juan* – This is Juan), **possessive (e.g.** *Es **mío*** – It's **mine), relative** (*Pedro, **que** era muy atrevido, le preguntó su nombre* – Pedro, **who** was very daring, asked her name), **indefinite** (***Alguien** viene* – Somebody is coming) and **negative** (***Nadie** se ha levantado todavía* – **Nobody** has got up yet).
Question words – *Interrogativos*	See **Interrogatives**.
Radical changing verbs – *Verbos con irregularidades que afectan a la raíz*	Verbs whose changes affect the stem or root.
Reciprocal – *Recíproco*	Grammatical term which indicates that an action is mutual, e.g. *Luis y Carmen se odian* (Luis and Carmen hate each other). There are reciprocal pronouns (*nos, os, se*) and reciprocal verbs (e.g. *quererse, odiarse (unos a otros)*).

Reflexive – *Reflexivo* Grammatical term which indicates that an action is performed by oneself on oneself, e.g. *Me voy a lavar* (I'm going to wash myself). There are reflexive pronouns (me, *te, se, nos, os, se)* and reflexive verbs (e.g. *ducharse*).

Register – *Registro* Linguistic variety or style. A register is characterised by the choice of expression, structures and in particular vocabulary. A register can be formal, standard or neutral, informal or colloquial, or vulgar.

Regular verb – *Verbo regular* Verb which follows the rules for a given tense. Some verbs are always regular, like *comer* (to eat), and others may be regular in some tenses but not in others, like *conducir* (to drive), which is regular in all tenses except the preterite and imperfect subjunctive. See also **Irregular verb**.

Relative clause – *Oración de relativo* A type of **subordinate clause** which takes the place of an adjective, and therefore qualifies a noun. *Las montañas **nevadas** son una maravilla* (The **snowy** mountains are wonderful) (adjective); *Los montes **que se ven desde aquí** son una maravilla* (The mountains **that you can see from here** are wonderful) (relative clause).

Relative pronoun – *Pronombre relativo* **Connector** which joins the relative clause to its **antecedent**. In *La niña de la foto **que lleva trenzas** soy yo* (The little girl in the photo <u>who has plaits</u> is me), *que* is the relative pronoun, which joins the relative clause to its **antecedent** *niña*.

Reported speech – *Discurso indirecto* See **Indirect speech**.

Simple sentence – *Oración simple* Sentence consisting of just one clause and which expresses a complete, independent and coherent thought, e.g. *Este niño se llama Ramón* (This boy is called Ramón).

Singular – *Singular* See **Number**.

Stem of the verb – *Raíz verbal* Also known as 'root'. What remains of the infinitive form of the verb after removing the ending *-ar*, *-er*, or *-ir*, and to which the conjugation endings are added, e.g. *vivir* → *viv-* (*viv*ía, **viv**irás, *viv*iéramos, etc.).

Subject – *Sujeto* The person or thing which performs the action denoted by the verb, e.g. **Daniel** *trabaja en el Ministerio de Educación* (**Daniel** works in the Ministry of Education).

Subjunctive – *Subjuntivo* The **mood**, or category of verb tenses, which expresses doubt, uncertainty or conjecture.

Subordinate clause – *Oración subordinada* **Clause** which does not express a complete thought and therefore cannot stand on its own, but must be part of a larger unit, a **complex sentence**, in which it is dependent on another clause called the **main clause**. For instance, the clause *el cual se puso a ladrar al vernos* (which started barking as soon as it saw us) does not have complete sense on its own, but it does as part of a complex sentence, e.g. *Nos salió un perro enorme, el cual se puso a ladrar al vernos* (A huge dog came out, which started barking as soon as it saw us). There are three types of subordinate clauses: **noun clauses, relative clauses** and **adverbial clauses**.

Subordination – *Subordinación*	Relationship of dependency that a **subordinate clause** has with its governing **main clause**. In *Si quieres, ven* (If you want, come along), the clause *si quieres* has a relationship of subordination to *ven*, i.e. it is dependent on *ven*.
Suffixes – *Sufijos*	See **Affixes.**
Superlative – *Superlativo*	Form of an adjective which indicates its quality as being of the highest degree, e.g. *la más bella del mundo* (**the most** beautiful in the world).
Synonym – *Sinónimo*	Term which has the same meaning as another term, e.g., *coger* and *tomar* are synonyms meaning 'to take'.
Syntax – *Sintaxis*	Part of grammar which sets the rules about how words are ordered in sentences.
Tag-question – *Coletilla interrogativa*	A **question** which follows a statement and which seeks confirmation, e.g., *¿no?, ¿verdad?, ¿cierto?,* as in *Vendrás a la fiesta, ¿verdad?* (You'll come to the party, won't you?).
Tense – *Tiempo verbal*	Grammatical category of verbs which indicates distinctions in time. All personal forms of the verbs must be conjugated in a tense form, e.g. present tense, perfect, future, preterite, imperfect, etc. For instance, *está mintiendo* (he's lying) is in the present continuous tense.
Transitive verb – *Verbo transitivo*	Verb which takes a direct **object**. This is because the meaning of the verb implies that the action influences a person, animal or thing. An example is *escribir* (to write), since when somebody writes, s/he must write something (even if this were not specified in the sentence): *Ha escrito un sinfín de novelas* (He's written no end of novels). See also **Intransitive verb**.
Triphthong – *Triptongo*	A combination of three vowel sounds that are pronounced as part of the same syllable, e.g. *in-si-nuáis, biau-ral*. (See Unit 1 Accentuation.)
Utterance – *Unidad de habla*	A general term for a string of speech produced by a speaker in a particular situation. It may be a full sentence, a clause, an exclamation, an order or just a single word.
Verb – *Verbo*	Word which indicates the action of a sentence, such as *llover* (**to rain**), *Pasaremos luego* (**We'll pop** in later), *Ha nacido esta mañana* (**It was born** this morning).
Voice – *Voz*	Term used to refer to the relationship between the subject of the verb and the action. When the subject of the verb is presented as the active 'doer', the verb is said to be in the active voice, e.g. *Juan cortó varios árboles deljardín* (Juan **cut down** several trees in the garden). When the object of the verb is given prominence as the recipient of the action, the verb is said to be in the passive voice, e.g. *Varios árboles del jardín fueron cortados* (Several trees in the garden **were cut down).**
Word order – *Orden de las palabras*	Order of the words in a sentence. Different languages have different orders. In Spanish the most common order for affirmative statements is: subject + verb + object, e.g. *María ha estudiado Empresariales* (María has done business studies).

1 Accentuation

Accentuation – *acentuación* – refers to the stress or relative emphasis in pronunciation that is given to a syllable in a word. In Spanish, like in any other language, all words have a stressed syllable – *sílaba tónica*. With one type of exception, in Spanish words carry just one stress, which is fixed, that is, it does not change depending on the place or function of the word in the sentence. Any syllable of the word can carry stress: the final syllable (*re**loj**, col**chón***), the penultimate syllable (*biblio**te**ca, auto**mó**vil*), the antepenultimate syllable (*o**cé**ano, te**lé**fono*) and the fourth-to-last syllable (*l**lé**vatelo, **dí**gamelo*).

1.1 General written accentuation rules in Spanish

Level 1

In the written language in Spanish there are general rules governing accentuation, so that it is obvious how a word should be stressed just by looking at it.

The basic general accentuation rules in Spanish are:

- All words ending in a vowel are stressed on the penultimate (last but one) syllable: *libro, ven**ta**na, arre**ci**fe.*
- All words ending in the consonants -n or -s are also stressed on the penultimate syllable: *co**men**, **ha**blas, **cam**pos, re**su**men, carca**ja**das.*
- All words ending in any other consonant are stressed on the final syllable: *bis**tec**, universi**dad**, re**loj**, unilate**ral**, aves**truz**.*

If words don't follow the rules above they will have a written accent called *acento ortográfico* or *tilde*, to indicate the syllable where the stress falls.

The following examples show words that end in a vowel, -n or -s but are not stressed on the penultimate syllable, and which therefore have a written accent on the stressed syllable:

col**chón**, **cán**taros, Pana**má**, in**glés**, **lám**para, termi**nó**, te**lé**fono.

Similarly, the following words ending in a consonant (other than -n or -s) are not stressed on the last syllable, and therefore also have a written accent:

*lá*piz, *cés*ped, *dé*ficit, *ár*bol, *ál*bum, *Ós*car, *crá*ter.

Double stress: adverbs ending in *-mente*

Adverbs that end in *-mente* have two stresses. They are formed from adjectives or adverbs and the ending *-mente* (corresponding to *-ly* in English). One of the stresses is placed on the adjectival or adverbial part of the word, and the second on the first syllable of *-mente*: gene**ral**men*te*, para**dó**jica**men**te, repe**ti**da**men**te, **fá**cil**men**te. Whether they have a written accent depends on the general rules explained above.

☞ For further information about adverbs ending in *-mente* go to Unit 10.

1.2 Diacritic accent (*tilde diacrítica*)

Sometimes accents are used to distinguish words that sound the same but have different meanings or grammatical functions. This type of accent is called a diacritic accent.

Diacritic accent with monosyllables

In the case of words of one syllable (*monosílabos*) the written accent is used with the word that carries more emphasis because of its meaning. Examples include: *él/el*, *mí/mi*, *tú/tu*, *sí/si*, *sé/se*, *té/te*, *dé/de*.

- **él** (personal pronoun): *Él es el hermano de Miguel.* (**He** is Miguel's brother.)
  el (definite article): *El libro es interesante.* (**The** book is interesting.)
- **mí** (personal pronoun): *La carta es para mí.* (The letter is for **me**.)
  mi (possessive adjective): *Mi madre se llama Inés.* (**My** mother's name is Inés.)
- **tú** (personal pronoun): *Yo estoy bien, ¿y tú?* (I am fine, and **you**?)
  tu (possessive adjective): *Me gusta tu casa.* (I like **your** house.)
- **sí** (adverb): *Sí, quiero café.* (**Yes**, I want some coffee.)
  si (conjunction): *Voy al parque si no llueve.* (I will go to the park **if** it doesn't rain.)
- **sé** (first person singular of verb *saber*): *¡No sé nada!* (**I** don't **know** anything.)
  se (personal pronoun): *Maribel se levanta muy tarde.* (Maribel gets up very late.)
- **té** (tea): *Me gusta mucho el té.* (I like **tea**.)
  te (personal pronoun): *Te llamo cuando llegue a casa.* (I will call **you** when I get home.)
- **dé** (first and third person singular of the present subjunctive and singular formal of the imperative of the verb *dar*): *Dé la vía a los peatones.* (**Give** way to pedestrians.)
  Notice that *dé* on its own needs an accent to distinguish its meaning, but not when it combines with an enclitic pronoun and it follows normal spelling rules: *deme*.
  de (preposition): *La mesa es de madera.* (The table is made **of** wood.)

Accent with interrogatives and exclamations

Question words such as *qué, cuál, cuánto, cuándo* and *(a)dónde* carry a written accent when used in questions and exclamations, as in the following examples:

> *¿**Dónde** está la llave?* (Where is the key?)
>
> *¡**Qué** horror!* (How awful!)
>
> *¿**Cuándo** llega tu madre?* (When does your mother arrive?)

☞ For more information about interrogatives and exclamations go to Units 11 and 13.

The same words don't have a diacritic accent if they function as relatives (*relativos*), as in:

> *La casa **donde** vive mi hermana es muy moderna.* (The house where my sister lives is very modern.)
>
> *Ese es el chico **que** canta en el coro de la escuela.* (That one is the boy who sings in the school choir.)
>
> *No sé **cuando** termina la exposición.* (I don't know when the exhibition ends.)

☞ For more information about relatives go to Section 26.4.

1.3 Vowel combinations

When vowels in Spanish are next to each other they can be either in the same syllable (*diptongos*) or in separate syllables (*hiatos*).

To understand how accents are used when vowels are together, note that vowels are classed either as **strong and open** (*fuertes/abiertas*) – **a, e, o** – or as **weak and closed** (*débiles/cerradas*) – **i, u**.

As you will see below, the combination of strong and weak vowels determines whether vowels are included in the same or in separate syllables.

Diphthongs (*Diptongos*)

A diphthong is a combination of two vowel sounds that are pronounced as part of the same syllable.

A diphthong is formed in one of two ways:

(a) when a strong vowel combines with a weak vowel, provided that there is no stress on the weak vowel: ***dais, seis, sois, aun**que, **Eu**ropa, no**ria**, **tier**no, pre**mio**, du**a**lidad, te**nue**, **cuo**ta.*

(b) when two weak vowels are in combination: ***viuda, cuidado, ruido, ciu**dadela.*

Words with dipthongs follow the general accentuation rules explained in 1.1 above.

Level
3

Hiatos

Hiatos are combinations of vowels that are pronounced as two different syllables. This happens when:

- the two vowels are strong: a + e, a + o, e + a, e + o, o + a, o + e (*caer, caoba, crear, veo, boa, roer*)
  Words with this type of *hiato* also follow the general accentuation rules explained in 1.1 above.
- one vowel is strong and the other one is weak **and** stressed: a + í, a + ú, e + í, e + ú, o + í, o + ú (*caí, baúl, leí, reúnen, oímos*).
  It is important to note that **all** words with this type of *hiato* have a written accent on the stressed vowel. They **do not** follow the general accentuation rules explained in 1.1 above.

Level
2

Triphthongs (*triptongos*)

A triphthong is a combination of three vowel sounds that are pronounced together as part of the same syllable: *actuéis, vaciáis, **huai**no, se**miau**tomático, **viei**ra.*

Words with tripthongs follow the general accentuation rules explained in 1.1 above.

Level
2

1.4 Accents with enclitic pronouns

When pronouns are added to the end of a verb form, the verb form itself may need to have an accent added in order to preserve the stress: *démelo* (give it to me), *cómpraselo* (buy it for him), *tómalo* (take it).

Level
1

1.5 Accents on upper case vowels

Words that have a written accent will also carry it if they are written in upper case (capital letters): *África, PERÚ, Los Ángeles, JAPÓN.*

Level
1

1.6 Diaeresis (*diéresis*)

In Spanish diaeresis is a pair of dots that appears above the vowel *u* to show that it should be sounded.

Remember that the letter *u* is used after *g* and before *e* or *i* to harden the sound, e.g. *guitarra, guerra*. If, after a hard g-sound, the *u* also needs to be sounded, a diaeresis is used: *Lingüística, agüero, contigüidad.*

Ejercicios

1 Highlight or underline the syllable that carries the stress in the following words.

> manzana, lámpara, corren, dices, floreros, pared, general, eficaz, albóndigas, cárcel

2 Look at the following words and explain why they have or do not have a written accent.

Ejemplo: *calle*

calle doesn't have a written accent because it ends in a vowel and is stressed on the penultimate syllable. It follows the accentuation rule.

a mamá
b delantal
c corazón
d respirar
e áspero

3 Add accents to the following words if you think they are needed.

a hablo (I speak)
b hablo (he/she spoke)
c continuo (constant)
d continuo (I continue)
e continuo (he/she continued)

4 Read the following poem and put the written accents where they are missing.

Cobardia (Amado Nervo)
Paso con su madre. ¡Que rara belleza!
¡Que rubios cabellos de trigo garzul!
¡Que ritmo en el paso! ¡Que innata realeza
de porte! ¡Que formas bajo el fino tul . . . !
Paso con su madre. Volvio la cabeza:
¡me clavo muy hondo su mirar azul!
Quede como en extasis.
Con febril premura,
«¡Siguela!», gritaron cuerpo y alma al par.
. . . Pero tuve miedo de amar con locura,
de abrir mis heridas, que suelen sangrar,
¡y no obstante toda mi sed de ternura,
cerrando los ojos, la deje pasar!

2 Nouns

Nouns – *sustantivos* – are words which stand for persons, things, places or abstract concepts. 'Laura', 'chair', 'Madrid' and 'freedom' are all nouns.

As you will see in the following sections, the concepts of gender and number are important in relation to the noun, which can be either masculine or feminine, and singular or plural.

<table>
<tr><td>Level
1</td></tr>
</table>

2.1 Natural gender

Nouns have gender. In Spanish all nouns, including those that signify an object, are either masculine or feminine. So, for instance, *mesa* (table) is a feminine noun, and *libro* (book) is a masculine noun.

It is important to know whether a noun is masculine or feminine as other words in a sentence have to agree with it in gender. Compare: *el niño alto* (the tall boy) and *la niña alta* (the tall girl). The article (*el* or *la*, 'the') and the adjective *alto* or *alta* ('tall') that accompany the noun (*niño*, 'boy', or *niña*, 'girl') have to **agree** in gender and number with the noun itself.

☞ See Unit 3 and Section 4.1 for more information on number and gender agreement.

Naming people and animals

The gender of most nouns used to name people or animals depends on whether the person or animal is male or female:

Masculine nouns	Feminine nouns
el padre (the father)	*la madre* (the mother)
el niño (the boy)	*la niña* (the girl)
el ingeniero (the (male) engineer)	*la ingeniera* (the (female) engineer)
el gato (the (male) cat)	*la gata* (the (female) cat)

Form

Nouns that name people or animals usually have a masculine and a feminine form. The most common masculine ending is *-o,* and the most common feminine one is *-a,* but there are others.

Masculine form	Feminine form	
Nouns that end in **-o**	Replace the **-o** with an **-a**.	*el secretario* → *la secretaria* (the secretary)
Nouns that end in **-d, -l, -n, -r, -s, -z**	Add an **-a** to the masculine form to make the feminine form.	*el profesor* → *la profesora* (the teacher). The main exceptions are: *el/la joven* (the youth), *el/la líder* (the leader)
Nouns that end in **-e**	Sometimes the **-e** is replaced by an **-a,** sometimes the ending remains the same.	*el jefe* → *la jefa* (the boss), *el estudiante* → *la estudiante* (the student) but note: *el tigre* (the tiger) → *la tigresa* (the tigress)
Nouns that end in **-ón** or **-ín**	Change to **-ona** or **-ina** respectively.	*el campeón* → *la campeona* (the champion); *el bailarín* → *la bailarina* (the ballet dancer)
Nouns that end in *-í* or *-ú*	Remain the same.	*el iraní* → *la iraní* (the Iranian) *el hindú* → *la hindú* (the Hindu)

Nouns that remain the same in the masculine and feminine

Some nouns ending in **-a** (and particularly **-ista)** can be used to refer to either males or females.	*el/la artista* (the artist) *el/la atleta* (the athlete) *el/la ciclista* (the cyclist) *el/la futbolista* (the footballer)	*el/la policía* (the police officer) *el/la taxista* (the taxi driver) *el/la tenista* (the tennis player) *el/la turista* (the tourist)
Other nouns that can be used for either males or females*	*el bebé* (the baby) *la persona* (the person) *la víctima* (the victim) *el personaje* (the character, e.g. in a book)	*el genio* (the genius) *la estrella* (the TV/film star) *el/la testigo* (the witness) *el/la modelo* (the model)

* 👁 Note that most of these only take one article (either masculine or feminine), so that for instance *el personaje* can be used to refer to a female character: *el personaje de lady Macbeth.*

Ejercicios

Level 1

1 First match each noun with its English translation, and then give the feminine form, remembering to use the feminine article, *la*.

a   el profesor
b   el campeón
c   el abogado
d   el iraquí
e   el atleta

i   the Iraqi
ii   the champion
iii   the athlete
iv   the teacher
v   the lawyer

Level 1

2 Give the masculine form of the following feminine nouns, remembering to use the masculine article, *el*.

a   la doctora
b   la presidenta
c   la ciclista
d   la bailarina
e   la policía
f   la estudiante

Level 1

3 Complete the missing word from each caption. See the table 'Nouns that remain the same in masculine and feminine'.

a	b	c	d	e
. . . Albert Einstein.	. . . de Shakespeare, lady Macbeth.	Alicia, . . . de mi hermana.	. . . más famosa.	. . . durante el juicio.

Level 1

2.2 Grammatical gender

In Spanish, nouns denoting things or abstract concepts also have a grammatical gender, which means that they too are either masculine or feminine. All nouns in Spanish are either masculine or feminine.

Nouns ending in -o and -a

In general, nouns ending in *-o* are masculine and those ending in *-a* are feminine (e.g. *el año* – the year, *la semana* – the week).

There are some important exceptions

Masculine nouns ending in -a	The main masculine nouns ending in -a (many of them ending in -ma) are: **el día** (the day), and some nouns of Greek origin: **el clima** (the climate), **el idioma** (the language), **el mapa** (the map), **el planeta** (the planet), **el poema** (the poem), **el problema** (the problem), **el programa** (the programme), **el sistema** (the system), **el tema** (the theme/topic).
Feminine nouns ending in -o	The main feminine nouns ending in -o are **la mano** (hand) and some words which are abbreviations: **la foto** (short for *fotografía,* photo) **la moto** (short for *motocicleta,* motorcycle)

Other endings

Many nouns do not end in either **-o** or **-a.** Nevertheless, there are consistent patterns. The following rules can help you to decide the gender of a noun.

(a) Nouns that are usually feminine

	Example
Nouns ending in **-dad, -tad** and **-ud**	*la ciudad* (the city), *la igualdad* (equality), *la libertad* (liberty), *la lealtad* (loyalty), *la virtud* (virtue), *la salud* (health)
Many nouns ending in **-ez**	*la estupidez* (stupidity), *la idiotez* (idiocy), *la sencillez* (simplicity)
Nouns ending in **-sis** and **-itis**	*la crisis* (the crisis), *la tesis* (the thesis), *la trombosis* (thrombosis), *la hepatitis* (hepatitis)
Nouns ending in **-ie**	*la serie* (the series)
Most nouns ending in **-ión**	*la acción* (the action), *la estación* (the station), *la excursión* (the excursion), *la revolución* (the revolution), *la pasión* (the passion), *la misión* (the mission) Two important exceptions are: *el camión* (the lorry) and *el avión* (the aeroplane).
The names of the letters of the alphabet are feminine.	*la a, la be, la ce, la de* *La eñe no existe en inglés.* (The letter 'ñ' doesn't exist in English.)

(b) Nouns that are usually masculine

	Example
Nouns ending in **-ón**	*el jamón* (ham)
Nouns ending in **-or**	*el amor* (love), *el valor* (courage or valour)
Nouns ending in **-aje**	*el garaje* (the garage), *el paisaje* (the landscape)

	Example
Nouns ending in a stressed vowel	*el sofá* (the sofa)
Names of the days and months	*el lunes* (Monday), *el abril pasado* (last April) 👁 Note that in Spanish the names of the days and months are written with an initial lower-case letter.
Numbers	*El tres es mi número favorito.* (Three is my favourite number.)
Colours are masculine when used as nouns.	*El rojo es mi color favorito.* (Red is my favourite colour.)
The names of rivers, seas and oceans	*el Amazonas*, *el Atlántico*, *el Mediterráneo*
The names of languages	*el español* (Spanish), *el francés* (French), *el inglés* (English), *el japonés* (Japanese) 👁 Note that in Spanish the names of languages are written with an initial lower-case letter.

(c) Gender of nouns that end in -e

The gender of nouns that end in *-e* or those that do not fit into any of the categories above is not easy to predict. When learning new vocabulary, it is important to learn the gender of the words too. The best way of doing this is always to learn the noun with its article, so that you remember if the word is masculine or feminine: *el coche* (the car), *la noche* (the night). If you look a noun up in the dictionary it will tell you its gender (usually masculine nouns are followed by the letter *m*, and feminine nouns by *f*).

Nouns which can be masculine or feminine, but with different meanings

There are some words which exist both in the masculine and in the feminine forms, but which mean different things depending on the gender. Some of the most common are:

el bolso (the handbag)	*la bolsa* (the bag/the stock exchange)
el capital (capital, i.e. money)	*la capital* (the capital city)
el guía (the (male) guide)	*la guía* (the (female) guide, but also the guide book)
el margen (the margin)	*la margen* (the river bank)

Ejercicios

1 Decide the gender of the following words and then write the correct definite article in the gap: *el* if they are masculine, *la* if they are feminine, or *el/la* if they can be either. Check the explanations above if you are not sure.

a	. . . multitud	d	. . . bronquitis
b	. . . enigma	e	. . . fraternidad
c	. . . capital	f	. . . reunión

2 Do the same as in 1, but this time do not consult the grammatical explanations.

a	. . . dentista	d	. . . mano
b	. . . apendicitis	e	. . . síntoma
c	. . . suposición	f	. . . juventud

3 Read each sentence and give the Spanish equivalent of the word in bold.

Ejemplo

I like living in **the capital.** la capital

a   I'd like to start a business but I haven't really got **the capital** I need.
b   **The guidebook** says the museum is closed on Mondays.
c   I wrote some notes in **the margin** of the document.
d   **The guide** told us about several restaurants and then took us to a very good one.

2.3 Number

'Number' – *número* – is a grammatical concept which categorises words as singular or plural. Nouns are said to be singular if they refer to one person or thing, or plural if they refer to several. 'Chair' is singular, whereas 'chairs' is plural. In Spanish, the plural is usually formed by adding *-s* or *-es*.

The articles, *el* and *la*, also have a plural form, *los* and *las*.

Formation of the plural

Nouns ending in a vowel (*-a*, *-e*, *-i*, *-o* or *-u*)	Add **-s.** If the vowel is an accented *í* or *ú,* add **-es.**	*la casa* → *las casas* (houses) *la estudiante* → *las estudiantes* (female students) *el libro* → *los libros* (books) *la tribu* → *las tribus* (tribes) *el iraní* → *los iraníes* (Iranians)
Nouns ending in a consonant	Add **-es.** If the vowel before the last consonant has an accent, the accent disappears in the plural.	*el doctor* → *los doctores* (doctors) *la nación* → *las naciones* (nations)

👁 Note that nouns ending in a stressed *-í* or *-ú* in the singular form their plural by adding *-es: el iraquí* → *los iraquíes* (Iraqis); *la hindú* → *las hindúes* (Hindu women). The exceptions are *el menú* → *los menús* (the menus), *el champú* → *los champús* (the shampoos). Note however that it is becoming acceptable simply to say *los iraquís, las hindús,* etc.

Masculine plural forms that include males and females

The masculine plural form can refer to both males and females:

los abuelos (grandparents)   *los hijos* (children, i.e. sons and daughters)
los hermanos (brothers and sisters)   *los primos* (male and female cousins)
los niños (children, i.e. boys and girls)   *los padres* (parents)
                                        los tíos (uncle(s) and aunt(s))

> *Los niños empiezan el colegio a los cinco años.* (Children start school at five.)

◉ Note that in the light of current debate about gender-inclusive language, the more politically correct form is:

> *Los niños y las niñas empiezan el colegio a los cinco años.*

Nouns that do not change in the plural

Nouns that end in an unstressed vowel plus 's' in the singular keep the same form in the plural: *el lunes* → *los lunes* (Mondays), *la crisis* → *las crisis* (crises), *la tesis* → *las tesis* (theses)

Foreign borrowings

Many borrowed nouns form their plural by adding an 's', regardless of their ending:

el modem → *los modems*   *el póster* → *los pósters*
el bit → *los bits*   *el camping* → *los campings* (the camp sites)

Ejercicios

1 Give the plural of the following nouns. Remember to use the correct article, *los* or *las*.

a	la estación	d	el actor	g	el tabú
b	la mesa	e	el virus	h	la estudiante
c	el lunes	f	el café	i	el atlas

2 Replace the words in bold with gender-inclusive expressions:

Ejemplo

Los padres de Alicia: La madre y el padre de Alicia.

a   En España **los niños** empiezan el colegio a las nueve.
b   **Los abuelos** de Mariana viven en Orense.
c   **Los profesores** trabajan mucho.

Level 1

3 Tick the relevant boxes to identify the gender and number of the following nouns. If in doubt, use your dictionary.

	Masculino	Femenino	Singular	Plural
a Mediterráneo				
b gas				
c problemas				
d crisis				
e ciclistas				

Level 1

2.4 Collective nouns

Collective nouns – *los sustantivos colectivos* – are used to refer to people, animals or things as a group. In English, some collective nouns such as 'people', or 'the police', are plural: 'People **are** selfish'; in Spanish; collective nouns are singular: *La gente **es** egoísta.*

Some of the most common collective nouns in Spanish

el comité (the committee)   *el gobierno* (government)

el ejército (the army)   *la policía* (the police)

la familia (the family)   *el rebaño* (the herd)

la gente (people)

Collective nouns in Spanish are used **in the singular** when they refer to a group:

> Mi ***familia*** *vive en Italia.* (My family lives in Italy.)

> La ***policía*** *detuvo a los terroristas.* (The police arrested the terrorists.)

When referring to several groups, collective nouns are used **in the plural**:

> *los* ***gobiernos*** *democráticos* (democratic governments)

> *las* ***familias*** *numerosas* (large families)

Ejercicios

Level 1

1 Circle the collective nouns in the following list.

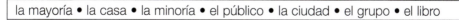

la mayoría • la casa • la minoría • el público • la ciudad • el grupo • el libro

Level 1

2 Decide if the subject is a collective noun or not, and then choose the correct verb form (third person singular or third person plural).

 a   La políca **encontró/encontraron** al ladrón.
 b   Los policías **lleva/llevan** pistola.
 c   El comité **tomó/tomaron** la decisión unánimemente.
 d   El ejército **realiza/realizan** maniobras.

2.5 Diminutive, augmentative and pejorative suffixes

In Spanish, diminutive, augmentative and pejorative **suffixes** – *sufijos diminutivos, aumentativos y peyorativos* – can be added to nouns (and sometimes to **adjectives** and even **adverbs).** These suffixes, or particles added at the end of the word, convey connotations of smallness or endearment (diminutives), or largeness, ugliness or clumsiness, but also admiration or aggrandisement (augmentatives). Pejorative suffixes convey negative connotations, such as contempt, although sometimes they can connote affection.

Diminutive suffixes added to nouns

The most common diminutive is *-ito/-ita.*

🌎 The use of diminutive suffixes is even more extended in Spanish America than in Spain.

Form

Drop the last vowel and add **-ito, -ita** generally if the noun ends in *-o* or *-a* 👁 Note in the examples, spelling changes occur when adding *-ito/-ita,* to preserve the same sound as in the original noun: *c → qu; g → gu.* Note also *z → c,* as in Spanish it is not usual to have *z* in front of *-e* or *-i.*	*el gato* (cat) → *el gat**ito*** *Ana → An**ita*** *Paco → Pa**quito*** *lago* (lake) → *la**guito*** *pinza* (peg) → *pin**cita***	*La gata ha dado a luz a cinco gatitos.* (The cat has given birth to five kittens.)
Add **-cito, -cita** if the noun ends in *-n, -r,* or if the noun ends in *-e* and has more than one syllable.	*el camión* (lorry) → *el camion**cito*** *el sabor* (flavour) → *el sabor**cito*** *la fuente* (fountain) → *la fuente**cita***	*Tiene un saborcito muy rico.* (It has a very pleasant taste.)
Add **-ecito, -ecita** if: the noun has two syllables, ends in *-o* or *-a,* and the first syllable contains *ie* or *ue;* or if the noun has one syllable and ends in a consonant. 👁 Note that the spelling change *z → c* occurs when adding *-ecito/-ecita,* as it is not usual to have *z* in front of *-e* or *-i.*	*el viento* (wind) → *el vient**ecito*** *la cuesta* (hill) → *la cuest**ecita*** *la flor* (flower) → *la flor**ecita*** *el pez* (fish) → *el pe**cecito***	*Sopla un vientecito muy agradable.* (There is a very pleasant little breeze.)

Other diminutive endings include:

-ico/-ica, a regional variation of *-ito/-ita,* is particularly common in Spanish America and Aragón and Navarre in Spain	*Pásame la mant**ica**, que tengo frío.* (Pass me the blanket. I'm cold.)
-illo/-illa is a less common and slightly old-fashioned alternative to *-ito/-ita* 👁 Note that it is sometimes used to add a note of contempt or sarcasm.	*las florec**illas** del campo* (the little wild flowers) *Eres un list**illo**.* (What a know-all you are!)
-uelo/-uela is less common than the other suffixes 👁 Note that it can also add a negative connotation (for instance, of contempt)	*Carlitos se ha convertido en un moz**uelo** muy guapo.* (Carlitos has a become a very handsome young man.) *Es una mujerz**uela**.* (She's a slut.)
-ete/-eta often indicates affection (Peninsular Spanish only)	*Es un chico muy guap**ete**.* (He is a nice-looking lad.)

All these endings add *-c-* or *-ec-* (or *-z-* or *-ez-* in the case of *-uelo/-uela*) in the same way that *-ito/-ita* does:

> *joven* → *joven**cita*** → *joven**cilla***   *flor* → *flor**ecita*** → *flor**ecilla***

Change of meaning by using diminutive suffixes

In many cases, the addition of a diminutive suffix has created a new noun with a different meaning.	*un bolso* (a bag) → *un bolsillo* (a pocket) Sometimes, the new word is also of the other gender: *un zapato* (a shoe) → *una zapatilla* (a slipper).

Diminutive suffixes added to adjectives and some adverbs

Adjectives	*pobre* → *pobre**cito*** *azul* → *azul**ito***	*Pobrecito, me da mucha pena.* (Poor thing, I feel really sorry for him.)
Adverbs	*ahora* → *ahor**ita*** *cerca* → *cer**quita*** *en seguida* → *en seguid**ita***	*Ahorita le llamo por teléfono.* (I'll phone him in a second.)

Augmentative suffixes

Augmentative suffixes can be added to nouns or adjectives to convey the idea of large size or intensity, often in conjunction with ugliness, excess or contempt, but sometimes as a term of endearment.

Form

Add **-ón/-ona** to give connotations of large size, or to add a hint of sarcasm.	*una casa → una casona* (a large, rambling house) *un drama → un dramón* (a melodrama: ironic or sarcastic) *inocente → inocentón* (gullible)	*¡Qué dramón se armó!* (What a melodrama!)
Add **-ote/-ota** to convey largeness, sometimes with negative connotations of clumsiness or ugliness, and sometimes to denote endearment.	*grande → grandote* (very large) *abrazo → abrazote* (big hug)	*Es un chico grandote, un poco torpe.* (He's a big, clumsy lad.) *¡Dame un abrazote!* (Give me a big bear hug!)
Add **-azo/-aza** to convey a positive meaning, sometimes associated with large size.	*un coche → un cochazo* (a great big car)	*Se ha comprado un cochazo impresionante.* (He's bought a great big car.)

Other meanings of the augmentative suffixes

Note that the suffix **-azo** can also be added to a noun to indicate that a blow is given with the thing referred to by the noun.	*un codo → un codazo* (a blow with the elbow) *un martillo → un martillazo* (a blow with a hammer)
The suffix **-ón/-ona** can also be used with some verbs and adjectives to mean 'given to doing' something.	*contestar → contestón, -ona* (given to answering back) *llorar → llorón, -ona* (cry baby) *mandar → mandón, -ona* (bossy boots) *comer → comilón, -ona* (glutton) *dormir → dormilón, -ona* (sleepy head)

Change of meaning by using augmentative suffixes

As with diminutives, in some cases the addition of an augmentative suffix has created a new word.	*una silla* (a chair) → *un sillón* (an armchair) *una caja* (a box) → *un cajón* (a drawer)

Pejorative suffixes

-ejo/-eja or **-ajo/-aja** denotes the idea of smallness, sometimes with a connotation of affection. (Peninsular Spanish only)	*Es una calleja que sale de la plaza.* (It's a narrow little street that leads from the square.) *Hola, pequeñajo, dame un abrazo.* (talking to a toddler: Hello little one, give me a hug.)
-ucho/-ucha conveys the idea of ugliness and smallness	*Ese cuartucho apenas tiene luz.* (That little room has hardly any light.) *Vivía en una casucha muy fea.* (He lived in an ugly little house.)

Ejercicios

Level
1

1 Write the diminutive of the following nouns using *-ito/-ita.*

a	la isla	**d**	el reloj	**g**	el cuenco
b	el abuelo	**e**	el pájaro	**h**	el bastón
c	el café	**f**	el pico	**i**	la mano

Level
1

2 Replace the words in bold by a diminutive or an augmentative, according to the meaning.

Ejemplo

Al bebé le compré un **traje** muy bonito.
Al bebé le compré un *trajecito* muy bonito.

a Me compré un monedero **pequeño** muy mono.
b El Real Deportivo marcó un **gol** fantástico en el último minuto.
c Después giras a la izquierda y verás una **calle** estrecha. Mi casa está al fondo.
d Tienen un **perro** enorme para que no les entre nadie en el jardín.

Level
1

3 Diminutives are often used when talking to children, and they are common in children's stories. Can you recognise any of the following titles?

a Caperucita Roja y el lobo feroz.
b Los tres cerditos.
c El patito feo.
d Blancanieves y los siete enanitos.
e Ricitos de oro.

Level
2

4 Read this extract from a novel by the Peruvian writer Mario Vargas Llosa. A woman writes to her lover, telling him she will look after him. You will see it uses an exaggerated number of diminutives for literary effect. Then rewrite it without any diminutives.

> **Menú diminutivo**
>
> Ya sé que te gusta comer poquito y sanito, pero riquito, y estoy preparadita para complacerte *también* en la mesita.
>
> En la mañanita iré al mercado y compraré la lechecita más fresquita, el pancito recién horneadito, y la naranjita más chaposita. Y te despertaré con la bandejita del desayuno, una florecita fragante y un besito. "Aquí está su juguito sin pepitas, sus tostaditas con mermeladita de fresita y su cafecito con leche sin azuquítar, señorcito."
>
> (Mario Vargas Llosa (1997), *Los cuadernos de Don Rigoberto,* Madrid: Alfaguara)

3 Articles

An article – *un artículo* – is a type of word that precedes a noun and signals whether that noun refers to a specific element, or to an unspecified one. In the case of a specific element, the definite article is used ('**the** house', '**the** apple'), and in the case of an unspecified element, the indefinite article is used ('a house', '**an** apple').

In Spanish, the number and gender of the article depend on the number and gender of the noun.

In many cases, the article in Spanish is used in the same way as in English, but there are some differences, and in this unit we have mainly focused on those instances where use differs in the two languages.

3.1 The definite article

In English, 'the' is an article. It is called the definite article – *el artículo definido* – because it is used to refer to something specific ('Pass me **the** pen'). In Spanish, the article has to agree in number and gender with the noun it accompanies: *el niño, la niña, los niños, las niñas.*

Form

	Masculine singular	Feminine singular	Masculine plural	Feminine plural
Definite article	*el* profesor	*la* profesora	*los* profesores	*las* profesoras

☞ See Unit 12 for more information on prepositions followed by articles, and Unit 2 for agreement with nouns.

The article with nouns starting with a stressed *a-* or *ha-*

When a feminine word starts with a stressed *a-* (or *ha-*), such as the word *águila* (eagle), the singular article is in the masculine form, although the noun itself remains feminine: *el águila*. In the plural, the article reverts to the feminine form: *las águilas.*

The most common feminine nouns beginning with a stressed *a-* or *ha-* are:

el agua (water)	*el arma* (the weapon)
el alma (the soul)	*el asma* (asthma)
el ancla (the anchor)	*el aula* (the classroom)
el área (the area)	*el hambre* (hunger)

The two exceptions are the names of the letters 'a' and 'h': *la a* and *la hache*.

👁 Note that any adjective accompanying these nouns, including the demonstrative adjective, agrees with the noun and is therefore in the feminine: *el agua fría* (cold water), *estas áreas* (these areas).

☞ See Section 4.1 on adjectival agreement and Unit 6 on demonstratives.

Use
Specific and general sense

In general, the definite article is used before:

A specific noun (this use is the same in English)	*Buenos Aires es **la** capital de Argentina.* (Buenos Aires is the capital of Argentina.) *Pon el plato en **la** mesa.* (Put the plate on the table.)
A noun used in a general sense. Note that in this case in English the article is not generally used	*Me gustan **los** perros.* (I like dogs.) ***El** chocolate engorda.* (Chocolate makes you fat.)

Use of the article with countries and places

The definite article is used before:

The names of some countries, although the tendency is increasingly to omit it	The article is always used with: *los Países Bajos, el Reino Unido, El Salvador.* Its use is optional with *(la) Argentina, (el) Brasil, (el) Canadá, (el) Ecuador, (los) Estados Unidos, (la) India, (el) Japón, (el) Paraguay, (el) Perú, (el) Uruguay.* 👁 Note that names of other countries are not usually preceded by an article, except when they are being modified by an adjective or an expression. The article helps to signal that the meaning is more specific: *España*, but: ***la** España democrática* (democratic Spain) *México*, but: ***el** México del siglo XIX* (19th-century Mexico)
The names of streets and squares	*Vivo en **la** Plaza de la Independencia.* (I live in Independence Square.)
The names of rivers, oceans, and mountains	***el** Amazonas* (the Amazon), ***el** monte Etna* (Mount Etna)

Use of the article with times, dates and periods

The definite article is also used in many expressions that refer to times, dates and periods, and some of these are often different from the way they are used in English. In particular it is used before:

The days of the week and dates	*El concierto es* **el** *lunes*. (The concert is on Monday.) *Su cumpleaños es* **el** *6 de enero*. (Her birthday is on 6 January.) 👁 Note that certain common expressions used for dates do not use the article: *Estamos a viernes, 23 de marzo*. (Today is Friday 23 March.)
Article + time period + *pasado,-a/ próximo,-a/que viene*	**el** *año que viene/***el** *próximo año* (next year) **la** *semana pasada* (last week) **la** *primavera que viene* (next spring)
The time of day	*El tren sale a* **las** *cuatro*. (The train leaves at four.) *Es* **la** *una y media*. (It's half past one.)

Uses that differ from English

The following are the main cases when the article is used in Spanish, although not in English:

Concepts	**la** *democracia* (democracy), **la** *libertad* (freedom), **la** *justicia* (justice)
Academic subjects	**la** *filosofía* (philosophy), **las** *matemáticas* (mathematics), **la** *literatura* (literature) *Me gusta la literatura francesa*. (I like French literature.) 👁 But note that after the verbs *saber* (to know), *enseñar* (to teach), *estudiar* (to study) and *aprender* (to learn), and the prepositions *en* and *de*, the article is omitted: **Estudia** *geografía*. (She's studying geography.); *un libro* **de** *física* (a physics book).
The names of languages	**el** *inglés* (English), **el** *japonés* (Japanese), **el** *chino* (Chinese) 👁 Note that names of languages are not capitalised in Spanish. 👁 Note also that after the verbs *hablar* (to speak), *saber* (to know), *aprender* (to learn), *enseñar* (to teach) and *estudiar* (to study) and the prepositions *en* and *de*, the article is omitted: **Hablo** *francés*. (I speak French.); *Es profesora* **de** *ruso*. (She is a teacher of Russian.); *una carta* **en** *inglés* (a letter in English).
The names of colours	*El rojo es mi color favorito*. (Red is my favourite colour.) 👁 But only when the colour is a noun, not when it is an adjective, or when it follows a preposition: *Tengo un coche rojo*. (I have a red car.); *La novia va vestida* **de** *blanco*. (The bride is dressed in white.)
The names of meals	**el** *desayuno* (breakfast), **la** *comida/***el** *almuerzo* (lunch), **la** *merienda* (snack), **la** *cena* (dinner)

The names of sports teams	*Juega **el** Sevilla contra **el** Atlético de Madrid.* (Sevilla and Atlético de Madrid are playing).
Titles of people	***el** Sr Ruiz, **el** capitán Araña, **el** rey Don Juan Carlos, **el** presidente Clinton* (Mr Ruiz, Captain Araña, King Juan Carlos, President Clinton) 👁 Note that the article is not used when addressing a person directly: *Sr Ruiz, le llaman al teléfono.* (Mr Ruiz, you are wanted on the telephone.)
Family relations (but not usually parents or siblings)	***La** tía Julia está en Córdoba.* (Aunt Julia is in Cordoba.) *Llama a **la** abuela.* (Call grandma.) But: *Mamá está trabajando.* (Mum is working.)
Qualified proper names	***el** pequeño Tomás* (young Thomas)
The direct object in verbs of feeling	*Me gusta la cerveza.* (I like beer.) *Odio las películas de miedo.* (I hate horror films.)
With nouns used to talk about measurements and quantities	*El café está a 8 euros el kilo.* (Coffee is 8 euros a kilo.) *Esta tela está a 10 euros el metro.* (This material costs 10 euros a metre.)

Use of the article to denote possession

👁 In Spanish the article is used on many occasions when in English a possessive (such as 'my', 'your', etc.) would be used instead:

To refer to parts of the body, including clothes currently worn	*¡Lávate **los** dientes!* (Brush **your** teeth!) *Se metió la mano en **el** bolsillo.* (He put his hand in **his** pocket.)
To refer to personal objects when the meaning is 'one each'	*El rector les entregó **el** título.* (The chancellor gave them **their** certificates.) *Nos sellaron **el** pasaporte.* (They stamped **our** passports.)

Casa, clase, misa

🌎 In Spain, the definite article is not used with the word *casa* when it means 'home', although in Spanish America it is.

casa ('home')	*estar en (la) casa* (to be at home); *sentirse como en (la) casa* (to feel at home); *ir a (la) casa* (to go home); *salir de (la) casa* (to leave the house); *quedarse en (la) casa* (to stay at home)
casa ('house')	*La casa de Rosa tiene un jardín muy grande.* (Rosa's house has a very large garden.)

The article is not used with *clase* and *misa* in expressions such as the following:

clase	*estar en clase* (to be in class); *ir a clase* (to go to class); *tener clase* (to have a class/lesson)
misa	*estar en misa* (to be at mass); *ir a misa* (to go to mass); *salir de misa* (to come out of mass); *decir misa* (to celebrate mass)

The neuter article *lo*

The neuter article *lo* never accompanies a noun, but is used as follows:

lo + adjective or past participle to express the English 'the thing that . . .'	**Lo** *difícil es encontrar dónde aparcar.* (The difficult thing is to find where to park.) *Tienes que cumplir* **lo** *prometido.* (You have to do what you promised.)
To refer to a part of a whole	*Lo puse en* **lo** *alto del armario.* (I put it on the top of the wardrobe.)
To refer to a series of things that share the same quality	*Le gusta* **lo** *rosa.* (She likes pink things.)

☞ See Section 26.4 for the use of *lo que*.

Ejercicios

1 What do you like? Make true sentences using the words in the box. Remember to add the correct article. If you are not sure of the gender of any of the nouns, look it up in the dictionary!

Ejemplo

If you like it you say: **Me gusta el chocolate.** (I like chocolate.)
If you dislike it you say: **No me gusta el chocolate.** (I don't like chocolate.)

> vino • agua • café • té • cerveza • sangría
>
> sal • pimienta
>
> ensalada • pollo • carne • verdura
>
> melón • flan • fruta • yogur

2 Complete each gap with the correct article.

a   . . . **lunes** siempre voy al gimnasio.
b   La moneda oficial en . . . **Reino Unido** es la libra esterlina.
c   El hotel está en . . . **Avenida de la Paz**, y el restaurante en . . . **calle Cuervo**.
d   . . . **semana que viene** me voy de vacaciones.

3 Now translate the expressions in bold in the previous activity into English. Notice which uses of the article are different in Spanish and English.

4 Fill each gap with a definite article if necessary.

    a . . . desayuno se sirve de 9 a 10.30, y . . . cena de 8.30 a 11.
    b Mi color favorito es . . . azul.
    c Tengo una chaqueta . . . azul.
    d Hablo . . . francés, . . . italiano y . . . español.

3.2 The indefinite article

Indefinite articles – *los artículos indefinidos* – are used to refer to an element that is not specific; in English 'a'/'an' is the indefinite article ('Pass me a pen', i.e. any pen, not a specific one, as opposed to 'Pass me **the** pen'). When used with plural nouns 'some'/'any' is used instead of 'a' (compare 'I need **some** apples' with 'I need **the** apples').

In Spanish, the indefinite article has singular, plural, masculine and feminine forms, and it has to agree in number and gender with the noun it accompanies: *un niño, una niña, unos niños, unas niñas.*

Form

	Masculine singular	Feminine singular	Masculine plural	Feminine plural
Indefinite article	*un* coche	*una* moto	*unos* coches	*unas* motos

As in the case of the definite article (☞ Section 3.1), when a feminine word begins with a stressed 'a-' (or 'ha-'), such as the word *águila* (eagle), the singular article is in the masculine form, although the noun itself remains feminine: *un águila*. In the plural, the article reverts to the feminine form: *unas águilas.*

Omission of the article in Spanish

👁 Unlike in English, no article is needed in Spanish in the following cases:

ser + profession hacerse + profession	*Es diputada del Congreso.* (She is a Member of Parliament.) *Es capitán del ejército.* (He is a captain in the army.) *Quiere hacerse cura.* (He wants to become a priest.)
Gender or sexual orientation	*¿Es niño o niña?* (Is it a boy or a girl?) *Es lesbiana.* (She is a lesbian.)
Nationality	*Es italiano.* (He is (an) Italian.)
Religion	*Es católica.* (She is a Catholic.)
Political persuasion	*Mi abuelo era comunista.* (My grandfather was a communist.)
Possessions or personal effects with the verb *tener*	*¿Tienes coche?* (Have you got a car?) *No tengo pasaporte.* (I haven't got a passport.)

Certain ailments with the verb *tener*	*Tengo tos/fiebre/dolor de cabeza/dolor de espalda.* (I've got a cough/a temperature/a headache/a bad back.)
A hundred, a thousand	*cien pesos* (a hundred pesos) *mil dólares* (a thousand dollars)
In the expression *¡Qué . . . !* (What a . . . !)	*¡Qué estúpido!* (What an idiot!) *¡Qué día!* (What a day!)

Indefinite article in English, definite article in Spanish

👁 In English, the indefinite article is used to talk about physical characteristics, as in the example below. In these cases, however, the definite article is usually preferred in Spanish.

He's got **a** round face. (*Tiene **la** cara redonda.*)

Ejercicios

Level 1

1 Look at the following ID card and make three sentences about the person's profession, gender and nationality.

REPÚBLICA DE COLOMBIA
NOMBRE: Teresa
APELLIDOS: Segura Ramos
FECHA DE NACIMIENTO: 15-6-54
SEXO: F
PROFESIÓN: Abogada
NACIONALIDAD: Colombiana

Level 1

2 Now write some sentences about yourself on some or all of the following.

profession • nationality • gender • sexual orientation • political persuasion

Level 1

3 Which of the following do you own? Say '*Tengo . . .*' or '*No tengo . . .*' .

coche • moto • fax • ordenador • modem • reloj • pasaporte • carnet de conducir • permiso de residencia • radio • televisor

Level 1

4 Look at the following people and animals and write a sentence about their physical appearance.

a

b

d

e

c

Ejemplo

a Tiene la cabeza muy grande.

4 Qualifying adjectives

Qualifying adjectives are words that modify or qualify a noun, i.e. they add specific information to a noun. Words such as *grande* (big), *amarillo* (yellow) or *simpático* (friendly) are qualifying adjectives.

Level 1

4.1 Agreement in gender and number

In Spanish, adjectives – *los adjetivos* – agree in number and gender with the noun they qualify.

Agreement in gender

Adjectives need to agree in gender with the noun they qualify: if the noun is masculine, the adjective that qualifies it needs to be masculine; if it is feminine, the adjective needs to be feminine.

    *un coche **rojo*** (a red car)   *una bicicleta **roja*** (a red bicycle)

 Note that when you look up an adjective in the dictionary, you will find it under its masculine singular form, which is followed by the feminine ending: *conservador, -ora*.

Formation of the feminine

Masculine adjectives ending in	Feminine form	Example Masculine	Feminine
-o	Replace *-o* with *-a*	*dinámico*	*dinámica*
-án, -ín, -ón, -or	Replace by *-ana*, *-ina, -ona, -ora* respectively	*charlatán* *parlanchín* *dormilón* *trabajador*	*charlatana* (talkative, chatty) *parlanchina* (talkative) *dormilona* (sleepy-head) *trabajadora* (hard-working)

Masculine adjectives	Feminine form	Example	
-ior (and the comparatives *mayor, menor, mejor* and *peor*) ☞ See Section 4.3.	Remains the same	*superior* *inferior* *anterior* *posterior* *mayor* *menor* *mejor* *peor*	*superior* *inferior* *anterior* *posterior* *mayor* (bigger/older) *menor* (smaller/younger) *mejor* (better) *peor* (worse)
-ete, -ote ☞ See Section 2.5.	Replace by **-eta** and **-ota** respectively	*regordete* *grandote*	*regordeta* (chubby) *grandota* (big)
Adjectives of nationality that end in a consonant	Add an **-a** (and remove the accent in the last syllable if there	*francés* *alemán* *español*	*francesa* (French) *alemana* (German) *española* (Spanish)
Adjectives of nationality that end in **-a, -e, -í** or **-ú**	Remain the same	*belga* *costarricense* *paquistaní* *hindú*	*belga* (Belgian) *costarricense* (Costa Rican) *paquistaní* (Pakistani) *hindú* (Indian)
-e	Remains the same	*fuerte*	*fuerte* (strong)
All the others	Remain the same	*difícil* *liberal* *capaz*	*difícil* (difficult) *liberal* *capaz* (able)

Agreement in number

👁 Adjectives have to agree in number with the noun they modify, i.e. if the noun is singular the adjective will be singular, and if the noun is plural the adjective will be plural. English speakers often forget to make this agreement, as adjectives in English are invariable.

> *un coche **rojo*** (a red car) → *dos coches **rojos***
> *una niña **pequeña*** (a little girl) → *dos niñas **pequeñas***

Formation of the plural

Singular adjectives ending in	Plural form	Example singular	plural
Vowel with no accent	Add **-s**	*importante* *estúpido* *atractiva*	*importantes* *estúpidos* *atractivas*

Singular adjectives ending in	Plural form	Example singular	plural
Consonant or accented vowel	Add -es	liberal hindú	liberales hindúes
-z	Replace by -ces	eficaz veraz	eficaces (effective) veraces (truthful)

Note that when a masculine noun and a feminine noun share the same adjective, the adjective is in the masculine plural.

*un hombre y una mujer **argentinos*** (an Argentinian man and woman)

Position of the adjective

 In Spanish the adjective often goes after the noun, whereas in English it usually goes before:

*un niño **simpático*** (a friendly boy)

☞ For adjectives whose meaning changes according to their position, see Section 4.2.

Ejercicios

Level 1

1 Do you know where these famous Hispanic people come from? Test your knowledge by completing each gap with the correct adjective of nationality. Remember to use the appropriate adjectival ending.

argentino, -na • chileno, -na • español, -la • guatemalteco, -ca • mexicano, -na

    a Antonio Banderas y Fernando Rey son dos actores . . .
    b Julio Cortázar y Jorge Luis Borges son dos escritores . . .
    c Rigoberta Menchú es una activista . . .
    d Isabel Allende y Gabriela Mistral son dos autoras . . .
    e Laura Esquivel, autora de *Como agua para chocolate*, es una escritora . . .
    f Frida Kahlo y Diego Rivera son dos pintores . . . muy famosos.
    g Pablo Neruda es un excelente poeta . . .

Level 1

2 Complete each sentence by selecting a noun and an adjective from each of the boxes. More than one combination is sometimes possible. When completing your sentences, make sure you make the adjective agree with the noun both in gender and in number. If you are not sure of a noun's gender, look it up in the dictionary.

Nouns	Adjectives
~~trabajo~~ • coche • lengua • hoteles • foto • aire	difícil • ~~interesante~~ • precioso, -a • fresco, -a • caro, -a • excelente

Ejemplo

Soy ingeniera. Es un *trabajo interesante.*

a Estoy aprendiendo alemán. Es una . . .
b Abre la ventana. Necesitamos un poco de . . .
c En algunas playas mexicanas hay . . .
d Mi padre se ha comprado un Mercedes. Es un . . .
e He encontrado una . . . de mi abuela cuando era pequeña.

Level 2

4.2 Shortened forms and change of meaning

Qualifying adjectives in Spanish normally follow the noun they modify. However, there are a number of adjectives that can also be placed before the noun. Some of them lose their last vowel or syllable when they are placed before the noun, and others change their meaning depending on their position.

Form

Rule	Example	Remarks
grande → *gran* in front of masculine or feminine singular nouns	un **gran** *acontecimiento* (a great event) una **gran** *mujer* (a great woman)	except when they are preceded by the adverb *más*: *el más* **grande** *acontecimiento del siglo XX* (the greatest event of the 20th century)
bueno → *buen* and *malo* → *mal* in front of masculine singular nouns	un **buen** *hijo* (a good son) un **mal** *viaje* (a bad journey)	but not in front of feminine nouns: **mala** *visibilidad* (bad visibility)
Santo → *San* in front of masculine proper nouns	**San** *Andrés* (St Andrew)	but not in front of: • feminine proper nouns: **Santa** *Teresa* (St Teresa) • masculine proper nouns beginning in *To-* or *Do-*: **Santo** *Tomás*, **Santo** *Domingo* (St Thomas, St Dominic) • common nouns: *el* **santo** *matrimonio* (holy matrimony)
primero → *primer* and *tercero* → *tercer* in front of masculine nouns ☞ See Section 8.2 for the use of ordinal numbers.	*el* **primer** *hombre en la luna* (the first man on the moon) *el* **tercer** *milenio* (the third millennium)	but not in front of feminine nouns: *la* **primera** *semana de agosto* (the first week in August) *la* **tercera** *puerta a la derecha* (the third door on the right)
alguno → *algún* and *ninguno* → *ningún* in front of masculine nouns ☞ See Unit 9 on the use of these indefinites.	*¿Has leído a* **algún** *escritor argentino?* (Have you read any Argentinian writers?) *No tengo* **ningún** *libro de Borges.* (I don't have any books by Borges.)	but not in front of feminine nouns: *¿Le queda* **alguna** *entrada?* (Have you got any tickets left?)

Meaning

The meaning of some of these adjectives can change depending on whether they go before or after the noun.

Adjective	Before the noun	After the noun
grande	una gran casa (a great house) un gran hombre (a great man)	una casa grande (a large house) un hombre grande (a large man)
antiguo, -a	un antiguo convento (a former convent)	un convento antiguo (an old convent)
medio, -a	medio grupo (half the group)	un grupo medio (an average group)
pobre	un pobre hombre (a wretched man)	un hombre pobre (a poor man, i.e. not rich)
simple	una simple excusa (a mere excuse)	una persona simple (a simple person)
único, -a	un único concierto (a single concert)	un concierto único (a unique concert)

Ejercicios

1 Fill each gap with the correct form of the adjective, which is given in brackets in the masculine.

    a   He tenido una . . . idea. (grande)
    b   Hoy puede ser un . . . día. (grande)
    c   Ana es una . . . amiga. (bueno)
    d   Pasé un . . . momento. (malo)
    e   Vivo en el . . . piso. (primero)

2 Read the following sentences and translate the expressions in bold into Spanish. Make sure the adjective is in the correct position!

    a   He lives in **a large house**. (casa)
    b   The headteacher was **a great man**. (hombre)
    c   The other day I met **a former colleague**. (colega)
    d   It's **an old university**. (universidad)
    e   Would you like **half an orange**? (naranja)

4.3 Comparison of adjectives

The following sentences express comparison:

    *Ana es **menos simpática que** Sara.* (Ana is less friendly than Sara.)

*Marina es **más sociable que** Emilia.* (Marina is more outgoing than Emilia.)

*Julián es **tan alto como** Pablo.* (Julián is as tall as Pablo.)

Comparatives – *los comparativos* – are said to be of inferiority (*menos . . . que*), superiority (*más . . . que*), or equality (*tan . . . como*).

Form

Superiority	*más* + adjective + *que*	*Julián es **más alto que** su padre.* (Julian is taller than his father.)
Inferiority	*menos* + adjective + *que*	*Esteban parece **menos abierto que** su hermano.* (Esteban seems less open than his brother.)
Equality	*tan* + adjective + *como*	*Isabel está **tan guapa como** su madre.* (Isabel is looking as beautiful as her mother.)

Level 2 The second term in the comparison can be one of the following:

a noun	*El gato es más listo que **el perro**.* (The cat is cleverer than the dog.)
another adjective	*El perro es más feroz que **inteligente**.* (The dog is fiercer than it is clever.)
an adverb	*El perro está más limpio que **antes**.* (The dog is cleaner than before.)
an adverb phrase	*En casa el perro está más tranquilo que **en la calle**.* (At home the dog is calmer than he is in the street.)
a verb clause	*El gato es más listo **de lo que parece**.* (The cat is cleverer than it seems.) ☞ To revise the comparative clause, go to Section 26.5(d).

In Spanish, as in English, the first term in the comparison can be omitted if it can be inferred from the context:

Isabel es inteligente y saldrá adelante. (Isabel) Es más trabajadora que su hermano.
(Isabel is clever and she'll go far. She is harder working than her brother.)

Similarly, the second term can be omitted too:

Las dos hermanas son muy listas, pero Concha es más trabajadora (que su hermana).
(Both sisters are very clever, but Concha is more hardworking (than her sister).)

Level 1

Irregular comparatives

The following adjectives can have irregular comparatives:

Adjective	Comparative	Example
bueno, -a, -os, -as	mejor, -es	En mi opinión el vino de Rioja es **mejor que** el de Burdeos. (In my opinion Rioja wine is better than Bordeaux.)
malo, -a, -os, -as	peor, -es	La carretera de la costa es **peor que** esta. (The road that goes along the coast is worse than this one.)
grande, -es	mayor, -es	El otro apartamento es **mayor que** este. (The other flat is larger than this one.) Note that mayor also means 'older': Juan es mayor que Silvia. (Juan is older than Silvia.)
pequeño, -a, -os, -as	menor, -es	El daño será **menor** si se lo dices. (The harm will be less if you tell him.) Note that menor also means 'younger': Silvia es menor que Juan. (Silvia is younger than Juan.)

👁 Note, however, that the regular form of the comparatives above is also possible, although the meaning is slightly different:

> Juan es **más bueno/más malo** que su hermano. (implies moral characteristics) (Juan is kinder/naughtier than his brother.)

> Juan es **mejor/peor** que su hermano. (implies physical or intellectual characteristics) (Juan is better/worse than his brother.)

Menor can be replaced by más pequeño:

> Juan es **menor/más pequeño** que Tomás. (Juan is younger/smaller than Tomás.)

But mayor can only be replaced by más grande to mean larger (not older):

> Juan es **más grande** que Enrique. (Juan is bigger than Enrique.)

Level 2

How to say 'more and more' and 'less and less'

'more and more' cada vez más	Es **cada vez más** antipático. (He is more and more unfriendly.)
'less and less' cada vez menos	Es **cada vez menos** amable. (He is less and less polite.)

Level 2 | **How to say 'the more'/'the less' . . . 'the more'/'the less'**

Expressions such as 'the more/the less . . . the more/the less . . .' are translated as:

the more . . . the more . . .	*cuanto más . . . más*	***Cuanto más*** *amable es* Juan, ***más*** *grosero parece José.* (The more polite Juan is, the ruder José seems.)
the less . . . the less . . .	*cuanto menos . . . menos*	***Cuanto menos*** *nos veamos,* ***menos*** *discutiremos.* (The less we see of each other, the less we'll argue.)
the more . . . the less . . .	*cuanto más . . . menos*	***Cuanto más*** *dinero gana,* ***menos*** *quiere gastar.* (The more he earns, the less he wants to spend.)
the less . . . the more . . .	*cuanto menos . . . más*	***Cuanto menos*** *gordo estés,* ***más*** *sano te encontrarás.* (The less overweight you are, the healthier you'll feel.)

Ejercicios

 Level 1 | **1** Fill in the gaps to make comparative sentences, using *más . . . que*:

Mi cama no es muy cómoda. La tuya es **más cómoda que** la mía.

   a Tu coche es muy pequeño. El mío es . . . el tuyo.
   b Este queso es caro. Es . . . el jamón.
   c Esta chaqueta roja es muy bonita. Es . . . el jersey.

Level 1 | **2** Now do the same, but this time using irregular comparatives:

   a Mi idea no es buena. La tuya es . . .
   b El colesterol es malo, pero el tabaco es . . .

 Level 1 | **3** Look at the picture of the Solís family. Then write six sentences using the adjectives provided saying in which way the daughter, Cristina, on the right, is just like each of her parents.

| rubia • alta • ~~deportista~~ • delgada • pecosa • aventurera |

Ejemplo

Cristina es tan deportista como su padre.

4.4 The superlative

The relative superlative

The forms 'the most . . .' and 'the least . . .' are called the relative superlative, because they identify a particular element as having the highest or lowest degree of a quality amongst a group.

> *El examen de fin de curso es el más difícil de todos.* (The end-of-year exam is the most difficult of all.)

definite article + comparative adjective (+ *de* + noun clause)	*el más rápido* (the fastest) *Juan es el menos hablador de los hermanos.* (Juan is the least talkative of the brothers.)
definite article + comparative adjective (+ *que* + verb clause)	*Tomás es el mejor pianista que conozco.* (Tomás is the best pianist I know.)

👁 Note that Spanish uses *de* where English uses *in* in expressions such as *el más grande de Europa* (the biggest in Europe).

The absolute superlative

The absolute superlative intensifies the quality. In English, the following are absolute superlatives: It's a **very funny** film. I have read a **most interesting** book.

In Spanish, the absolute superlative is formed as follows:

muy + adjective	*Es una película **muy** divertida.* (It's a very funny film.)
adjective + *-ísimo/-ísima/-ísimos/-ísimas*	*Es una película divertid**ísima**.* (It's a very funny film.)

Irregular absolute superlatives

The following irregular forms can be used as absolute superlatives:

Adjective	Comparative	Absolute superlative	Example
bueno	*mejor*	**óptimo**	*Está en condiciones **óptimas**.* (He is in peak condition.)
malo	*peor*	**pésimo**	*Está de un humor **pésimo**.* (She is in a dreadful mood.)
grande	*mayor*	**máximo**	*Le otorgaron el **máximo** galardón.* (She was awarded the highest honour.)
pequeño	*menor*	**mínimo**	*No tengo el **mínimo** interés en saber de su vida.* (I haven't got the slightest interest in knowing anything about his life.)
alto	*superior*	**supremo**	*Tiene autoridad **suprema**.* (He has supreme authority.)
bajo	*inferior*	**ínfimo**	*Lo compré por una cantidad **ínfima**.* (I bought it for a negligible amount.)

Informal absolute superlatives

The following prefixes are used in colloquial language to express the absolute superlative:

super-	*Es una chica* **super***guapa*. (She's a really pretty girl.)
extra-	*Fuma cigarrillos* **extra***largos*. (He smokes extra long cigarettes.)
archi-	*Es* **archi***millonario*. (He's a multimillionaire.)
requete-	*El pastel estaba* **requete***bueno*. (The cake was really good.)

Ejercicios

1 What do you know about world records? Transform the prompts on the left to make the title of each world record, and then match each title with the correct answer from the second column.

Ejemplo

Edad/licenciado/joven/del mundo
La edad del licenciado más joven del mundo.

a Edad/licenciado universitario/joven/del mundo
b Nación con/número de aparatos telefónicos por cabeza
c Altura/montaña/alta del sistema solar
d Longitud/tendedero de ropa/largo del mundo
e Edad/persona/vieja del mundo
f Estatura/persona/alta del mundo
g Temperatura/fría/jamás registrada en el mundo

i 25 km
ii Mónaco
iii 24.160 km
iv 89,2 grados bajo cero
v 10 años y 4 meses
vi 122 años
vii 2,72 metros

Level 2

2 Read the following headlines from the Spanish newspaper *El País* and underline the irregular superlatives.

> ### Un informe avisa del pésimo estado de las infraestructuras de EEUU

> El gobierno elimina la distancia mínima entre gasolineras en carretera

> La Bolsa de Tokio cae a un mínimo de 16 años

> Hollywood asume con impotencia y máxima expectatión la temida huelga de actores

4.5 Comparison of adverbs, nouns and verbs

Adverbs, nouns and verbs can be used in comparative structures, as well as adjectives.

Adverbs

Adverbs are compared in the same way as adjectives:

Superiority	*más* + adverb + *que*	*Camina **más lentamente que** yo.* (She walks more slowly than I do.)
Inferiority	*menos* + adverb + *que*	*Canta **menos fuerte que** yo.* (She sings less loudly than I do.)
Equality	*tan* + adverb + *como*	*Habla **tan deprisa como** yo.* (She talks as fast as I do.)

Irregular comparatives of adverbs

The following adverbs have irregular comparatives:

bien → *mejor*	*Habla inglés **mejor** que tú.* (He speaks English better than you do.)
mal → *peor*	*Se ha portado **peor** de lo que me esperaba.* (She behaved worse than I expected.)

Nouns

Nouns are compared as follows:

Superiority	*más* + noun + *que*	*Tiene **más** dinero **que** yo.* (She has more money than I have.)
Inferiority	*menos* + noun + *que*	*Hay **menos** niños y niñas **que** antes.* (There are fewer children than before.)
Equality	*tanto, -ta, -tos, tas* + noun + *como*	*No hay **tanto** vino **como** creía.* (There isn't as much wine as I thought.) *Han venido **tantas** personas **como** ayer.* (There have been as many people as (there were) yesterday.)

Verbs

Verbs are compared as follows:

Superiority	verb + *más que*	*Habla **más que** yo.* (He talks more than I do.)
Inferiority	verb + *menos que*	*Come **menos que** antes.* (He eats less than (he did) before.)
Equality	verb + *tanto como*	*Sabe **tanto como** cualquier otro experto en el tema.* (He knows as much as any other expert on the subject.)

The more . . . the more . . .

Expressions such as *the more . . . the more . . .* with adverbs or verbs follow the same construction as those expressions with adjectives, e.g. *Cuanto menos come, más adelgaza.* (The less he eats, the more weight he loses.)

☞ To revise the comparison of adjectives go to Section 4.3.

Note that with nouns, *cuanto* needs to agree in gender and number with the noun it modifies: *Cuantas más tonterías dice, más caso le hacen.* (The more silly things he says, the more they listen to him.)

Ejercicios

Level 2

1 Complete the following mini-dialogues with comparatives of adverbs as in the example.

Ejemplo

–Yo toco **mal** el piano, pero tú tocas peor que yo.
–No, no es verdad. Yo no toco el piano (mal/tú) tan mal como tú.

a   –Yo hablo **rápido**, pero mi hermana habla . . .
    –No, no es verdad, no habla (deprisa/tú)

b   –Yo como **despacio**, pero mi hijo come . . .
    –No, no es verdad, nadie come (despacio/tú)

c   –Mi marido habla **bien** italiano, pero yo hablo . . .
    –No, no es verdad. No hablas (bien/él)

Level 2

2 Compare the place you live in or where you come from with a Spanish-speaking town you know. Use the nouns in the box.

> cines • museos • pubs • parques • jardines • tráfico • contaminación • sol • frío

Ejemplo

En mi ciudad hay menos cines que en Madrid.

Level 2

3 Write 5 sentences comparing members of your family. Use comparatives of verbs, adverbs or nouns as in the example.

Ejemplo

Mi hija duerme más que yo, y se levanta más tarde. ¡Pero no duerme tanto como mi hijo!

Level 2

4 Translate the following into Spanish.

The more I learn the more I forget.
The more I forget the less I know.
The less I know, the more I have to study.
But the more I study, the more I forget . . .

5 Personal pronouns

Personal pronouns – *los pronombres personales* – are words which can take the place of a noun (e.g. 'The mechanic is looking at the car. **He** needs to find out what's wrong with **it**': 'He' and 'it' are pronouns which stand for 'the mechanic' and 'the car' respectively). The following sections deal with the different types of personal pronouns, which are summarised in the following table. The symbol ☞ shows you which sections to consult for further information on each type of pronoun.

Person	Subject pronoun	Direct object pronoun	Indirect object pronoun	Reflexive pronoun
	☞ Section 5.1.	☞ Section 5.3.	☞ Section 5.4.	☞ Section 22.5.
First person singular	*yo*	*me*		
Second person singular	*tú* (vos)	*te*		
	usted	*lo/le/la*	*le*	*se*
Third person singular	*él* *ella*	*lo/le* *la*	*le*	*se*
First person plural	*nosotros* *nosotras*	*nos*		
Second person plural	*vosotros* *vosotras*	*os*		
	ustedes	*los/les/las*	*les*	*se*
Third person plural	*ellos* *ellas*	*los/les* *las*	*les*	*se*

5.1 Subject pronouns

Subject pronouns – *los pronombres sujeto* – as their name indicates, are pronouns that stand for the subject of a sentence.

Form

(🌍) Subject pronouns are an area where Peninsular Spanish differs slightly from American Spanish varieties.

☞ You can find more information about this in Section 5.2, Forms of address.

Regional varieties

Second person pronouns are slightly different in Spain and Spanish America. Within Spanish America itself there are also two trends. These varieties have been summarised in the table below. Note that all other persons (other than the second person singular and plural) **are the same** in all varieties of Spanish.

	Spain	Spanish America	
		Tuteo	Voseo
First person singular (I)	*yo*		
Second person singular (you)	*tú* (familiar) *usted* (formal)	*tú* (familiar) *usted* (formal)	*vos* (familiar) *usted* (formal)
Third person singular (he/she/it)	*él/ella*		
First person plural (we)	*nosotros/nosotras*		
Second person plural (you)	*vosotros/vosotras* (familiar) *ustedes* (formal)	*ustedes* (familiar and formal)	*ustedes* (familiar and formal)
Third person plural (they)	*ellos/ellas*		

(🌍) Note that in many parts of Andalucía, in Southern Spain, and in the Canaries, the system used is the same as in most of Spanish America.

☞ For more information on the *vos* form, see Section 5.2.

Él/ella expressing he/she/it

(👁) Notice that in English there are three third person singular pronouns: 'he', 'she' and 'it'. In Spanish, as all nouns are either masculine or feminine, 'he', 'she' and 'it' can only be rendered by two forms, *él* and *ella* respectively, which can refer to things as well as to people.

(👁) In Spanish there is a neuter subject pronoun, *ello*, which can be used to refer to an idea rather than a thing. However, it is rarely used, and if a neuter pronoun is necessary, it is better to use *esto* or *eso*:

Esto sucedió el martes pasado. (It happened last Tuesday.)

Verb form for *usted/ustedes*

Notice that although *usted* and *ustedes* refer to the second person ('you'), they take third person verb endings, which is why they usually appear with *él/ella* in verb tables.

> *Usted habla español. Ustedes hablan español.* (You speak Spanish.)

☞ See the verb tables in the Appendix to see how *hablar* is conjugated. It is a regular verb ending in -*ar* so it follows the same pattern as *atar*.

Abbreviation of *usted* and *ustedes*

In writing, and especially in formal documents such as business letters, *usted* and *ustedes* are often abbreviated. Notice that these abbreviations always have capital letters:

> usted: Ud./Vd.
> ustedes: Uds./Vds.

Nosotros/vosotros/ellos to include both masculine and feminine

Notice that, as with nouns, the masculine plural of the subject pronouns is used to refer to groups that contain both male and female elements:

> *Nosotros somos peruanos.* (We are Peruvian.)

Nosotros could refer to men, or to both men and women.

> *Ellos no quieren venir.* (They don't want to come.)

Here too, *ellos* could refer to men or to both men and women.

Use

👁 In Spanish, subject pronouns are rarely used in everyday conversation. In English, subject pronouns show who or what the subject of the verb is referring to, but in Spanish the verb endings provide this information, so the pronoun is not necessary:

> *Tengo dos hermanos.* (**I** have two brothers.)

> *¿Tienes frío?* (Are **you** cold?)

In Spanish, subject pronouns are used for four main purposes:

To show emphasis	*¿**Tú** qué opinas?* (What do *you* think?) *¿**Ella** te dijo eso?* (Did *she* tell you that?)
For contrast	***Ella** habla tres idiomas, pero **yo** sólo uno.* (She speaks three languages, but I only speak one.)

For clarity	*–Tiene mucho dinero.* *–¿Quién, **ella?*** *–No, **él**.*
To avoid confusion when the same verb ending corresponds to more than one grammatical person	*Mi hermana y yo éramos muy distintas:* **yo era** *rubia y **ella era** morena.* (My sister and I were very different: I was blonde and she was dark.)

Subject pronouns with *ser*

 Notice that with the verb *ser* in expressions such as *Soy yo,* the subject pronoun is used in Spanish. In English, the object pronoun would be used, e.g. 'It's me'.

Ejercicios

Level
1

1 Identify the subject of each verb in the present indicative. If there is more than one possible subject pronoun for that verb form, give all of them.

Ejemplo

canta: él, ella, usted

a   Estamos en casa.
b   ¿Viven en París?
c   Eres mi amigo.
d   Tengo tres hijos.

Level
1

2 Your sister and you are very different. Make sentences comparing yourselves as in the model:

Ejemplo

Yo tengo los ojos azules pero ella tiene los ojos verdes.

Yo . . .	Mi hermana . . .
tengo los ojos azules	tiene los ojos verdes
tengo un gato	tiene un perro
vivo en Madrid	vive en Miami
estoy casado, -a	está divorciada
soy rubio, -a	es morena

Level
1

3 Read the following sentences in English, and then look at the Spanish translations. Add the subject pronoun if it is needed to show emphasis or contrast.

Ejemplo

I am a doctor, but he is a dentist.
Yo soy médico, pero él es dentista.

a   Do you speak Italian?
    ¿ . . . hablas italiano?
b   Most people seem to have a computer. Do *you* have one?
    La mayoría de la gente tiene ordenador. ¿ . . . tienes uno?

c I work from 9 to 5, but he works only in the mornings.
    . . . trabajo de 9 a 5, pero . . . trabaja sólo por la mañana.
d I leave the house at 8 o'clock and I arrive in the office at 9.
    . . . salgo de casa a las 8 y . . . llego a la oficina a las 9.
e *She* told you that? She's mad!
    ¿ . . . te dijo eso? ¡ . . . está loca!

5.2 Forms of address

Spanish has two forms of address equivalent to the English 'you', *tú* (or *vos* in some parts of Spanish America) and *usted*.

The use of *tú* (or *vos*) and *usted*, and *vosotros*, *-as* and *ustedes*, is different in Spain and Spanish America. However, throughout the Spanish-speaking world, the choice between the different forms of address, *tú* (or *vos*) and *usted*, depends on a number of variables:

* the level of familiarity between the speakers;
* courtesy (resulting from differences in age, for instance);
* the closeness/distance between the speakers (which can be psychological or affective);
* the level of informality/formality of the situation;
* the feeling of solidarity that may exist between the speakers (e.g. between people who share the same social class, ideological belief, profession or social group, such as a sports team or school);
* issues of power (such as differences in status or authority).

In general, people who are familiar with each other, who are close to each other, who have an informal relationship or who share some feeling of solidarity use the 'familiar' *tú* (or *vos* – see below), whereas *usted* is used by interlocutors to indicate distance, courtesy, formality or differences in the power relation.

Except in the case of interaction between children and older people, where the child might use *usted* and the older person *tú*, the form of address is usually reciprocal. Calling someone *tú* is called *tutear*, using *vos* is called *vosear*, and calling someone *usted* is called *tratar de usted*.

The Spanish norm

The Peninsular norm used in most parts of Spain is as follows:

To convey familiarity, closeness, informality or solidarity	*tú*	*vosotros, vosotras*
To convey distance, courtesy, formality or a power relation	*usted* (+ verb in the third person singular)	*ustedes* (+ verb in the third person plural)

🌐 Note however that in Andalucía, in Southern Spain, and in the Canary Islands, *ustedes* is often used instead of *vosotros/as*. Also, in Andalucía *ustedes* is often used with the verb form for *vosotros/as* (second person plural): **¿Ustedes queréis** comer algo? (Would you like something to eat?). In Peninsular Spanish the form would be **¿Vosotros queréis** comer algo? (informal) or **¿Ustedes quieren** comer algo? (formal).

The Spanish American norm

There are two main norms in Latin America, that of the countries where *tú* is used, and that of the countries where *vos* is used.

(a)   Spanish American countries using *tú (la América tuteante)*

Tú is predominant throughout Spanish America.

To convey familiarity, closeness, informality or solidarity	*tú*	*ustedes* (+ verb in the third person plural)
To convey distance, courtesy, formality or a power relation	*usted* (+ verb in the third person singular)	

(b)   Spanish American countries using *vos (la América voseante)*

Vos is used in many parts of Spanish America, but is especially common in the area of the River Plate (Argentina, Uruguay, Paraguay).

To convey familiarity, closeness, informality or solidarity	*vos*	*ustedes* (+ verb in the third person plural)
To convey distance, courtesy, formality or a power relation	*usted* (+ verb in the third person singular)	

The forms of the verb with *vos* vary slightly from area to area, but in the main region using *vos,* the area of the River Plate, the verb forms in the three conjugations are:

		-ar	-er	-ir
Indicative	Present	*cantás*	*comés*	*venís*
	Past simple	*cantaste*	*comiste*	*viniste*
	Future	*cantarás*	*comerás*	*vendrás*
Subjunctive	Present	*cantes/cantés*	*comas/comás*	*vengas/vengás*
Imperative		*cantá*	*comé*	*vení*

Ejercicios

Level 1

1 Read the following sentences and decide if the forms of address correspond to the Spanish norm, the Latin American norm, or both. If the form of address corresponds to the Latin American norm, decide if the use is from the *América tuteante* or from the *América voseante*.

    a   Pilar y Juan, vosotros venís en mi coche.
    b   ¿Vos sabés dónde está Eduardo?
    c   (Un padre hablando a sus hijos) He dicho que ustedes no pueden ir al cine esta noche, así que no hay más de que hablar.
    d   ¿Tienes fuego?
    e   Ustedes son colombianos, ¿no es cierto?

Level 2

2 Read the following extract from the story *El Sordo* by Argentinian author Roberto Fontanarrosa. Underline the examples of the use of *vos*, as well as the verbs in the *vos* form.

> El tipo apareció de improviso, ante la indiferencia general, por detrás de la columna. Se inclinó por sobre el hombro del sordo, lo tocó en un brazo y le dijo "Quiero hablar con vos". El sordo levantó la vista, lo miró con el ceño fruncido como si no lo conociera, pegó una ojeada sobre los otros componentes de la mesa y amagó una evasiva. [. . .]
>
> —Yo a vos . . . ¿te conozco?
>
> —Sí, me conocés . . .
>
> —Porque, vos acá aparecés . . . —sobrevoló la información del Sordo— . . . me venís a buscar a la mesa, me presionás para que venga a hablar con vos . . . Me hacés levantar de la mesa donde . . .
>
> —Sí me conocés . . .
>
> (Roberto Fontanarrosa (1995), 'El sordo', en *La mesa de los galanes y otros cuentos*, Ediciones de la Flor, SRL)

Level 2

3 Now read the previous extract and change the text so that you use *tú* (and its corresponding verb form) instead of *vos*.

Level 1/2

5.3 Direct object pronouns

Direct object pronouns – *los pronombres de objeto directo* – are pronouns that are used to replace the direct object:

> *Veré a **Enrique** mañana.* (I will see **Enrique** tomorrow.) → ***Lo** veré mañana.* (I will see **him** tomorrow.)

> *María ha comprado **una moto**.* (María has bought **a motorcycle**.) → *María **la** ha comprado.* (María has bought **it**.)

In the previous sentences, *Enrique* and *una moto* are the direct objects, and *lo* and *la* are the direct object pronouns.

Form

In Spanish, the direct object pronouns are:

me	*Ana **me** ve*. (Ana can see **me**.)
te	***Te** veo*. (I can see **you**.)
lo (for masculine people and things) *le* (for masculine people in some parts of Spain) *la* (for feminine people and things)	***Lo** veo*. (I can see **him/it/you**.) ***Le** veo*. (I can see **him/you**.) ***La** veo*. (I can see **her/it/you**.)
nos	*Juan **nos** ve*. (Juan can see **us**.)
os	***Os** veo*. (I can see **you**.)
los (for people and things) *las* (for feminine people and things) *les* (for people in many parts of Spain)	***Los** veo*. (I can see **them/you**.) ***Las** veo*. (I can see **them/you**.) ***Les** veo*. (I can see **them/you**.)

As you have seen, in many parts of Spain it is common to use the pronouns *le* and *les* instead of *lo* and *los,* a practice known as *leísmo*. Notice that this is only acceptable when the pronoun refers to males, but not to things or animals:

> ***Le** vi esta mañana.* → ***Lo** vi esta mañana.* (I saw him this morning.)
> *No puedo ver**les** hoy.* → *No puedo ver**los** hoy.* (I can't see them (or you) today.)

For the use of *ustedes* see Section 5.2.

Use

General rule	
In most cases, the direct object pronoun is placed before the verb whose object it is. Notice that in English, on the other hand, the direct object pronoun is placed after the verb.	***Te** veo*. (I can see **you**.) *No **los** compres*. (Don't buy **them**.)

Exceptions	
In the following cases, the direct object pronoun goes **after** the verb and is **attached to it** (these are called '**enclitic** pronouns'):	
Affirmative commands	*¡Ábre**lo**!* (Open it!)
Constructions with the infinitive	*Tengo que ver**la***. (I need to see her.)

Exceptions	
Constructions with the gerund	*Estoy llamándolos ahora.* (I am calling them now.) 👁 Notice how the pronoun is attached to the verb, but notice also that a written accent needs to be added so the stress on the main part of the verb remains the same: gerund: *llamando* (stress on -*an*) gerund + pronoun: *llamándolos* (stress and written accent on -*án*)
If the infinitive or gerund is preceded by a **finite** verb, the pronoun can be placed **before** the finite verb.	*Tengo que verla.* → **La** *tengo que ver.* *Estoy llamándolos ahora.* → **Los** *estoy llamando ahora.* *No quiero hacerlo.* → *No **lo** quiero hacer.*

Personal *a* before the direct object

If a direct object refers to a thing, it follows the verb directly, without using the personal *a*.	*Estoy viendo la televisión.* (I'm watching television.)
If it refers to a specific person, it is preceded by personal *a*.	*Estoy buscando **a** mi hija.* (I'm looking for my daughter.) 👁 But note that the personal *a* is not used with nouns referring to people who are not specific: *Estoy buscando un carpintero.* (I'm looking for a carpenter.) 👁 Note that the personal *a* is not usually used with *tener*: *Tengo tres hermanos.* (I have three brothers.)
The personal *a* is also used with:	
alguien, *nadie*, *alguno*, *ninguno* and *cualquiera*	*No veo **a** nadie.* (I can't see anyone.) *¿Conoce **a** alguien que pueda instalar la cocina?* (Do you know anyone who can plumb in the cooker?)
A number that refers to people	*¿A cuántas personas has invitado? **A** veinte.* (How many people have you invited? Twenty.)

👁 Note that when the direct object is a pronoun, the personal *a* disappears:

Estoy llamando a Ana. (I'm phoning Ana.) → *La estoy llamando.*

☞ See Unit 12 for more on the preposition *a*.

Ejercicios

1 Assert your authority over these unruly children! Tell them to do it right now, as in the example.

Ejemplo

—Lava los platos.
—No tengo ganas.
—¡Lávalos ahora mismo!

a —Haz los deberes.
  —Estoy viendo la tele.
  —¡ . . . ahora mismo!
b —Recoge tu ropa.
  —Es que estoy escuchando música.
  —. . .
c —Apaga la luz.
  —No, es que estoy leyendo.
  —. . .

Level 1/2

2 Answer the following questions using the prompt in brackets, as in the example:

Ejemplo

¿Quién está leyendo este libro? (yo). Lo estoy leyendo yo/Estoy leyéndolo yo.

a ¿Quién está viendo la tele? (nosotros)
b ¿Quién está preparando los bocadillos? (Miguel)
c ¿Quién está ordenando estas fotos? (Cristina)
d ¿Quién está haciendo un café? (yo)
e ¿Quién está cortando el césped? (Raquel)

Level 1/2

3 You are a bit behind with your chores. Answer the questions following the example.

Ejemplo

¿Compraste la leche? No, todavía tengo que comprarla/No, todavía la tengo que comprar.

a ¿Llamaste a Enrique?   e ¿Viste a Teresa?
b ¿Recogiste el paquete?   f ¿Terminaste la colada?
c ¿Fregaste los platos?   g ¿Escribiste las cartas?
d ¿Mandaste el mensaje?   h ¿Pagaste los recibos?

Level 1/2

5.4 Indirect object pronouns

Indirect object pronouns – *los pronombres de objeto indirecto* – are pronouns that stand for the indirect object, i.e. the person or object that benefits from an action or receives something as a result of it.

> *¿Mandaste una tarjeta **a Esther**?* (Did you send Esther a postcard?) → *¿**Le** mandaste una tarjeta?* (Did you send her a postcard?)

Note that a direct object pronoun and an indirect object pronoun can appear in the same sentence: I gave **it** to **her.**

☞ For information on the order of object pronouns go to Section 5.6.

Form

In Spanish, the indirect object pronouns are:

| me | **Me** *escribió una carta.* (He wrote me a letter.) |
| te | **Te** *mandó un ramo de rosas.* (He sent you a bunch of roses.) |

le	**Le** *di un beso.* (I gave him a kiss (or her, or you (formal)).
nos	**Nos** *cantaron una canción.* (They sang us a song.)
os	**Os** *mandé las fotos de la boda.* (I sent you the wedding photos.)
les	**Les** *conté la noticia.* (I told them (or you) the news.)

Use

General rule	
In general, the indirect object pronoun goes before the verb. 👁 Notice that in English, on the other hand, it goes after the verb.	**Me** *regaló un libro.* (He gave **me** a book.)

Exceptions	
In the following cases, the indirect object pronoun goes **after** the verb and is **attached to it** (these are called '**enclitic** pronouns'). You will notice that these rules are the same as those that apply to the direct object pronouns. (☞ Section 5.3.)	
Affirmative commands	*¡Dame el libro!* (Give me the book!)
Constructions with the infinitive	*Tengo que daros la dirección.* (I need to give you the address.)
Constructions with the gerund	*Estoy contándole el chiste.* (I am telling her the joke.) 👁 Notice how the pronoun is attached to the verb, but notice also that a written accent needs to be added so the stress of the main part of the verb remains the same: gerund: *contando* (stress on *-an*) gerund + pronoun: *contándole* (stress and written accent on *-án*)
If the infinitive or gerund is preceded by a finite verb, the pronoun can be placed **before** the finite verb.	*Tengo que darte las fotos.* → **Te** *tengo que dar las fotos.* (I have to give you the photos.)

Ejercicios

Level
1/2

1 Replace the indirect object in brackets with an indirect object pronoun.

Ejemplo

Escribió una carta (a su madre) → *Le escribió una carta.*

  a Contó un secreto (a mí).
  b Luisa, quiero pedir un favor (a ti).
  c Mandaron un paquete (a sus tíos).
  d Regalaste unas flores (a la abuela).

Level
1/2

2 Now do the same, but remember that all these sentences are imperatives:

Ejemplo

Cuenta qué te pasó (a Marta) → *Cuéntale qué te pasó.*

a   Recuerda que tengo que ir al dentista (a mí).
b   Da el libro (a Juan).
c   Explica cómo se llega a la estación (a ellos).
d   Enseña las fotos (a nosotras).

5.5 Object pronouns with prepositions

When a pronoun follows a preposition (e.g. *con él* (with him), *para mí* (for me), etc.), some special forms are used in Spanish, notably *mí* and *ti* for 'me' and 'you':

> *para mí* (for me)
> *de ti* (from you)

Form

After a preposition use the following personal pronouns:

	Preposition	Object pronoun	Example
First person singular	*a*	*mí*	*¿Es **para mí?*** (Is it for me?)
Second person singular	*de* *en* *hacia* *para* *sobre*	*ti* *(vos)* *usted*	*Estoy pensando **en ti/en usted**.* (I'm thinking about you.)
Third person singular		*él* *ella* *(ello)*	*Caminó **hacia él**.* (She walked towards him.)
First person plural		*nosotros* *nosotras*	*Nos está hablando **a nosotros**.* (He is talking to us.)
Second person plural		*vosotros* *vosotras* *ustedes*	*Estamos hablando **de vosotras**.* (We are talking about you.)
Third person plural		*ellos* *ellas*	*Me acuerdo mucho **de ellos**.* (I think about them a lot.)

Use of *sí*

The third person reflexive *sí* is used when the subject and the object pronouns refer to the same person. It can be followed by *mismo, -ma*.

> —*Siempre está pensando **en sí misma**.* (She's always thinking **about herself**.)
> —*No es cierto, dijo **para sí**.* ('It's not true', he said **to himself**.)

Use of *yo* and *tú* after some prepositions and adverbs

With the following prepositions and adverbs, you should use *yo* and *tú* rather than *mí* and *ti*. The rest of the **persons** are the same as for other prepositions.

como	Es **como yo**. (She is like me.)
según	**Según tú**, no había mucha gente. (According to you there weren't many people.)
salvo/excepto/menos	Todos vinieron **menos tú**. (They all came except for you.)
entre	**Entre él y yo** no hay nada. (There is nothing going on between him and me.)

Level 3

The preposition *con*

The preposition *con* functions like other normal prepositions (*con él, con nosotros,* etc.), except in the following cases:

First person singular	*conmigo*: with me *conmigo (mismo, -ma):* with myself	Ven **conmigo**. (Come with me.) Estoy hablando **conmigo misma**. (I'm talking to myself.)
Second person singular	*contigo*: with you *contigo (mismo, -ma):* with yourself	Quiero ir contigo. (I want to go with you.)
Reflexive use	*consigo (mismo/misma)*: with himself/herself/yourself (formal) *consigo (mismos/mismas)*: with themselves/yourselves	Está enfadado consigo mismo. (He is angry with himself.) ¿Está usted hablando consigo mismo? (Are you talking to yourself?) Están irritados consigo mismos. (They are annoyed with themselves.)

Ejercicios

Level 2

1 Fill in the gaps using the object pronoun given in the prompts.

    a Quiere escribir un libro sobre . . . (me)
    b No me esperaba eso de . . . (you)
    c Nadie me escucha salvo . . . (you)
    d Dicen que piensan mucho en . . . (me)
    e Estas flores son para . . . (you)
    f Decoramos el salón entre mi hermana y . . . (me)

Level 2

2 Fill in each gap by translating the prompt in brackets into Spanish.

    a Quiere hablar . . . (with them)
    b ¿Quieres casarte . . . ? (with me)
    c Estamos muy contentos . . . (with her)
    d ¿Señorita, puedo bailar . . . ? (with you)

Level 3

3 Now do the same, but beware that these are all reflexive cases.

    a Alicia está muy contenta . . . (with herself)
    b Estoy enfadada . . . (with myself)
    c Están furiosos . . . (with themselves)
    d Veo que estáis furiosos . . . (with yourselves)

Level 2

5.6 Order of object pronouns

Verbs often have a direct and an indirect object pronoun. In the sentence *Compró un regalo para vosotras* (He bought a present for you), *un regalo* (a present) is the direct object (DO), and *para vosotras* (for you) the indirect object (IO). If the objects are replaced by object pronouns, the sentence becomes *Os lo compró* (He bought it for you) (order: IO + DO + verb).

◉ Notice how in Spanish, when there are two object pronouns together, the indirect object comes before the direct one. In English, the order is reversed.

Se replacing *le* or *les*

The **indirect object** pronouns *le* and *les* become *se* **before the direct object** pronouns *lo, la, los* and *las*.

Escribí	*una carta*	*a mi madre* →	*Le*	*escribí*	*una carta*	→	*Se*	*la*	*escribí.*
	DO	IO		IO	DO		IO	DO	

I wrote	my mother	a letter →	I wrote	her	a letter	→ I wrote	it	to her.
	IO	DO		IO	DO		DO	IO

Se: avoiding ambiguity

A sentence such as *Se lo dije* can be ambiguous, as it could mean any of the following: *a ella, a él, a usted, a ellos, a ellas* or *a ustedes*.

In such cases, it is common to clarify the meaning of *se* as in the following example: *La doctora **se** lo explicó **a ella*** (The doctor explained it to her).

Order of object pronouns

When different object pronouns appear in a group, they go in the following order:

1	2	3	4
se	te, os	me, nos	lo, la, los, las, les

Examples

Se lo expliqué. (I explained it to him/her/them/you (polite).)
Te lo avisé. (I warned you about it.)
Mi madre me las regaló. (My mother gave them to me.)
¡Dímelo! (Tell me (it)!)
¡No te nos vayas! (Don't go!) (expresses familiarity and endearment)

Affirmative commands, and constructions with the infinitive and the gerund

Double object pronouns follow the same rules as direct and indirect object pronouns in affirmative commands and in constructions with the infinitive and the gerund.

☞ For more information go to Section 5.3 and 5.4.

👁 Notice that a written accent is needed for the stress to remain on the same syllable as it would be on without the pronouns.

Affirmative commands	¡Dá**selos**! (Give them to him/her!)
Constructions with the infinitive	Tengo que explicár**telo**. (I need to explain it to you.)
Constructions with the gerund	Está enseñándo**melo** ahora. (She is showing it to me now.)
If the infinitive or gerund is preceded by a finite verb, the pronoun can be placed **before** the finite verb.	Tengo que decír**selo**. → **Se lo** tengo que decir. Estoy mandándo**tela** ahora. → **Te la** estoy mandando ahora. No quiero explicár**oslo**. → No **os lo** quiero explicar.

Ejercicios

Level 2

1 People are so demanding! But you are really efficient: tell them you've already done it, by filling in the gaps with the correct indirect and direct object pronouns, as in the example.

Ejemplo

—¿Cuándo le vas a decir a Juan que no vienes?
—Ya **se lo** he dicho.

a —¿Cuándo vas a darle el mensaje a Cristina?
   —Ya . . . he dado.
b —¿Cuándo vas a prestarle las herramientas a Juan?
   —Ya . . . he prestado.
c —¿Cuándo va a explicarle el problema a los niños?
   —Ya . . . he explicado.
d —¿Cuándo vas a entregarle el trabajo a tu jefe?
   —Ya . . . he entregado.

Level 2

2 Children can be so spoilt – and parents so strict! Fill the gaps with the indirect and direct object pronouns, as in the example.

Ejemplo

—Quiero esta muñeca. ¡Cómpra**mela**!
—No, no voy a comprár**tela**./No, no **te la** voy a comprar.

a —Quiero este juego. ¡Cómpra . . . !
   —No, . . .

b   —Quiero estas patatas fritas . . .

—No, . . .

c   —Carlitos y yo queremos esta bicicleta . . .

—No, . . .

d   —Carlitos y yo queremos unos videojuegos . . .

—No, . . .

6 Demonstratives

Demonstratives are words that indicate the person or thing referred to. There are two sorts of demonstratives – demonstrative adjectives: *este coche* (**this** car); and demonstrative pronouns: *¿Qué es esto?* (What's **this**?).

In English, 'this' (and 'these') is used to refer to things or people that are close to the speaker, and 'that' (and 'those') is used for things and people that are distant. In Spanish, there are three types of demonstratives: *este, ese* and *aquel* (with their respective feminine and plural forms).

<table>
<tr><td>Level 1</td><td colspan="4">**Form**</td></tr>
</table>

Masculine singular	este	ese	aquel
Feminine singular	esta	esa	aquella
Masculine plural	estos	esos	aquellos
Feminine plural	estas	esas	aquellas
Example	Me gustan **estos** cestos. (I like these baskets.) **Este** es mi favorito. (This is my favourite.)	¿Me pasas **ese** plato? (Could you pass me that plate?) **Esos** son distintos. (Those are different.)	Prefiero **aquel** jarrón. (I prefer that vase (over there).) **Aquel** es muy bonito. (That one (over there) is very pretty.)

<table>
<tr><td>Level 2</td><td>**The neuter demonstrative pronoun**</td></tr>
</table>

There is also a neuter demonstrative, which functions only as a pronoun:

　　esto　　　*eso*　　　*aquello*

It is used to refer to inanimate things without specifying their gender (meaning 'this thing'):

　　Esto es una brújula. (This is a compass.)

It is also used to talk about ideas, concepts or abstract things:

　　Eso es lo que yo quiero. (That's what I want.)

👁 The neuter form (*esto, eso, aquello*) can only be a pronoun. The masculine and feminine can be either a pronoun or an adjective, although in either case they are spelt the same. Note, however, that in the past demonstrative pronouns had an accent to differentiate them from demonstrative adjectives:

> *Estos cuadros son muy interesantes, pero el que más me gusta es **aquél**.*
> (These paintings are very interesting but I like that one better.)

Nowadays it is only necessary to write the accent on the demonstrative pronoun if the sentence might be ambiguous, but that is not very likely. You will still, however, come across the accent on the pronouns in many written texts.

Use
Reference to space and time

Level 1

The three demonstratives (*este, ese* and *aquel*) refer to different relationships in terms of space and time.

Demonstrative	Relation to space		Relation to time	
este, esta, estos, estas	**Close to the speaker in space**	*Este libro es interesante.* (This book is interesting.)	**Close to the speaker in time**	*No puedo ir este jueves.* (I can't make it this Thursday.)
ese, esa, esos, esas	**Close to the listener in space**	*¿Cómo se llama ese libro?* (What's that book called?)	**Close to the listener in time**	*Ese día no me conviene.* (That day is not convenient for me.)
aquel, aquella, aquellos, aquellas	**Remote from the speaker and listener in space**	*Aquellos coches hacen mucho ruido.* (Those cars (over there) are very noisy.)	**Remote from the speaker and listener in time**	*Aquellos años fueron estupendos.* (Those years were fantastic.)

Derogatory connotations

Level 3

The demonstratives can be used to convey derogatory connotations, as they can convey a psychological distancing from the referent:

> *Por ahí viene **ese** imbécil.* (Here comes that idiot.)
> *Esa es una bruja.* (She's a real witch, that one.)

With this derogatory meaning, the demonstrative adjectives can also be placed **after** the noun (notice that the noun will then need an article):

> *No me hables de **las** chicas **esas**.* (Don't talk to me about those girls.)
> *No me vengas con **la** excusa **esa** de que no tienes tiempo.* (Don't come to me with that excuse about not having time.)

How to say 'the latter' and 'the former'

Este and *aquel* can be used to mean 'the latter' and 'the former' respectively:

> *El director y el secretario general asistieron a la reunión. **Este** habló mucho, mientras que **aquel** no dijo nada.* (The director and the general secretary attended the meeting. The latter talked a lot, whereas the former did not say a word.)

Notice that *este* refers to the noun that is closer to it (i.e. *el secretario general*), and *aquel* to the one that is further away (i.e. *el director*).

Ejercicios

Level 1

1 Put the following sentences in the plural by making the words in bold plural.

  a **Ese niño está** en clase de Inés.
  b **Esta es mi prima**.
  c Pruébate **esa falda**.
  d **Aquella chica que viene** por ahí **es mi vecina**.

Level 1

2 Alicia is shopping for clothes and her friend Clara is helping her decide what to buy. Read the following dialogue between the two friends and fill in each gap with the correct demonstrative using the prompts in brackets:

> Alicia: ¿Qué te parece . . . (this) vestido?
> Clara: Es mono, pruébatelo. Pero, ¿por qué no te pruebas también . . . (that) falda?
> Alicia: ¿Cuál?, ¿ . . . (this one) de rayas?
> Clara: No, . . . (that one) de flores que está detrás.
> Alicia: Ah, sí, es bonita. Mira, y me voy a probar también . . . (this) otro vestido rojo.

7 Possessives

Possessives – *los posesivos* – are words that indicate possession or belonging, such as **mis** *libros* (**my** books) or *Es **mío*** (It's **mine**).

7.1 Possessive adjectives

Possessive adjectives – *los adjetivos posesivos* – agree in gender and number with the nouns they accompany.

Possessive adjectives before a noun

Possessives can replace the article to express possession: *el coche* (the car) → **mi** *coche* (my car).

Possessive adjective	Example
mi, mis	**mi** *coche* (my car), **mis** *amigos* (my friends)
tu, tus	**tu** *casa* (your house), **tus** *cosas* (your things)
su, sus	**su** *trabajo* (= *el trabajo de él*: his job; = *el trabajo de ella*: her job; = *el trabajo de usted*: your job) **sus** *hijos* (= *los hijos de él*: his children; = *los hijos de ella*: her children; = *los hijos de usted*: your children)
nuestro, nuestra, nuestros, nuestras	**nuestro** *dinero* (our money); **nuestra** *salud* (our health); **nuestros** *amigos* (our friends); **nuestras** *bicicletas* (our bicycles)
vuestro, vuestra, vuestros, vuestras	**vuestro** *dinero* (your money); **vuestra** *salud* (your health); **vuestros** *amigos* (your friends); **vuestras** *bicicletas* (your bicycles)
su, sus	**su** *trabajo* (= *el trabajo de ellos*: their job; = *el trabajo de ellas*: their job; = *el trabajo de ustedes*: your job) **sus** *hijos* (= *los hijos de ellos*: their children; = *los hijos de ellas*: their children; = *los hijos de ustedes*: your children)

👁 Notice that in Spanish, unlike in English, possessive adjectives agree with the gender and number of the thing possessed:

nuestras *bolsas* → our bags (because the thing possessed is feminine and plural).

nuestro *equipaje* → our luggage (because the thing possessed is masculine and singular).

Su: avoiding ambiguity

Su can have several possible meanings. If the context is not clear, this can lead to ambiguity.	The sentence: *¿Cuál es **su** coche?* could mean any of the following: Which is ***his/her/your*** (*de usted* or *de ustedes*)/**their** car?
To ensure there is no ambiguity, *su* can be replaced by one of the following.	***de él/de ella*** (or ***de* + the owners**): *el coche de él/el coche de José/el coche de ella/ el coche de mi madre* ***de usted***: *el coche de usted* ***de ellos/de ellas/de ustedes*** (or ***de* + the owners**): *el coche de ellos/el coche de mis padres/el coche de mis hermanas*

Cases in which the possessives are not used

👁 The most common cases are with items of clothing and parts of the body. Note that in such cases, the possessives are used in English.	*Se pusieron **los** abrigos.* (They put **their** coats on.) *Ponte **los** guantes.* (Put **your** gloves on.) *Se rompió **la** pierna.* (He broke **his** leg.) *Me lavé **el** pelo.* (I washed **my** hair.)
👁 Similarly, the possessive adjective is used to denote 'one's own' in English, but the article is preferred in Spanish.	*Enseñaron **los** pasaportes.* (They showed **their** passports.)

☞ See Section 3.1 for these uses of the definite article.

Possessive adjectives after a noun

When the possessive adjective is used after the noun, the noun has to keep its article: ***un** amigo **mío*** (a friend of mine).

Form

Adjective	Example
mío, mía, míos, mías	*unos libros **míos*** (some books of mine)
tuyo, tuya, tuyos, tuyas	*la pluma **tuya*** (your pen)
suyo, suya, suyos, suyas	*el coche **suyo*** (his/her/your car)
nuestro, nuestra, nuestros, nuestras	*las cosas **nuestras*** (our things)
vuestro, vuestra, vuestros, vuestras	*un amigo **vuestro*** (a friend of yours)
suyo, suya, suyos, suyas	*una hija **suya*** (one of their/your daughters)

Use

Possessive adjectives after a noun are used as follows:

To emphasise who the owner is	*Este libro **mío** no lo cojáis.* (Don't take this book of mine.)
To emphasise the fact that the thing possessed is one of a group	*Es un amigo **mío**.* (He is a friend of mine, i.e. I have several friends, and he is one of them.)
When the noun is preceded by *algún, ningún, cualquier, cada, mucho, poco, varios, más, menos* ☞ See Unit 9.	*Cualquier idea **suya** suele ser interesante.* (Any idea of his is usually interesting.) *He conocido a muchos amigos **suyos**.* (I have met many of his friends.)
Before *nada* and *algo* ☞ See Units 9 and 25.	*No quiero nada **suyo**.* (I don't want anything of his.) *Creo que tienes algo **nuestro**.* (I think you have something of ours.)

Ejercicios

1 Fill in the gaps with the correct possessive adjective.

    a ¿Te gusta . . . piso? (my)
    b Elisa ha perdido . . . maletas. (her)
    c Lo más importante es la salud de . . . hijas. (our)
    d No entiendo a . . . madre. (his)

2 Translate the following sentences into Spanish.

    a Some friends of mine are coming.
    b This handbag is yours.
    c I haven't got anything of hers.
    d You have many books of mine.

7.2 Possessive pronouns

Possessive pronouns – *los pronombres posesivos* – replace a noun (and the possessive adjective that may accompany it) and indicate possession:

> *Mi casa es más grande que **la tuya*** (i.e. *que tu casa).* (My house is bigger than yours (i.e. than your house).)

Form

In Spanish, possessive pronouns have the same form as the possessive adjective after a noun (☞ see Section 7.1), but without the noun that the adjective accompanies:

Possessive pronouns	
el mío, la mía, los míos, las mías (my)	el nuestro, la nuestra, los nuestros, las nuestras (our)
el tuyo, la tuya, los tuyos, las tuyas (your)	el vuestro, la vuestra, los vuestros, las vuestras (your (Spain))
el suyo, la suya, los suyos, las suyas (his, her, its, your (formal))	el suyo, la suya, los suyos, las suyas (their, your (formal, Spain; formal and informal, Latin America))

👁 Possessive pronouns agree in gender and number with the possessed thing, not with the person that possesses them:

–*El coche de Juan es muy grande, ¿y **el de Ana?*** (Juan's car is very big. And Ana's?)

–***El suyo** también.* (Hers too.) *(El suyo is masculine because coche is masculine.)*

Level 2

Lo mío/tuyo/suyo . . .

The neuter article *lo* can be used with a possessive pronoun, as in the following examples.	***Lo nuestro*** *tiene que acabar.* (Our relationship/affair has to finish.) ***Lo vuestro*** *está en el coche.* (Your things are in the car.) ***Lo suyo*** *es la música clásica.* (His thing is classical music.)

Ejercicios

Level 1

1 Fill in the gaps with a possessive pronoun, as in the example.

Ejemplo

Estás contento con tu trabajo, pero yo no estoy contento con **el mío.**

 a Este es tu periódico. . . . está en la cocina.
 b Estas son tus gafas. . . . no las encuentro.
 c ¿Me prestas tu diccionario? . . . me lo dejé en casa.
 d Tus hijas son buenas estudiantes, pero . . . no.

Level 1

2 Answer the questions following the example. You may want to revise the units on the comparative before you do this exercise.

Ejemplo

—Mi pueblo es muy bonito. ¿Y el tuyo?
—**El mío es más bonito que el tuyo.**

 a —Mi casa es muy grande. ¿Y la tuya?
 b —Mi jardín tiene muchas flores. ¿Y el tuyo?
 c —Mi calle es muy agradable. ¿Y la tuya?
 d —Nuestros vecinos son muy simpáticos. ¿Y los vuestros?

8 Numerals

There are two types of numerals: cardinal numbers – *los numerales cardinales* – which correspond to a series *(uno, dos, tres . . . : one, two, three . . .)*, and ordinal numbers – *los numerales ordinales* – which refer to the order in a series *(primero, segundo, tercero . . . : first, second, third . . .)*.

Numerals can be adjectives or pronouns:

> *Tiene tres coches.* (He has three cars.): adjective

> *Los tres están en el garaje.* (All three are in the garage.): pronoun

8.1 Cardinal numbers

<table>
<tr><td>Level
1</td></tr>
</table>

0 cero	10 diez	20 veinte	30 treinta
1 uno	11 once	21 veintiuno	31 treinta y uno
2 dos	12 doce	22 veintidós	32 treinta y dos
3 tres	13 trece	23 veintitrés	33 treinta y tres
4 cuatro	14 catorce	24 veinticuatro	40 cuarenta
5 cinco	15 quince	25 veinticinco	50 cincuenta
6 seis	16 dieciséis	26 veintiséis	60 sesenta
7 siete	17 diecisiete	27 veintisiete	70 setenta
8 ocho	18 dieciocho	28 veintiocho	80 ochenta
9 nueve	19 diecinueve	29 veintinueve	90 noventa

100 cien	500 quinientos, -tas	1.000 mil
101 ciento uno	600 seiscientos, -tas	2.000 dos mil
200 doscientos, -tas	700 setecientos, -tas	10.000 diez mil
300 trescientos, -tas	800 ochocientos, -tas	1.000.000 un millón
400 cuatrocientos, -tas	900 novecientos, -tas	

Gender

> *El número ganador es **el 625**.* (The winning number is 625.)
>
> *El uno no toca nunca.* (Number one never wins.)

In general, numbers are masculine in Spanish, but see below for further information.

Uno, un, una

Uno becomes *un* when it appears before a masculine noun or a feminine noun beginning with a stressed *a-* or *ha-*.	*¿Cuántos libros quieres? Uno.* (How many books would you like? One.) *Quiero un libro y tres cuadernos.* (I would like one/a book and three notebooks.) *Solo hemos visto un águila.* (We have only seen one eagle.)
When *uno* is part of another number, it becomes *un* before a masculine noun or a feminine noun beginning with a stressed *a-* or *ha-*.	*Hay treinta y un niños en la clase.* (There are thirty-one children in the class.)
'One' takes the feminine form if accompanying or referring to a feminine noun.	*una cerveza y una bolsa de patatas fritas* (a/one beer and a/one packet of crisps) *¿Cuántas cervezas, una o dos? Una.* (How many beers, one or two? One.)
Other numbers ending in 'one' also take the masculine or the feminine form.	*treinta y un invitados* (31 guests)/*treinta y una entradas* (31 tickets)

One word or two?

Note that from 16 to 29, numbers are contracted to one word.	16: *dieciséis*
After 29, they are written separately.	34: *treinta y cuatro*

Hundreds

When counting, the number 100 is *cien*.	*los números del uno al **cien*** (numbers 1 to 100)
👁 Unlike in English, *cien* is not preceded by an article.	*Había **cien** personas.* (There were a hundred people.)
In numbers from 101 to 199, the word used is *ciento*.	***ciento** un dálmatas* (101 dalmatians) 150: ***ciento** cincuenta*
Ciento is also used to express percentages.	*cincuenta por ciento de descuento* (50% discount) Except in the expression '100%': ***cien por cien***
Numbers in the hundreds agree in gender with the noun they accompany.	*doscient**os** niños* (two hundred boys) *doscient**as** casas* (two hundred houses)

Thousands

The word *mil* (one thousand) is invariable, as in English.	*dos mil* (two thousand)
It can appear in the plural in the expression *miles de*, 'thousands of', as in English.	*miles de turistas* (thousands of tourists)
👁 Unlike English, *mil* is not preceded by an article.	*Cuesta mil dólares*. (It costs a thousand dollars.)
In the expression 'one hundred thousand', the shortened form *cien* is used. Other hundreds of thousands revert to the form ciento.	*cien mil; doscientos mil* (or **doscientas mil**)

Millions

👁 Although 'million' is invariable in English (e.g. two million), in Spanish the plural form is used in expressions of two million or more.	*dos millones* (two million)
👁 Note that the expression 'one million + noun' is *un millón de + noun*.	*un millón de personas* (one million people) *cuatrocientos millones de hispanoparlantes* (400 million speakers of Spanish)

🌍 In Spain, *un billón* is a million million, although in Spanish America it is often the same as a US billion (i.e. a thousand million).

Punctuation of numbers

👁 In Spain, numbers in the thousands are separated by a full stop, not a comma, as they are in English.	*mil quinientos* is written *1.500* (not 1,500 as in English)
👁 Conversely, in decimals, commas are used in Spain where full stops are used in English.	*0,5 (cero coma cinco)* (as opposed to 0.5 (nought point five) in English)
🌍 However, in parts of Latin America, the same convention as in English is applied.	

Expressing dates

👁 Dates in Spanish are expressed in cardinal numbers, not in ordinal numbers as in English. ☞ For the use of the article, see Section 3.1.	*Mi cumpleaños es el dos de junio.* (My birthday is on 2nd June.) *el 25 (veinticinco) de abril* (25th April)

Saying telephone numbers

In Spanish, telephone numbers are said in tens whenever possible.	82 07 50: *ochenta y dos, cero siete, cincuenta* 575 68 16: *cinco setenta y cinco, sesenta y ocho, dieciséis* 091: *cero noventa y uno*

Ejercicios

Level 1

1 Read aloud the following shopping list, using the masculine or feminine as appropriate.

```
1 kilo de naranjas
1 bolsa de patatas
100 gramos de paté
1 paquete de té
1 botella de vino
200 gramos de queso
1 docena de huevos
1 barra de pan
```

Level 1

2 Say the following telephone numbers in Spanish:

81 62 17   257 46 14   94-886 83 24   00-34-91-250 77 28

Level 1

3 Now say your own telephone number in Spanish.

Level 1

4 Match the date with the historical event, and then say the date out loud.

(a) 12 de octubre de 1492	(i) Se firma el armisticio y termina la Primera Guerra Mundial.
(b) 23 de abril de 1616	(ii) Los Estados Unidos lanzan una bomba atómica sobre Hiroshima.
(c) 11 de noviembre de 1918	(iii) Muere Miguel de Cervantes, autor de El Quijote.
(d) 6 de agosto de 1945	(iv) Cristóbal Colón llega a América.

Level 1

8.2 Ordinal numbers

Ordinal numbers are those that indicate order or succession: *primero, segundo, tercero . . .* (first, second, third . . .).

Form

The most common ordinal numbers in Spanish are:

| primero | segundo | tercero | cuarto | quinto |
| sexto | séptimo | octavo | noveno | décimo |

General remarks

| Ordinal numbers agree in gender and number with the noun they accompany. | *la primera puerta a la izquierda* (the first door on the left)
el segundo libro del autor (the second book by the author) |

The masculine forms *primero* and *tercero* drop the 'o' in front of a noun.	*su primer hijo* (his first son) *el tercer milenio* (the third millennium)
Although there are ordinal numbers larger than *décimo*, they are seldom used in Spanish. Usually cardinal numbers are preferred.	*el piso doce* (the 12th floor) *el cincuenta aniversario* (the 50th anniversary) *su setenta y cinco cumpleaños* (her 75th birthday)

Use

Ordinals are used in Spanish in the following cases:

Naming kings, queens and popes (👁 Note that in Spanish they are written in Roman numerals.) • Numbers from 1 to 9 • With the number 10, the ordinal or the cardinal is possible • After 11, cardinal numbers are used	*Isabel II* (*Isabel segunda*) *Alfonso X* (*Alfonso décimo/diez*) *Pío XII* (*Pío doce*)
Naming centuries (👁 Note that in Spanish they are written in Roman numerals.) • from the 1st to the 9th AD, and from the 9th to the 1st BC • With the number 10, the ordinal or the cardinal is possible. • After 11, cardinal numbers are used.	*el siglo I a.C.* (*el siglo primero antes de Cristo*) *el siglo V* (*el siglo quinto*) *el siglo X* (*el siglo décimo/diez*) *el siglo XX* (*el siglo veinte*)

👁 Remember that in Spanish, cardinals are used to express the date:

el 23 de marzo (el veintitrés de marzo) 23rd March

☞ To revise this, go to Section 8.1.

Ejercicios

Level 1

1 Fill each gap with one of the words in the box.

> primer • primero • primera • segundo • segunda • tercero • tercera

    a   Tiene tres hermanas: la mayor se llama Sofía, la . . . Karen y la . . . Raquel.
    b   Juan es un niño muy inteligente. Siempre es el . . . de su clase.
    c   A ver, ¿en qué piso vive Pedro? Hay que subir tres pisos, y su puerta es la del medio, así que vive en el tercer piso. En el . . . B.
    d   Es la . . . vez que Carlitos va al circo.
    e   Febrero es el . . . mes del año.
    f   Le hizo mucha ilusión el nacimiento de su . . . nieto, porque quería ser abuela.

Level 1

2 Which of the following are Popes? Say their names aloud in Spanish:

a	León X	**d**	Pío XII	**g**	Luis XIV
b	Enrique VIII	**e**	Julio II	**h**	Juan XXIII
c	Luis XVI	**f**	Juan Pablo I		

8.3 Collective numbers and fractions

Collective numbers

Some common collective numbers – *numerales colectivos* – are:

un par (a couple/a pair)

una treintena (thirty, thirty-odd)

una decena (about ten)

un centenar/una centena (around a hundred)

una docena (a dozen)

un millar (around a thousand)

una veintena (twenty, twenty-odd)

When accompanying a noun, collective numbers are followed by *de*.	*una veintena **de** invitados* (twenty-odd guests) *un centenar **de** personas* (about 100 people) *dos docenas **de** huevos* (two dozen eggs)
Collective numbers, like any other collective noun, are usually singular.	***Viene** una docena de invitados*. (A dozen guests are coming.) 👁 Note that in Spanish the verb is in the third person singular.
However, because in meaning collective numbers imply more than one, they are often considered plural.	***Vienen** una docena de invitados*. 👁 Note that here the verb is in the third person plural.

Fractions

Fractions – *fracciones* – are expressed as follows:

$\frac{1}{2}$: *medio/media* (adjective) *la mitad* (noun)	*medio limón* (half a lemon) *media naranja* (half an orange) *la mitad de los niños* (half the children)
$\frac{1}{3}$: *un tercio* or *una tercera parte*	*un tercio de la población* (a third of the population) *dos tercios del total* (two thirds of the total)
$\frac{1}{4}$: *un cuarto* or *una cuarta parte*	*un cuarto de litro* (a quarter of a litre) *tres cuartas partes de los entrevistados* (three-quarters of those interviewed)
$\frac{1}{5}$: *un quinto* or *una quinta parte*	*una quinta parte de la herencia* (a fifth of the inheritance)
$\frac{1}{6}$: *un sexto* or *una sexta parte*; $\frac{1}{7}$: *un séptimo* or *una séptima parte*; $\frac{1}{8}$: *un octavo* or *una octava parte*; $\frac{1}{9}$: *un noveno* or *una novena parte*; $\frac{1}{10}$: *un décimo* or *una décima parte*	

With larger numbers, the suffix *-avo* is added to the number to make the fraction, e.g.

$\frac{1}{11}$: *un onceavo* $\frac{5}{12}$: *cinco doceavos*

Ejercicios

1 How many are there?

Ejemplo

cinco botellas	→	media **decena** de botellas
doce huevos	→	una . . . de huevos
seis niños	→	media . . . de niños
diez personas	→	una . . . de personas
ocho zapatos	→	cuatro . . . de zapatos
dos calcetines	→	un . . . de calcetines

2 Rephrase the following sentences so you express the quantities using a collective number with the same meaning.

a   Hay **unos 20 niños** en la clase.

b   **Unas cien personas** vinieron a la boda.

c   Había **unos treinta cuadros** del museo en la exposición.

d   Tengo **dos libros** nuevos muy buenos.

e   Tiene **40 zapatos** en el armario.

f   Para esta receta se necesitan **24 huevos**.

9 Indefinites

Level 1/2/3 Indefinite adjectives, pronouns or adverbs – *los indefinidos* – are types of word that refer to persons, animals, things, etc., which are not specific or clearly defined, e.g. *alguien* (somebody), *algo* (something), *alguna* (some). Many indefinites are quantifiers expressing greater or lesser degrees of imprecision, such as *bastante* ('enough' or 'quite') or *varios* ('several'). They are listed in alphabetical order in a common list for greater convenience.

Indefinite	Uses	Remarks
algo	*Tengo **algo** en el zapato.* (I have something in my shoe.) *¿Quieres **algo** de beber?* (Do you want anything to drink?)	An invariable pronoun that means 'something' or, in questions, 'anything'. It can also mean 'a bit': *Es algo coqueta.* (She is a bit of a flirt.)
alguien	*Necesito que **alguien** me acompañe.* (I need someone to come with me.) *¿Ha llamado **alguien**?* (Has anybody phoned?)	An invariable pronoun, always masculine and singular, which refers to an indeterminate person in the way 'somebody' or 'someone' (or 'anybody' or 'anyone' in questions) would in English.
alguno, -a, -os, -as	*Mira estos libros y dime si hay **alguno** que te interese.* (Have a look at these books and tell me if there is any that interests you.) ***Algún** día lo comprenderás.* (You'll understand it one day.) *He visto **alguna** de sus películas.* (I've seen some of his films.)	Pronoun or adjective. *Algún* is the shortened form when it is used as an adjective before a masculine noun. Followed by '*de* + noun phrase' it means one or several of a group.
bastante, -s	*Había **bastantes** coches.* (There were plenty of cars.)	Adjective or pronoun which can mean 'enough' or 'plenty'. The adverb *bastante* also exists, meaning 'enough' or 'quite a bit': *Ya he trabajado bastante por hoy.* (I have worked enough for today.)

Indefinite	Uses	Remarks
cada *cada uno/una* *cada cual*	***Cada*** *empleado tenía su propio despacho.* (Each employee had their own office.) ***Cada uno*** *fue en su propio coche.* (Each one went in their own car.) ***Cada cual*** *que haga lo que quiera.* (Let each one do their own thing.)	*Cada* is an invariable adjective, meaning 'each'. The forms *cada uno/una* and *cada cual are* pronouns, meaning 'each person'.
cualquiera	*Hoy en día* ***cualquiera*** *sabe programar el vídeo.* (Anyone knows how to programme a video recorder these days.) *¡****Cualquiera*** *se atreve!* (Who would dare!) ***Cualquier*** *niño sabe esas cosas.* (Any child knows that.) ***cualquier*** *niña* (any girl) ***Cualquiera*** *que sea su intención, no me fío de él.* (Whatever his intention, I don't trust him.) ***Cualesquiera*** *que sean sus intenciones . . .* (Whatever his intentions . . .)	Adjective or pronoun used to refer to an indeterminate person, animal or object, which doesn't need to be specific, similar to the meaning conveyed by 'anyone (from a group)'. The shortened form, *cualquier*, is used before a masculine or feminine noun. *Cualquiera que* is always followed by a verb in the subjunctive. Note that the plural, *cualesquiera*, can also be used in this construction.
demás	*Los* ***demás*** *ya han comido.* (The others have already eaten.) *Lo* ***demás*** *no me interesa.* (The rest doesn't interest me.)	An invariable form meaning 'the rest' or 'the other(s)', which must be preceded by a neuter or a plural definite article. Used with the neuter article (*lo*) it refers only to things, never to people.
demasiado, -a, -os, -as	*Tengo* ***demasiados*** *problemas.* (I have too many problems.)	Adjective or pronoun, meaning 'too', 'too much' or 'too many'. The adverb *demasiado* also exists meaning 'too much': *He comido demasiado.* (I've eaten too much.)
igual, -es	*Tenía* ***igual*** *afecto a todos sus nietos.* (She had the same affection for all her grandchildren.)	Adjective or pronoun meaning 'the same', 'equal' or 'similar'. The adverb *igual* exists as a variant of *igualmente*, e.g. *Pienso igual.* (I think the same (in the same way).)
mismo, -a, -os, -as	*Vinieron otra vez los* ***mismos*** *chicos.* (The same boys came again.)	Adjective or pronoun, meaning 'the same' or 'similar'. It must always be preceded by an article. Note the change of meaning if it follows the noun, when it is used to emphasize the identity of the noun it refers to: *La jefa misma está de acuerdo.* (The boss herself agrees.)

Indefinite	Uses	Remarks
mucho, -a, -os, -as	*Tiene **muchas** amigas.* (She has a lot of friends.)	Adjective or pronoun meaning 'much', 'many', 'a lot (of)'. It must precede the noun and can be followed by *de* (e.g. *muchos de mis amigos*). Except for very specific cases, it is not preceded by an article. The adverb form *mucho* exists, meaning 'a lot' or 'much', as in *Me gusta mucho.* (I like it a lot.)
nadie	***Nadie** se acercó a saludarla.* (Nobody came to say hello to her.)	An invariable pronoun meaning 'nobody' or 'no one' (or 'not . . . anyone/anybody' in negative or interrogative constructions). ☞ You can revise its use as a negative in Unit 25.
nada	*No quiero **nada** de comer.* (I don't want anything to eat.)	An invariable pronoun meaning 'nothing' or 'anything' (in negative or interrogative constructions). ☞ You can revise its use as a negative in Unit 25.
ninguno, -a, -os, -as	*He visto algunos vídeos interesantes, pero no me he comprado **ninguno**.* (I've seen some interesting videos, but I haven't bought any.) *No tengo **ningún** libro de Vargas Llosa.* (I haven't got any book by Vargas Llosa.) *No me gusta **ninguna** de sus películas.* (I don't like any of his films.)	Adjective or pronoun, meaning 'no' (+ noun), 'none' or 'any' (in negative or interrogative constructions). *Ningún* is the shortened form when it is used as an adjective before a masculine noun. Followed by '*de* + noun phrase' it means 'none of', 'neither of' or 'any of' (a group). ☞ You can revise its use as a negative in Unit 25.
otro, -a, -os, -as	*Vino el cartero y trajo **otra** carta de tu madre.* (The postman came and brought another letter from your mother.) *La **otra** carta llegó ayer.* (The other letter arrived yesterday.)	Adjective or pronoun, meaning 'another' or 'other(s)'. 👁 Note that it is never used with an indefinite article, although it can be used with a definite one. The definite article is used when referring to somebody or something specific.
poco, -a, -os, -as	*Había **pocos** peces en el río.* (There were few fish in the river.) *Tengo unos **pocos** ahorros.* (I have a few savings.)	Adjective or pronoun meaning 'little', 'few' or 'a few'. 👁 Notice the difference between *pocos* (few) and *unos pocos* (a few). It can be followed by *de*, as in *un poco de azúcar* (a bit of sugar), *Pocos de mis amigos se atrevieron a saltar.* (Only a few of my friends dared to jump.) The adverb *poco* exists, meaning 'a little', e.g. *Me duele poco.* (It hurts only a little.)

Indefinite	Uses	Remarks
semejante, -es	No entiendo **semejante** cosa. (I don't understand such a thing.)	Adjective or pronoun, which can mean 'similar' or 'such (a)'.
tal, -es	Había **tales** colas en todas partes que nos fuimos. (There were such queues everywhere that we left.) Te ha llamado un **tal** Fernando. (A certain Fernando called you.)	Most commonly an adjective. It means 'such (a)'. Very frequent in the construction 'tal + noun + que . . .' to express intensity. Used with an indefinite article before a person's name it means 'a certain'.
todo, -a, -os, -as	He leído **todo** el libro. (I have read all the book.) He leído **todos** sus libros. (I have read all of his books.) **Toda** persona ha de ser respetada. (Every person has to be respected.) Es **todo** un hombre. (He's a real man.) Al llegar a casa estaba **toda** mojada. (When she got home she was all wet.)	Adjective and pronoun, meaning 'every', 'all' or 'the whole'. Most commonly followed by an article, a demonstrative or a possessive. Before a noun, todo/toda is a synonym of cualquier (toda persona = cualquier persona). In this idiomatic use, todo un . . . / toda una . . . means 'a real . . .' In this colloquial use, todo + adjective is a synonym of completamente.
uno, una	En esos casos, **uno** no sabe qué hacer. (In those cases, one doesn't know what to do.)	Pronoun with impersonal value, meaning 'one'. ☞ For its use in impersonal sentences see Section 23.1.
unos (cuantos), unas (cuantas)	He comprado **unas cuantas** revistas para el viaje. (I have bought a few magazines for the journey.)	Adjective or pronoun, meaning 'a few', similar to algunos, -as.
varios, -as	He visto **varios** vestidos bonitos, pero no he comprado ninguno. (I've seen several nice dresses, but I haven't bought any.)	Adjective or pronoun, most commonly used in plural, meaning 'several'. They precede the noun.

Ejercicios

Level 1

1 Fill in the gaps with the correct indefinite expression from the box.

mucho • todo • misma • poca • mismo • todos • uno

a   He visto cuatro veces la . . . película.
b   El verano que viene quiero veranear en el . . . sitio que el año pasado.
c   Cuando hace tanto frío, . . . ya no sabe ni qué ponerse.
d   He llegado tarde porque había . . . tráfico.
e   Había muy . . . gente en el cine.
f   He invitado a . . . mis amigos a la fiesta.
g   He preparado yo . . . el menú.

2 Select the correct alternative for each gap.

a ¡ . . . le pide al jefe que nos deje la tarde libre!
cada uno • cualquiera • cada cual

b . . . que suena el teléfono, me despierta.
cada vez • cada una • cualquiera

c . . . tiene que pensar en sí mismo.
cualquiera • cada • cada uno

d . . . que organice su propia vida.
cualquiera • cada cual • cada

3 What do the following proverbs mean? First underline the indefinites in each, then translate them literally into English, and finally give an equivalent proverb in English.

a Cada mochuelo a su olivo.
b Mucho ruido y pocas nueces.
c De tal palo tal astilla.
d No todo el monte es orégano.

10 Adverbs

Level 1/2 Adverbs – *los adverbios* – are invariable words that modify verbs, adjectives or other adverbs by saying how, where, when, how often or how much. The following are adverbs:

> *Es **muy** caro.* (It is very expensive.) (*muy* modifies the adjective, and says how expensive it is.)
>
> *Se levanta **demasiado temprano**.* (He gets up too early.) (Both *demasiado* and *temprano* are adverbs. *Temprano* modifies the verb *se levanta*, and explains when he gets up, and *demasiado* modifies the adverb *temprano*, and explains how early he gets up.)

In this unit you will find some of the most common adverbs. You will find it useful to learn them as vocabulary items.

Adverbs of quantity

Level 1

casi	*Casi no hay leche.* (There is **hardly** any milk.)
muy/mucho	*Está **muy** caliente.* (It's **very** hot.) *Amparo fuma **mucho**.* (Amparo smokes **a lot**.) Notice that *muy* is used before adjectives, participles or other adverbs and that *mucho* is used after verbs or before nouns.
poco	*María come **poco**.* (María eats **(very) little**.)
demasiado	*Hablas **demasiado**.* (You talk **too much**.)
más	*Sabe **más** que yo.* (She knows **more** than I do.)
menos	*Ahora llueve **menos**.* (Now it is raining **less**.)
tan/tanto	*¡Estoy **tan** cansada!* (I am **so** tired!) *¡Me gusta **tanto**!* (I like it **so much**!) Notice that *tan* is used before adjectives, participles or other adverbs, whereas *tanto* is used after verbs.

☞ Refer to Sections 4.3 and 26.5(d) for the use of *más, menos* and *tan/tanto* to express comparisons.

Adverbs of place

aquí	*Aquí hay demasiada gente*. (There are too many people **here**.)
acá	Ven *acá*. (Come **here**.) 🌎 In Spain, *acá* is more imprecise than *aquí*, and it is used mainly with verbs of movement and always after *más*: *más acá* (further over here). However, it is widely used in Latin America, where it is more common than *aquí*.
ahí	*Ponlo ahí*. (Put it **there**.)
allí	*Ponlo allí*. (Put it over **there**.) 👁 *Allí* implies that it is further than *ahí*, and that it is away from the speaker and the listener.
allá	*Ponlo allá*. (Put it over **there**.) 🌎 In Spain, as with *acá*, *allá* is more imprecise than *allí*, and it is used mainly with verbs of movement, and always after *más*: *más allá* (further over there). However, it is widely used in Latin America, where it is more common than *allí*. *Allá* can also signal distance in time: *allá por los años treinta* (**back** in the 1930s). It can also denote lack of interest: *Allá tú si no tienes un plan de jubilación*. (It's your problem if you don't have a retirement plan.)
dentro/adentro	*Miguel estaba dentro*. (Miguel was **inside**.) *Miguel volvió adentro*. (Miguel went back **inside**.) 🌎 In Spain, *adentro* is used with expressions of motion. In Latin America, *adentro* is used both with static positions (*Estaba adentro*) and with expressions of motion (*Volvió adentro*).
fuera/afuera	*Está esperando fuera*. (He is waiting **outside**.) *Vete afuera a ver qué es ese ruido*. (Go **out** and see what that noise is.) 🌎 As with *dentro* and *adentro*, in Spain *fuera* is used for static position, and *afuera* is used with expressions of motion. In Latin America, *afuera* is used with both.
arriba	*Vete arriba a buscar una toalla*. (Go **up** and get a towel.)
abajo	*Vete abajo a buscar un martillo*. (Go **down** and get a hammer.)
cerca	*La casa de Juan está muy cerca*. (Juan's house is very **near**.)
lejos	*Está demasiado lejos para ir andando*. (It's too **far** to walk.)
delante/adelante	*Si te pones delante, no puedo ver nada*. (If you stand **in front**, I can't see anything.) *Así no podemos ir adelante*. (We can't go **ahead** like that.) 🌎 As in previous cases, in Spain *delante* is used for static position, and *adelante* is used with expressions of motion. In Latin America, *adelante* is used with both.

Adverbs of time

ayer, hoy, mañana	*Vuelva usted mañana*. (Come back **tomorrow**.)
ahora	*Ahora mismo voy*. (I'll come **right away**.)
antes	*Antes no había tanto tráfico*. (**Before** there wasn't so much traffic.)

después	*Después del concierto fuimos a cenar*. (**After** the concert we went to have dinner.) *Primero fuimos al cine y después fuimos a cenar*. (First we went to the cinema and **afterwards** we went for dinner.)
entonces	*Entonces sonó el timbre*. (**Then** the bell rang.)
luego	*Luego me llamó por teléfono*. (**Then/Afterwards** he phoned me.)
nunca	*Nunca está en casa cuande le llamo*. (He's **never** at home when I call him.) Note that you can also say: *No está nunca en casa cuando le llamo*. ☞ See Unit 25 for more information on the negative construction.
siempre	*Siempre está ocupada*. (She's **always** busy.)
mientras (tanto)	*Yo preparo la ensalada y mientras (tanto), tú pon la mesa*. (I'll prepare the salad and **in the meantime** you lay the table.)
recientemente/ recién	*Se ha quedado viuda recientemente*. (She is **recently** widowed.) 🌎 In Spanish America, *recién* means 'just' or 'recently'. *Recién vino de México*. (He **just** arrived from Mexico.) In Spain, it only means 'recently' when used before a past participle: *La pared está recién pintada*. (The wall has **just** been painted.)
todavía	*Todavía falta mucho para las ocho*. (There is **still** some time to go before 8 o'clock.)
ya	*Ya he llamado a Inés*. (I have **already** called Inés.)

☞ For more information on these adverbs as connectors of time, go to Sections 26.5(h) and 26.6.

Todavía and ya

Level 1/2

 Todavía and *ya*, which can mean 'still', 'already' and 'yet', are often difficult for students of Spanish. The following tips might help you:

English	Spanish	Example
still	*todavía*	*Todavía está en casa*. (He is **still** at home.)
already	*ya*	*Ya está en casa*. (He is **already** home.)
yet	*ya*	*¿Ya has comido?* (Have you had lunch **yet**?)
not yet	*no . . . todavía*	*No he comido todavía*. (I haven't had lunch **yet**.)
no longer, no more	*ya no*	*Ya no tengo hambre*. (I am **no longer** hungry.)

☞ For the use of *ya* and *todavía* with the perfect tense, see Section 18.5.

Adverbs of manner

Level 1

así	*No me hables así*. (Don't talk to me **like that**.)
bien	*Canta muy bien*. (She sings very **well**.)

mal	*Cocino muy **mal**.* (I cook very **badly**.)
deprisa	*Conduces muy **deprisa**.* (You drive very **fast**.)
despacio	*Come más **despacio**, por favor*. (Eat more **slowly**, please.)

Bien, bueno, mal and malo

| *Bueno* and *malo* look similar to the adverbs *bien* and *mal*.
 👁 A common mistake for foreigners is to confuse adjectives and adverbs and use *bueno* for *bien*, *malo* for *mal*, and vice versa. | *Baila muy **bien** pero canta muy **mal**.* (He dances very **well** but he sings very **badly**.)
 *La comida es **buena**. Cocina muy **bien**.* (The food is **good**. She cooks very **well**.)
 *La carretera es **mala** y él conduce muy **mal**.* (The road is **bad** and he drives very **badly**.) |

Adverbs in -mente formed from adjectives

Many adverbs of manner in Spanish are formed by adding the **suffix** *-mente* to the feminine singular form of the adjective (or to the singular form in the case of invariable adjectives).		*rápido → rápida → rápidamente* (quickly) *fuerte → fuerte → fuertemente* (strongly) 👁 Note that when the adjective has a written accent, it is retained in the adverb.
Adverbs in *-mente* can sound clumsy in Spanish if too many are used together, so their meaning is often conveyed in other ways.	*de forma/de manera* (+ feminine adjective), *de modo* (+ masculine adjective), *con* (+ noun)	*Se comportó inteligentemente. → Se comportó de forma inteligente.* (He behaved intelligently.) *Nos habló groseramente. → Nos habló de modo grosero.* (He talked to us in a rude way.) *Nos contestó cortésmente. → Nos contestó con cortesía.* (He replied politely.)
Very often, usually in the spoken language and in some set phrases, some adjectives function as adverbs. In these cases, the masculine singular form of the adjective is used.		*Llegó rápidamente. → Llegó **rápido**.* (He arrived **fast**.) *Me lo dijo muy claramente. → Me lo dijo muy **claro**.* (He told me very **clearly**.) *hablar **alto*** (to talk loudly) *trabajar **duro*** (to work hard) *jugar **limpio*** (to play fairly) *jugar **sucio*** (to play unfairly)

Two adverbs in -mente together

| When two adverbs in *-mente* follow each other in a sentence and are joined by *y, o, ni, pero, sino*, the first one loses the suffix *-mente*. | *Me lo dijo **sencilla y claramente**.* (He told me **plainly and clearly**.)
 *Le contestó **firme pero cortésmente**.* (He answered her **firmly but courteously**.) |
| In English, an adverb in '-ly' can modify another adverb in '-ly'. In Spanish, an adverb in *-mente* should never be used to modify another adverb in *-mente*. | He spoke wonderfully clearly.
 Habló de un modo maravillosamente claro. (NOT: ~~maravillosamente claramente~~) |

Comparison of adverbs

☞ See Section 4.5 on the comparison of adverbs.

Ejercicios

1 Make the following adjectives into adverbs with *-mente*.

> elegante • especial • silencioso • tranquilo • sincero • profundo

2 Now write a sentence for each of the adverbs in the previous exercise.

3 Read the following text and fill each gap with an adverb from the box. Note that there are more adverbs than there are gaps.

> siempre • delante • mal • nunca • demasiado • rápidamente • mucho • despacio
> • casi • tarde • dentro

Martina **siempre** conducía . . . deprisa. Aquella mañana salió de casa más . . . que de costumbre. Dio un portazo al salir de casa, y se metió . . . en el coche. . . . le gustaba llegar tarde, y menos aún cuando tenía que ir a ver a algún cliente importante. Unos metros antes del cruce vio un camión que señalaba con el indicador para pararse . . . del supermercado. Lo adelantó sin mirar y ¡zas!, se dio con un coche que venía en sentido contrario. Afortunadamente, no le pasó nada. Menos mal que el otro iba bastante . . . Si no, podía haber sido más grave.

4 Cecilia and Miguel are getting things ready, as some friends are coming round for dinner. Fill the gaps with *ya* or *todavía*.

–¿ . . . has puesto la mesa?

–No, . . . no he terminado.

–Pero la cena . . . está preparada, ¿verdad?

–Sí, . . . está todo listo.

–Acaba de llamar a Elena y dice que . . . no han salido de casa.

–Menos mal, pensé que . . . estarían casi aquí.

–Bueno, pues entonces, déjame que te ayude a poner la mesa.

–Vale.

–Bueno, . . . está.

–. . . no hay nada más que hacer hasta que lleguen los demás.

11 Interrogatives

Interrogatives – *los interrogativos* – sometimes called 'question words', are special words which are used in questions to elicit specific information. Examples in English are 'who?', 'what?', 'where?', 'when?', 'how?', 'why?', 'whom?', 'which?', etc.

The main interrogatives in Spanish are presented in the following table. Notice that they always carry an accent.

¿Qué? (What?)	*¿Dónde?/¿Adónde?* (Where?/Where to?)
¿Cuál?/¿Cuáles? (Which?)	*¿Quién?/¿Quiénes?* (Who?)
¿Cómo? (How?)	*¿Por qué?* (Why?)
¿Cuándo? (When?)	*¿Para qué?* (What for?)
¿Cuánto?/¿Cuánta?/¿Cuántos?/¿Cuántas? (How much?/How many?)	

Word order

In interrogative sentences word order is normally inverted so that the verb comes before the subject. However, word order is quite free in Spanish and there are also regional differences.

In direct questions the interrogative is placed at the beginning of the sentence. (☞ See Unit 24 for more on the simple sentence.)	*¿**Adónde** va ese tren?* (Where's that train going to?) *¿**Por qué** me preguntaste el nombre de mi jefe?* (Why did you ask me my boss's name?)
In indirect questions the interrogative stands at the head of the subordinate clause.(☞ See Unit 26 to find out more about subordinate clauses; see Unit 27 for more on indirect speech.)	*No se sabe **quién** fue Juanito el Destripador.* (Nobody knows who Jack the Ripper was.) *No recuerda **dónde** escondió el testamento.* (He doesn't remember where he hid his will.)

¿Qué?

As a pronoun, *¿qué?* ('what?') refers to nouns as yet unidentified, unspecified or unknown. It has the sense 'what thing?', 'what object?' or 'what idea?' (but never 'what person?' in the sense of 'who?' – that is always *¿quién?*).	*¿**Qué** tienes en la mano?* (What have you got in your hand?) *No comprendo **qué** me estás diciendo.* (I don't understand what you're telling me.)

¿Qué? can combine with prepositions.	¿**En qué** estás pensando? (What are you thinking about?)
As an adjective, ¿qué? is used with nouns, and can refer to people as well as things, objects, ideas, etc. It can mean 'what type/sort of thing/object/idea/person', etc.	¿**Qué** ciudad es esa? (What city's that?) Queremos saber **qué** perfil tiene el consumidor de ese producto. (We want to know the profile of the consumer of that product.)

¿Quién?/¿Quiénes?

¿Quién?/¿quiénes? can only refer to people.	¿**Quién** no conoce el cuento de la liebre y la tortuga? (Who's never heard the story of the tortoise and the hare?)
The plural form ¿quiénes? shows the speaker expects, or knows there to be, more than one individual concerned.	¿**Quiénes** asistieron a la conferencia? (Who attended the lecture?)
¿Quién?/¿quiénes? can combine with prepositions. Note that they can be expressed in various ways in English, e.g. 'who', 'whom', 'whose' – ¿de quién? is the standard way of asking 'whose?' in Spanish.	¿**A quién** has visto en el supermercado? (Who(m) did you see in the supermarket?) ¿**Para quién** has comprado el chocolate? (Who(m) have you bought the chocolate for?) ¿**De quién** es el Rolls Royce amarillo? (Whose is the yellow Rolls-Royce?)

¿Cuál?/¿Cuáles?

¿Cuál?/¿cuáles? can refer to people or objects. It is used like ¿qué? but refers to specific nouns, i.e. which are either mentioned or understood by both speaker and listener(s).	—Esta semana pasada hemos visto ocho o nueve casas, pero todavía no hemos decidido **cuál** nos agrada más. —¿**Cuál** tiene mejores vistas? ('We've seen eight or nine houses in the last week, but we still haven't decided which we like best.' 'Which has got the best views?')
¿Cuál?/¿cuáles? is used when asking about options between specific nouns.	¿**Cuál** es la diferencia entre un policía nacional y un guardia civil? (What's the difference between a national police officer and a Civil Guard? – i.e., out of the range of possible differences?)
¿Cuál?/¿cuáles? can combine with prepositions.	¿**A cuáles** de los suministradores se ha enviado un pedido últimamente? (Which of the suppliers have been sent an order lately?)

¿Qué? or ¿cuál?

English speakers can sometimes find the difference between ¿qué? and ¿cuál? confusing. The following guidelines will help clarify their uses.

When dealing with pronouns, ask yourself what the sentence actually means	
• If the interrogative has the sense 'which of a range (of possible objects/people/ideas, etc.)', use ¿cuál?	No recordábamos **cuál** era más antigua, la civilización griega o la asiria. (We couldn't remember which was the older, Greek civilisation or Assyrian.)

• If, however, it does not restrict its frame of reference to a particular group or range (whether overtly stated or merely implied), use *¿qué?*	*¿Qué* desea? (What would you like? – i.e., anything is possible) Compare this example with the following: *¿Cuál* desea? (Which would you like? – i.e., the range of choice is specified in or by the context)

🌐 In Spain *¿cuál?* is not used as an adjective; *¿qué?* is always used in this position: *¿Qué consejos me daría?* (What advice would you give me?) *No habían decidido* **qué** *casa comprar.* (They hadn't decided which house to buy.) (*cuál* in Spanish America)

¿Cómo?

¿Cómo? means 'how?' 👁 It is a common mistake to take *¿cómo?* to mean 'how much . . .?/how many . . .?', etc. Note that for these *¿cuánto?* should be used.	*¿Cómo funciona el lavaplatos?* (How does the dishwasher work?) *No nos explicamos* **cómo** *sobrevivieron al terremoto.* (We can't understand how they survived the earthquake.)
When enquiring about characteristics, or the intrinsic nature of something, *¿cómo?* corresponds to the English 'what . . . like?'	*¿Cómo es su marido?* (What's her husband like?)
In the spoken language, *¿cómo?* can sometimes mean 'why?' or 'how come?' Note that this usage is colloquial and that the tone conveyed is normally one of frustration, anger or rebuke.	*¡Que has perdido el documento! ¿Cómo no me llamaste para decírmelo?* (You've lost the document! Why didn't you phone and tell me?) *¿Cómo dejaste el bolso en el autobús?* (How come you left your handbag on the bus?)

¿Cuándo?

¿Cuándo? means 'when?'	*No se sabe con exactitud* **cuándo** *se extinguió el último dinosaurio.* (It's not known exactly when the last dinosaur died out.)
Cuándo can combine with prepositions.	*¿Hasta cuándo te vas a quedar?* (When are you going to stay till?)

¿Dónde?/¿Adónde?

¿Dónde? means 'where?' and refers to position in space as well as motion towards a place.	*¿Dónde está la biblioteca?* (Where's the library?)
¿Dónde? can combine with prepositions.	*¿De dónde venimos, adónde vamos?* (Where do we come from, where are we going to?)
¿Adónde? can only mean motion towards a place, in the sense of 'where to?'	*¿Adónde fueron de vacaciones?* (Where did they go for their holiday?)

¿Cuánto?/¿Cuánta?/¿Cuántos?/¿Cuántas?

¿Cuánto? means 'how much?' or 'how many?', and can be used as a pronoun or an adjective. When used as an adjective it agrees in number and gender with the noun(s) which it describes.	*¿Cuánto vale este cinturón de cuero?* (How much is this leather belt?) *¿Cuántas personas esperas invitar?* (How many people are you hoping to invite?)

Cuánto can combine with prepositions.	*Le preguntamos al viejo marinero **en cuántos** barcos había servido, pero no lo recordaba.* (We asked the old sailor how many ships he had served on, but he couldn't remember.)

¿*Por qué*? and ¿*para qué*?

¿*Por qué*? is the principal way of asking 'why?' in Spanish. It differs from the lesser used ¿*para qué*? in that it refers to the cause of an action or event, whilst ¿*para qué*? alludes to its purpose, intention or objective. Compare the following pairs of questions and answers.	*–¿**Por qué** has comprado un nuevo coche? –Porque el viejo ya no funciona.* ('Why did you buy a new car?' 'Because the old one doesn't work any more.') *–¿**Para qué** has comprado un nuevo coche? –Para ir de viaje por Europa, como siempre he soñado con hacer.* ('What did you buy a new car for?' 'To travel around Europe, like I've always dreamt of doing.')

Algunos chistes
¿Cuál es el santo que menos ve?
(Casimiro)
¿Qué le dijo un pez al otro?
(Nada, hijo, nada.)
¿Qué le dijo la cuchara a la
gelatina? (¿Por qué tiemblas,
cobarde?)

Ejercicios

1 Form complete, meaningful sentences by selecting one element from each of the three columns.

Los mismos físicos no comprenden	por qué	costó el proyecto
El pirata no recordaba	dónde	ganaron los Premios Nóbel
El director explicó	cómo	había escondido la plata
No hemos oído ninguna noticia sobre	quiénes	había decidido dimitir
El gobierno no sabe	cuánto	funciona la luz

2 Complete the following sentences with either *qué, cuál* or *cuáles*.

a ¿ . . . libro vas a comprar?
b ¿ . . . de estos libros vas a comprar?
c ¿Usted se acuerda de . . . coche estaba aparcado delante de la joyería justo antes del robo?
d ¿A . . . público está dirigido el producto?
e ¿ . . . has elegido, las rojas o las verdes?

3 Look at the following statements, which are all answers to questions. Write the questions.

   a Fuimos a las Baleares.
   b Decidimos comprar la más moderna.
   c Pues, es blanca, fría y se derrite con el calor.
   d Creo que fue Gabriel García Márquez.
   e Lo compré para poder hablar algo cuando vaya a Italia en verano.

4 Imagine that you could put any five questions to any person, alive or dead, real or fictional. Whom would you choose? And what five questions would you ask him/her? Try to use different interrogatives for each question.

12 Prepositions

A preposition – *una preposición* – is a word which is placed before (literally, pre-posed) another word or phrase in order to show the relationship between the words which come before or after it, e.g. *El gato está durmiendo **sobre** la mesa* (The cat is sleeping **on** the table.). Prepositions can express all sorts of relationships: figurative or literal, temporal or spatial.

In this unit the main prepositions in Spanish are treated in alphabetical order, followed by an overview of the most common compound prepositions.

A

Personal a: this must be used when referring to specific people as direct objects. It has the effect of 'humanising' them, showing some kind of emotional bond between the subject and object of a verb.	*¿Conoces **a mi mujer**?* (Do you know my wife?)
It is also used with pronouns (negative and indefinite) denoting people, even if their identity is not specified.	*No encontré **a nadie**.* (I didn't meet anyone.)
It is used with animals that are personalised, but not when they are viewed dispassionately, or as commodities.	*Dorotea quiere mucho **a sus perros**.* (Dorotea really loves her dogs.) (Compare with *Odio los perros* – I hate dogs.)
To express the idea of motion, in whichever direction	*Fueron **al teatro**.* (They went to the theatre.) *Subió **al Aconagua** el año pasado.* (He climbed Mount Aconagua last year.)
To show the idea of direction towards something or someone	*'Salida **a la calle**'* ('Exit to the street')
To introduce an indirect object	*Alberto lanzó una piedra **a la ventana**.* (Alberto threw a stone at the window.)
To express manner	*Lo pinté **a mano**.* (I painted it by hand.)
In time phrases: 'at'	*La ópera comienza **a las siete**.* (The opera starts at 7.)

To refer to smell, taste or sound	*Esta camisa huele **a pintura***. (This shirt smells of paint.)
To show rate or distance	*El primer coche iba **a siete kilómetros** por hora*. (The first car went at 7 km per hour.)
To indicate action at a point in time ('on (do)ing'): *a* + article + infinitive 👁 Note that *a* followed by the article *el* contracts to *al*, e.g. ***al*** *campo*.	*Le pagaré **al salir***. (I'll pay him on leaving.)
☞ See Section 26.6 for more on time relations.	

Ante

Ante translates the English 'before' in the sense of 'faced with'. It can be literal or figurative in meaning.

To describe a physical or literal situation: 'in front of', 'before'	*Se arrodilló **ante el altar***. (She knelt down in front of the altar.)
To describe a figurative situation: 'faced with', 'in respect of', 'respecting'	*¿Cómo ha de actuar una empresa **ante el reto del ambiente económico internacional**?* (How should a company act when faced with the challenge of the international economic environment?)
To indicate preference: 'before', 'over', 'above'	*Siempre elegiría un Seat **ante cualquier otra marca***. (I would always choose a Seat over any other make.)

Bajo

Bajo literally means 'under'. It tends to be more formal than *debajo de,* and has more the register of the English word 'beneath'. It is also less spatially accurate, and is often used in a figurative sense.

To show a more or less accurate position in space: 'under', 'underneath', 'beneath'	*Se sentó **bajo el árbol***. (He sat down under the tree.)
To show submission or acceptance: 'under' used figuratively	*Las actividades clandestinas proliferaron **bajo la dictadura***. (Clandestine activities proliferated under the dictatorship.)
To express the idea of 'less than' or 'below' with measurements and temperatures	*Las temperaturas en Siberia pueden llegar a 55 grados **bajo cero***. (Temperatures in Siberia can reach 55 degrees below zero.)

Con

Con is the near equivalent to 'with', but it also has uses that are not found in its English counterpart.

Meaning 'with', to express the idea 'in the company of', to show means or instrument or the manner in which something is done. (Note the forms *conmigo* (with me), *contigo* (with you) and *consigo* (with himself/herself/yourself).) ☞ See Section 5.5 for object pronouns with prepositions.	*Fui al teatro **con mis padres***. (I went to the theatre with my parents.) *Cortó la carne **con un cuchillo especial***. (She cut the meat with a special knife.) *Murió **con dignidad***. (He died with dignity.)
In certain structures, to show reciprocal actions (*escribir, hablar, comunicar, charlar*, etc.)	*¿No te gustaría **escribirte con Luisa***? (Wouldn't you like to correspond with Luisa?)
To show an encounter, literal or figurative, between two people or objects	*De vacaciones en la playa nos tropezamos **con una profesora de tu colegio***. (On the beach on holiday we bumped into a teacher from your school.)
To express an attitude or disposition towards another person or people	*Siempre es muy atento **con las personas mayores***. (He is always very attentive to older people.) (Positive attitudes can also take *para con*: *Es amable para con todos*. (She's kind to everyone.))
With an infinitive, to translate the English 'by (do)ing . . .'	*Le harías muy feliz solo **con enviarle una tarjeta***. (You'd make her really happy just by sending her a card.)
To express the idea 'containing'	*Llevaba una bolsa **con fruta***. (She was carrying a bag of fruit.)
To express the idea 'in spite of', 'despite'	***Con todas las ventajas** que dicen que ofrece el producto, no es nada especial.* (Despite all the advantages they say the product offers, it's nothing special.)
To express a state or condition	*Está ocupada por completo **con su nuevo empleo***. (She's completely taken up with her new job.)
To convey the idea 'when it comes to'	*Es muy estricto **con la calidad***. (He's very strict when it comes to quality.)

Contra

Contra conveys most usages of the English word 'against'. However, when referring to reasons, opinions or arguments against something, *en contra de* is more normal. It is also used with verbs of throwing, firing, attacking, hitting, striking, etc., where English would normally use 'at' or 'into'.

To translate 'against' in a literal or physical sense	*Los muchachos esperaban apoyados **contra la pared***. (The boys were leaning against the wall, waiting.)
To translate 'against' in a figurative sense (often interchangeable with *en contra de* in this context)	***Contra la opinión** de los demás directores, el presidente optó por vender la empresa.* (Despite what the rest of the directors thought, the chief executive opted to sell off the company.)

With verbs of throwing, firing, attacking, hitting, striking, etc.	*Arrojaron piedras **contra las unidades policiales**.* (They threw stones at the police units.)

De

The nearest equivalent in English to *de* is 'of', although it has a wide range of uses which 'of' would not cover sufficiently.

To show possession: 'belonging to'	*Este es el abrigo **de mi abuelo**.* (This is my grandfather's overcoat.)
To express origin: 'from'	*Es **de Venezuela**.* (She's from Venezuela.)
To show material: 'made from', 'consisting of', often in the phrases *ser de* and *estar hecho de*	*Este juego de damas es **de plástico**.* (This draughts set is (made of) plastic.)
To show the cause of an action: 'out of', 'with'	*Se cayó de la silla **de la risa**.* (She fell out of her chair with laughter.)
To introduce the starting point in time or space: 'from'	***de ahora en adelante*** (from now onwards) ***de aquí en adelante*** (from here onwards)
With verb + noun: to indicate a person's role: 'as a . . .'	*Hoy día ya no trabaja **de enfermera**.* (Nowadays she no longer works as a nurse.)
To introduce a subject: 'about' (often interchangeable with *sobre*)	*¿Qué sabe **de este** tema?* (What do you know about this subject?)
To indicate price	*Compró la camisa **de diez euros**.* (He bought the ten-euro shirt.)
With *más/menos* to show number, quantity and age	*Tiene **más de ochenta años**.* (He's over eighty.) *Hace **menos de diez grados** fuera.* (It's less than 10 degrees outside.)
In certain adverbial phrases of manner (*de paso, de antemano, de balde, de pie*, etc.)	*La visitamos **de paso** por Sevilla.* (We visited her when passing through Seville.)
With an infinitive, to indicate a condition: 'if'	***De seguir así**, no va a durar mucho.* (If it carries on like that, it's not going to last long.)
To mean 'by' in verbs of seizing, taking, etc.	*El policía le agarró **del brazo**.* (The policeman seized him by the arm.)
To show content or specification	*Nos llevó una botella **de leche**.* (He brought us a bottle of milk.)
To show the agent in some passive constructions	*Llegó al tribunal acompañada **de su abogado**.* (She went to court accompanied by her lawyer.)
In some set time phrases (*de vacaciones, de día, de noche, de la madrugada*)	*Fueron al Perú **de vacaciones**.* (They went to Peru on holiday.)
To show a part of: 'some of', 'one of'	*Guárdame uno **de los pasteles**, que voy a llegar un poco tarde.* (Save me one of the cakes, I'm going to be a bit late.)
To show superlatives: 'in the . . .'	*Júpiter es el mayor planeta **del sistema solar**.* (Jupiter is the biggest planet in the solar system.)

To show position (*de* can be 'on', 'in' or 'by', depending on context; it can also introduce compound prepositions, e.g. *el banco de al lado* (the bank next door)).	*El banco **de la esquina** cierra a las tres.* (The bank on the corner closes at three o'clock.)
To show how someone dresses: 'as' (occupation or role), 'in' (colour)	*Siempre anda vestida **de negro**.* (She always dresses in black.)
Between adjectives and infinitives that govern them	*Es fácil **de ver**.* (It's easy to see.)
To show characteristics	*El hombre **del sombrero** empezó a seguirnos.* (The man in the hat began to follow us.)

👁 Note that *de* followed by the article *el* contracts to *del,* e.g. *del campo.*

Desde

Desde translates the English word 'from', although not in all senses, e.g. only *de* can be used to talk about personal origins (*Soy de Sevilla* – I'm from Seville). *Desde* is used instead of the more common word *de* when greater emphasis is required or when there is a possibility of ambiguity.

To show starting point in space	***Desde lo alto del rascacielos** se puede ver toda la extensión del estado.* (You can see the whole of the state from the top of the skyscraper.)
To show starting point in time	*Hemos vendido más de 10.000 ejemplares **desde mediados de abril**.* (We've sold more than 10,000 copies since mid-April.)
In the set phrase *desde . . . hasta*	***Desde San Sebastián hasta Sevilla, y desde Vigo hasta Valencia**, todo el estado se verá afectado.* (From San Sebastián to Seville, and from Vigo to Valencia, the whole country will be affected.)
In the phrase *desde hace/hacía* ('since') to show length of time	*Vivimos en esta casa **desde hace 10 años**.* (We've been living in this house for 10 years.)

☞ See also Section 26.6 for more examples of *desde* used to define limit in time.

Durante

Durante denotes a particular span of time, and means 'during' in the sense of 'while (the time specified) lasts' or 'for a specified length of time'	***Durante el verano** pasa mucho tiempo en el jardín.* (Throughout the summer he spends a lot of time in the garden.) *Perdieron contacto con el transbordador espacial **durante 24 horas**.* (They lost contact with the space shuttle for 24 hours.)

Note that *durante* contrasts with *por,* which can also refer to a specified length of time. But whereas *durante* refers to a duration of time, *por* tends only to refer to a brief moment or instant, e.g. *Perdieron contacto solo por un instante* (They only lost contact for an instant). ☞ See this use of *por* below.

En

En has a number of usages in Spanish, and can translate the ideas 'in', 'on', 'at', 'into' and 'onto', in addition to some other English prepositions, according to the context.

Position above: '(up) in'	*La bandera ondeaba **en el aire**.* (The flag fluttered in the air.)
Position against: 'on'	*Colgó un nuevo cuadro **en la pared** de su alcoba.* (She hung a new picture on her bedroom wall.)
Position inside: 'in', 'inside'	*Guardaba sus alhajas **en un cajón** sin cerrar con llave.* (She kept her jewels inside an unlocked drawer.)
Action within a time frame	*Siempre vamos a esquiar **en invierno**.* (We always go skiing in the winter.)
Point in space: 'at', 'in'	*Habíamos quedado **en el bar Hemingway** pero me dejó plantado.* (We arranged to meet in the Bar Hemingway but she stood me up.)
Action within a period of time: 'in', 'within'	*Completamos toda la documentación **en dos horas**.* (We filled in all the documentation in two hours.)
Movement into	*Entró **en el aula**.* (He went into the classroom.) *(Entró al aula* in Spanish America)
Means of transport: 'by'	*Llegamos a Cádiz **en coche**.* (We went to Cadiz by car.)
With measurements, value and prices: 'by', 'at'	*El cambio está **en 230** soles.* (The exchange rate's 230 soles.)
Manner	*Se la reconoce **en su forma de andar**.* (She can be recognised by the way she walks.)

Entre

Entre translates the idea 'between' or 'among', although this can be in a much looser sense than the English words would presuppose; sometimes it has the much vaguer sense of 'in the midst of' or 'through the midst of'. There are also a number of special uses that do not have direct equivalents in English.

To indicate an intermediate position, literally or figuratively: 'between'	*Me puso **entre la espada y la pared**.* (It put me between the devil and the deep blue sea.)
To indicate a vague, unspecified or unknown point in space, including movement through: 'among', 'in the midst of', 'through the midst of'	*Las tropas avanzaron en silencio **entre la maleza**.* (The troops advanced silently through the undergrowth.)
To indicate association with a group, literally or figuratively: 'among'	*Lorca y Alberti destacan **entre la llamada Generación del 27**.* (Lorca and Alberti stand out in the so-called 'Generation of 27'.)

To indicate a sense of co-operation within a group: 'together', 'between (them, us, etc.)'	**Entre todos**, *sí que somos capaces de llevar a cabo un proyecto de tal complejidad.* (Between us all, of course we're able to deliver a complex project like that.)
Used with verbs of choice: 'between'	*Es difícil elegir* **entre los dos candidatos**. (It's difficult to choose between the two candidates.)
To indicate a reflexive or a reciprocal action, especially speaking or writing ☞ See Section 22.5 to learn about reciprocal verbs.	*Los chicos susurraban* **entre sí** *al fondo del aula.* (The boys whispered to each other at the back of the classroom.)
Finally, note its idiomatic use with the word *semana* to mean 'weekdays and Saturdays'.	*El supermercado está abierto* **entre semana** *pero no los domingos.* (The supermarket is open all week except Sundays.)

👁 Note that *entre* takes the subject pronouns rather than the object pronouns: *entre nosotros, entre tú y ella.*

Hacia

Hacia conveys the idea of '(approximate) direction towards' in space, and 'about' or 'approximately' in time. It also translates 'towards' when referring to attitudes or emotions.

To show (imprecise) movement: 'towards'	*No sé adónde iba, se dirigió* **hacia el río**. (I don't know where she went, she headed towards the river.)
To show approximate time: 'about', 'around', 'approximately'	*Llegamos a la fiesta* **hacia medianoche**. (We got to the party about midnight.)
To show an attitude or emotional stance: 'towards'	*Tiene una postura ambigua* **hacia la religión organizada**. (He has an ambiguous attitude towards organised religion.)

Hasta

Hasta conveys the idea of 'until' or '(up) to' in time, and 'as far as' or '(up) to' in space. It can also mean 'as much/many as' when referring to numbers or quantities. When used with nouns, it has the meaning 'even', 'including'.

Hasta is used in a number of idiomatic expressions, mainly to do with saying good-bye	**Hasta luego**, **Hasta la vista**, **Hasta mañana**, **Hasta ahora**, **Hasta el sábado**, etc.
To express a limit in time: 'until', '(up) to'	*Tenemos* **hasta finales de la semana** *para completar la documentación.* (We've got until the end of the week to fill in the documentation.)

To express a limit in space: 'as far as', '(up) to'	*Los huelguistas marcharon* **hasta la barrera** *pero no la pudieron pasar.* (The strikers marched up to the gate but they couldn't pass through.)
To express a limit in number or quantity: 'up to', 'as much/many as'	*En el estanque pueden caber* **hasta 50 peces**. (You can get up to 50 fish in the pond.)
To indicate the greatest possible extent of inclusion: 'even', 'including'	*Parece que* **hasta el presidente** *anda involucrado en el escándalo.* (It seems even the president is implicated in the scandal.)

Hasta with infinitives and subjunctives

| *Hasta* can be followed by an infinitive or (with *hasta que*) by an indicative or subjunctive to convey the idea of 'until (do)ing . . .' or 'until (I, you, he, she, etc.) do(es)'
 👁 Note that in some subordinate clauses *hasta que* allows the use of *no* without changing the meaning of the clause. | *Trabajó* **hasta terminar** *el informe.* (He worked until he finished the report.)
 No nos quería pagar **hasta que (no) hubiéramos arreglado** *todos los detalles finales.* (He didn't want to pay us until we had sorted out the final details.) |

☞ See Section 26.6 on *hasta* to express limit of time in time relations.

Mediante

| *Mediante* expresses the idea 'by means of', 'by using' or 'by adopting'. It introduces the means by which, the implement with which or the course of action through which something is done or achieved. | *El gobierno ha podido evitar una crisis económica* **mediante una política rigurosa**. (The government has managed to avoid an economic crisis by adopting a stringent policy.) |

👁 *Mediante* highlights the means used, and can be replaced by the compound preposition *por medio de*.

When the means is not important, or the speaker does not wish to emphasise it, *mediante* can often be replaced with *con* or *por*: *Lo pude solucionar* **con** *una llamada telefónica.* (I managed to solve it with a telephone call.)

Para

Para is a very common preposition with several uses, most of which are connected with the idea of destination, or even destiny, in a figurative or literal sense. It is often translated as 'for', but be careful – the English word can also be translated as *por*.

👁 See '*Por* or *para*?' below.

| To indicate purpose or use | *Esta herramienta es* **para sacar clavos**. (This tool is for pulling out nails.) |

To indicate a recipient	*Ha comprado un hermoso collar de perlas **para su esposa**.* (He's bought a lovely pearl necklace for his wife.)
Movement or direction towards, again with an idea of 'destination to'	*El barco va **para Buenos Aires**.* (The ship is bound for Buenos Aires.)
Duration of predetermined period of time (*por* in Spanish America)	*Mis padres van a Canarias **para una quincena**.* (My parents are going to the Canaries for a fortnight.)
To show the holder of an opinion (notice that subject pronouns are used)	***Para nosotros**, las vacaciones son importantísimas.* (For us, holidays are extremely important.)

Por

To express cause or motive: 'because of', 'with a commitment to'	*Murió **por su fe**.* (He died for his faith.) *No trabajo **por amor al arte** sino por dinero.* (I don't work for the love of it but for money.)
To express price, equivalence or substitution: 'in exchange for', 'in (the) place of', 'on behalf of'	*Vendió el cuadro que descubrió en la buhardilla **por un dineral**.* (He sold the painting that he found in his loft for a fortune.) *La embajadora firmó el tratado comercial **por el presidente**.* (The ambassador signed the business pact on the president's behalf.)
To express a means or an instrument, including transportation: 'using', 'via', 'by'	*Ayer hablé con él **por teléfono**.* (I spoke to him yesterday on the phone.) *Finalmente le envié las piezas **por avión**.* (Finally I sent him the parts by plane.)
To express the manner or way in which something is done: 'using', 'by'	*Solo se puede obtener **por la fuerza**.* (It can only be obtained by force.)
To express a sense of personal involvement or commitment: 'as for', 'as far as [. . .] is concerned' (Note that in these cases *por* is usually at the head of the sentence.)	***Por ella** iríamos mañana.* (As far as she's concerned, we'd go tomorrow.)
To express speed, rate, or the idea of distribution in time or among a group: 'per'	*El límite de velocidad en las autopistas españolas es 120 km **por hora**.* (The speed limit on Spanish motorways is 120 kilometres per hour.)
To express transitional movement: 'along', 'up', 'down', 'in', 'into', 'through', 'throughout', depending on context	*Bajaba **por la escalera** cuando nosotros subíamos.* (She was coming down the stairs when we were going up.)
To express approximate duration: 'for the duration of' ☞ See also *Durante*, above.	*Dudó **por algunas horas** antes de tomar una decisión.* (He hesitated for several hours before making a decision.)
To introduce the agent in a passive construction: 'by' ☞ You can revise the passive in Section 23.2.	*Ahora parece que ese cuadro no fue pintado **por Romero de Torres**, sino **por otro artista desconocido**.* (It now seems that this picture was not painted by Romero de Torres, but by another unknown artist.)

◉ *Por* or *para*?

Sometimes the choice between *por* and *para* can be confusing for English speakers, since both words can be translated as 'for'.

When faced with a choice, try to decide whether the meaning looks forward to a destination or objective (in which case choose *para*), whether it refers back to a cause or motive (choose *por*), or whether it expresses substitution (again, choose *por*).

Examples

* *Puso un comedero en el jardín **por** sus hijos.* (He put a bird-feeder in the garden for his children.) *Por* is causal: the children are the reason, or cause, of his placing the feeder in the garden.
* *¿Podrías llamar a tu hermana **por** mí?* (Could you call your sister for me?) *Por* expresses substitution; the speaker is really saying 'Could you call her on my behalf'.
* *Compró un comedero **para** su madre.* (He bought a bird-feeder for his mother.) 'His mother' is the recipient of the gift, i.e. she is the gift's destination.

Según

Según means 'according to' or, when followed directly by a verb, 'according to what'.	***Según los médicos**, es peligroso fumar.* (According to doctors, it's dangerous to smoke.)
Sometimes *según* has more the sense of 'in accordance with' or 'depending on'.	***Según el contexto**, la palabra 'cola' se traduce de forma muy distinta al inglés.* (Depending on the context, the word *cola* is translated very differently into English.)

(☞ See Section 26.6 for *según* + verbs expressing actions in progress; see Section 26.5 (e) for *según* as a connector of manner.)

Sin

Sin translates the English 'without' quite straightforwardly. ◉ Note that when followed by a non-conjugated verb, *sin* is followed by the infinitive.	*Quisiera vivir **sin tener que trabajar**.* (I'd like to live without having to work.)
However, there are a number of cases where *sin* would not be translated as 'without'.	***sin plomo** (lead-free) una botella **sin abrir** (an unopened bottle) un edificio **sin terminar** (an unfinished building)*

Sobre

The basic meaning of *sobre* is 'on top of', although it can translate 'on', 'over', 'above', 'near', and even 'about' or 'approximately', according to the context.

To show position with physical contact: 'on', 'on top of'	*Puso la bandeja **sobre la mesa***. (He put the tray on the table.)
To show position without physical contact: 'above', 'over'	*Cuentan que la estrella se paró **sobre el pesebre***. (They say the star stopped above the crib.)
To show hierarchy: 'above' in a figurative sense	*No puedo hacer nada: ella es mi jefa y está **sobre mí***. (I can't do anything: she's my boss and she's above me.)
To show the subject or theme: 'about', 'on the subject of' ☞ See also *de*, in this unit.	*Tenemos que preparar un escrito de 500 palabras **sobre el papel del poder nuclear en la economía actual***. (We have to prepare a 500-word text on the role of nuclear power in today's economy.)
To show approximation of time: 'about', 'around', 'approximately'	*Llegó **sobre las ocho***. (She arrived around eight.)

Tras

Tras means 'after', 'following' or 'behind', and can replace *después de* and *detrás de*. ☞ See Prepositional phrases, below.	*La luna se levantó **tras el perfil esquelético** de los árboles*. (The moon rose up behind the skeletal outline of the trees.) (*detrás de* is also possible.)
Note that *tras* is much more common in the written language, particularly journalese. *Después de* and *detrás de* are far more likely to be heard in the spoken language.	*Todo el mundo aplaudió con entusiasmo **tras la charla** del experto*. (Everyone applauded enthusiastically following the expert's talk.) (*después de* is also possible.)
However, *tras* must be used when linking together pairs of nouns in phrases such as 'year after year', 'week after week', and so on.	*hora tras hora* (hour after hour), *día tras día* (day after day), *año tras año* (year after year), etc.

Prepositional phrases

Prepositional phrases, sometimes called compound prepositions, consist of one or more prepositions combined with an adverb or a noun.

Spanish has an enormous range of prepositional phrases, the most common of which are described below.

Prepositional phrase	Examples	Phrase refers to
Al lado de	*El banco está **al lado de la panadería***. (The bank's next to the baker's.)	Physical position: 'next to'

Prepositional phrase	Examples	Phrase refers to
Alrededor de	Hay huertos **alrededor de la casa**. (There are orchards surrounding the house.)	Physical position: 'surrounding' (Note also the expressions *a su alrededor* and *alrededor suyo.*)
Antes de	**Antes de acostarse** *hay que lavarse los dientes*. (Before going to bed you have to clean your teeth.)	Relative time: 'before'
Cerca de	*El Museo del Prado está* **cerca de la Puerta del Sol**. (The Prado is near the Puerta del Sol.)	Physical position: 'near'
Debajo de	*El gato está durmiendo* **debajo de la mesa**. (The cat is asleep under the table.)	Physical position: 'underneath'
Delante de	*Hay una plaza espléndida* **delante de la catedral**. (There's a splendid square in front of the cathedral.)	Physical position: 'in front of'
Dentro de	*Todas sus alhajas están* **dentro de una caja fuerte**. (All her jewels are inside a strongbox.)	Physical position: 'inside'
Después de	**Después de despertarse** *no suele acordarse de sus sueños*. (After waking up she doesn't usually remember her dreams.)	Relative time: 'after'
Detrás de	**Detrás de las cortinas** *no se veía nada*. (Nothing could be seen behind the curtains.)	Physical position: 'behind'
En contra de	*Estamos* **en contra de su opinión**. (We are opposed to her opinion.)	Figurative position: 'against', 'opposed to'
Encima de	*Puso la bandeja* **encima de la mesa**. (He put the tray on the table.)	Physical position, with or without contact: 'on top of', 'above'
Enfrente de/frente a	*El mercado está* **enfrente del/ frente al ayuntamiento**. (The market is opposite the town hall.)	Physical position: 'opposite'
Fuera de	**Fuera de la iglesia oscura**, *todo estaba soleado y luminoso*. (Outside the dark church, everything was light and sunny.)	Physical position: 'outside'
Lejos de	*Las Canarias están* **lejos de la Península**. (The Canaries are a long way from the Peninsula.)	Physical position: 'far (away) from'

Prepositional phrase	Examples	Phrase refers to
(Por) debajo de	*Hay muchas corrientes fuertes que fluyen **por debajo de los océanos***. (There are lots of strong currents flowing under the oceans.)	Physical motion: 'under', 'underneath'
(Por) delante de	*Pasamos **por delante de su casa** sin reconocerla.* (We went past her house without recognising it.)	Physical motion: 'in front of', 'past'
(Por) detrás de	*El río fluye **por detrás del castillo**; no se ve de aquí enfrente.* (The river flows behind the castle; you can't see it from the front here.)	Physical motion: 'behind'
(Por) encima de	*El avión voló **por encima de las nubes**.* (The plane flew above the clouds.)	Physical motion: 'over', 'above'

Ejercicios

Level 1/2

1 Insert a personal *a* in the gaps if you think it is necessary.

   a Busco . . . un profesor que ayude a mi hijo en matemáticas.
   b Busco . . . la profesora de matemáticas de mi hijo.
   c ¿ . . . quién viste primero al bajar del tren?
   d Fuimos al teatro anoche pero no conocíamos . . . nadie.
   e Cría . . . conejos en su jardín desde hace muchos años.

Level 1/2

2 Complete the gaps using the most appropriate preposition from the list below.

> a • con • de • en • para • por

   a Cuando llegó . . . casa tuvo que entrar . . . una ventana entreabierta porque había dejado las llaves . . . el bolsillo de la chaqueta.
   b Este vaso . . . cristal está diseñado . . . sangría. . . . preparar esta, tómese una botella . . . vino tinto, añádase zumo . . . naranja, un poquito . . . ron y trocitos . . . fruta, mézclese todo y sírvase bien fría.
   c . . . el calor que hace, me voy a tomar una gaseosa . . . hielo.
   d Entraron . . . la embajada uruguaya porque querían ir . . . vivir . . . ese país.
   e Ese libro se lo arrebató Pablo . . . la mano . . . Lucía.

Level 2

3 Complete the following sentences with an appropriate preposition or prepositional phrase, using the prompts.

   a Anduvieron . . . (*along*) la calle . . . (*in front of*) la librería.
   b El ratón corrió . . . (*under*) la cama y salió cerca de la puerta.
   c . . . (*behind*) el telón todo se cambió muy rápido para la siguiente escena.
   d La estación espacial circula continuamente . . . (*above*) la Tierra.
   e En una estructura no jerárquica, nadie debería estar . . . (*above*) nadie.

Level 2

4 Complete the gap with *para* or *por*, as appropriate.

a La semana que viene mis padres van a ir a Menorca . . . una quincena.

b Yo no volvería a votar nunca . . . los conservadores.

c Se ha construido una nueva cárcel . . . el aumento en el número de delincuentes en la ciudad.

d El sha Jahan hizo construir el Taj Mahal como sepultura . . . su querida esposa.

e Mi colega no ha podido venir al congreso . . . circunstancias imprevistas, pero me ha pedido que presente la ponencia . . . ella.

Level 2

5 Translate the sentences in exercise 4 into English. In those cases where you have translated *por* and *para* as 'for', try to think of the general sense of the word. Note it in brackets after your translation.

Level 3

6 Look at the following newspaper extract. Complete the gaps with the appropriate prepositions from the list below.

a • a través de • de • en • para • por

Ayuda a las víctimas del terremoto

(a) . . . las personas interesadas (b) . . . aportar su ayuda (c) . . . los damnificados (d) . . . el terremoto ocurrido (e) . . . El Salvador: Lo pueden hacer (f) . . . la siguiente manera: (g) . . . cuentas (h) . . . los siguientes bancos:

Banco Salvadoreño

Banco Agrícola

(*El Noticiero*, San Salvador, 29/1/01, http://www.elnoticiero.com.sv) (30/1/01)

13 Interjections

An interjection – *una interjección* – is a word or a short phrase which stands apart from – literally, is interjected into – the syntax and meaning of the rest of an **utterance** (what is being said). Examples in (current British) English include 'Aha!', 'Wicked!', 'Help!', 'No way!' and 'Great!'

In speech, an interjection is recognised by its markedly different intonation; it is usually also preceded and followed by a short pause. In written Spanish, this is normally signalled by placing the interjection between exclamation marks (¡ ! – note that Spanish uses an upside-down form before an interjection or exclamation).

☞ See section (b) of this unit for more on exclamatory sentences.

The function of the interjection is usually to express some kind of emotional reaction to whatever idea is being conveyed in the rest of the utterance or sentence, such as surprise, hope, disgust, agreement, anger, etc.

In Spanish there are different types of interjection:

(a)   Interjections proper
(b)   Derivative interjections and exclamatory phrases

There is an enormous range of interjections in Spanish. Those given in this unit are just a selection of the most common.

👁 Be very careful when using interjections. Their **register** – that is, the tone they convey – can change quite markedly over a relatively short period of time. They are also frequently associated with particular social groups and/or regions of the Spanish-speaking world.

> *Nada resulta más ridículo que un individuo que, supuestamente está furioso, diciendo: "¡Córcholis! ¡Menuda faena me habéis hecho!" Si está furioso de verdad, no dirá "córcholis" o "cáscaras"; soltará un exabrupto.*
>
> (Nothing is more ridiculous than someone who is supposed to be furious saying: 'Good lord! A fine one you've played on me!' If he is

really furious he won't say 'Good lord!' or 'Well I'm blowed!'; he'll use an expletive.)

(Rodolfo Martínez, 'Algunas notas sobre los diálogos', BEM,
http://www.bemmag.com/dialogos.htm) (8/3/01)

Notice that a particular interjection may convey different meanings, depending on the situation. You will need to rely on the context to identify the precise feeling or meaning expressed.

(a) Interjections proper

These are single sounds unrelated to particular words. They are often onomatopoeic, and serve to reinforce the message.

Interjection	Meaning/usage	Example
¡Ah!	Expresses realisation, sudden understanding.	— Que te digo que no te voy a poder acompañar. —¡**Ah**! Entonces, iré sola. ('I'm telling you I won't be able to go with you.' 'Oh, I see. I'll go by myself, then.')
¡Ajá!	Expresses approval, agreement.	—¡Ya entiendo! ¡Por eso no querías verlo! —¡**Ajá**! ('I see! That's why you didn't want to see him!' 'That's it.')
¡Ay!	Expresses sudden surprise, sorrow, anguish, pain.	—¡**Ay**, qué daño! ¡Me he pinchado con las rosas! (Ow, that hurt! I've pricked myself on the roses!)
¡Bah!	Expresses a dismissive or negative reaction (disbelief, scorn, refusal, etc.).	—¡Qué disgusto! Magda se ha enfadado conmigo por lo que he dicho. —¡**Bah**! No le hagas caso. Seguro que para mañana ya se le habrá pasado. ('I'm very upset. Magda is angry with me because of what I said.' 'Huh, don't take any notice of her. I'm sure she'll have got over it by tomorrow.')
¡Eh!	Attracts attention.	—¡**Eh**, señorita! ¡Se deja la tarjeta! (Hey, miss, you've forgotten your credit card.)
¡Hale!	Gives encouragement, hurries along.	¡**Hale**!, todos a comer. (Come on, everyone, time to eat.)
¡Huy!	Expresses (pleasant) surprise.	— Yo también me apunto. —¡**Huy**!, qué bien! Cuantos más, mejor. ('I'm coming as well.' 'Wow, that's great! The more, the merrier.')

Interjection	Meaning/usage	Example
¡Olé!	Expresses enthusiasm, warm approval (most common in Southern Spain)	—*¡Olé! ¡Bien dicho, niña!* (Brilliant! Well said, lass!)
¡Psss!/¡Pse!	Expresses indifference.	—*¿Qué te parece el cuadro?* —**Psss**. ('What do you think of the picture?' 'It's OKish . . .')
¡So!	Orders to stop (used with horses or donkeys), like the English 'whoa!'	*¡So, caballo, so!* (Whoa, boy, whoa!)
¡Uf!	Expresses relief or used during hot weather	*¡Uf, qué alivio!* (Phew! What a relief!)
¡Zas!	Imitates the sound of a blow or a swift movement; equivalent of English 'crash!', 'bang!', 'whack!', 'wham!', etc.	*Dejé que se posara, y ¡zas! la maté con la zapatilla.* (I let it land, then whack! I killed it with my slipper.)

(b) Derivative interjections and exclamatory phrases

This group of interjections consists of set, idiomatic expressions and single recognisable words, whose meaning may or may not correspond to non-exclamatory usage (e.g. *¡Auxilio!* always means 'help' whether or not it is an interjection, whereas *¡Hombre!* means something quite different from 'man' when used as an interjection).

The following interjections have been grouped according to the emotion or feeling that they express.

Interjections which are very colloquial or slang have been marked with a star (*). (There are also a number of rude or offensive interjections in Spanish – called *tacos* or *exabruptos* – but they have not been included here.)

Most of the interjections in this selection are heard on both sides of the Atlantic. However, there are some that are only used in Spain or Spanish America. They have been marked with (S) and (Sp.Am.) respectively.

Interjection	Meaning/usage	Example
¡Adelante!, ¡Ánimo!, ¡Valor!, ¡Dale!, ¡Vamos!, ¡Sigue!, ¡Así, así!	Expresses encouragement and support.	*¡Ánimo, que ya falta poco!* (Keep it up, not far to go now!)
¡Venga!, ¡Vamos!	Expresses encouragement or hurries along.	*¡Venga!, todos a firmar la tarjeta.* (Come on, everyone sign the card.)
¡Viva!, ¡Arriba!, ¡Bravo!, ¡Hurra!	Expresses exultation, enthusiasm and support.	*¡Viva! ¡Ya estamos de vacaciones!* (Hooray, we're now on holiday!) *¡Bravo, Miguel! ¡Bien hecho!* (Brilliant, Miguel! Well done!)

Interjection	Meaning/usage	Example
¡Estupendo!, ¡Fenomenal!, ¡Fantástico!, ¡Muy bien!, ¡Qué bien!	Expresses satisfaction and approval.	—Nos han concedido el préstamo. —¡**Estupendo**! ('They've given us the loan.' 'Great!')
¡Abajo (con) . . . !	Expresses disapproval.	¡**Abajo** la dictadura! (Down with dictatorship!)
¡Anda ya!, ¡Venga ya!, ¡Tonterías!, ¡Qué va!	Expresses incredulity or irony.	—Dicen que su madre es una bruja. —¡**Anda ya**! Eso no se lo cree nadie. ('They say his mother's a witch.' 'Oh, come off it! No one believes that one.')
¡Ni hablar!, ¡Ni pensarlo!, ¡Narices!(*), ¡Y un cuerno!(*)	Expresses refusal or rejection.	—¿Te importa cambiarme la guardia el lunes? —¡**Ni hablar**! ('Do you mind swapping for my duty on Monday?' 'No way!')
¡Qué pena!, ¡Qué mal!, ¡Vaya por Dios!	Expresses disappointment.	—No he podido conseguir entradas para el concierto. —¡**Qué pena**! ('I couldn't get tickets for the concert.' 'That's a shame!')
¡Ay de mí!, ¡Pobre de mí!	Expresses fear for oneself or self-pity.	¡**Ay de mí**! ¡Mi hija me va a matar cuando se entere! (Oh, no! My daughter's going to kill me when she finds out!)
¡Ojo (con) . . . ! ¡Ojito (con) . . . ! ¡Cuidado (con) . . . !	Expresses warning or threat.	Podéis salir, pero, ¡**ojo**!, que si llegáis tarde otra vez, mañana no salís. (You can go out, but watch out!, if you get back late again you won't go out tomorrow.)
¡Toma!, ¡Ahí va!, ¡Vaya!, ¡Atiza!, ¡Arrea! (old-fashioned), ¡Mi madre!, ¡Dios mío!, ¡Virgen Santa!, ¡Válgame Dios!, ¡Santo Cielo! (these last three old-fashioned)	Expresses surprise or shock.	¡**Ahí va**! ¡Si no he traído los papeles! (Oh, no! I haven't brought the papers.) ¡**Dios mío**, he dejado la sartén en el fuego! (Oh, my God! I've left the frying pan on the heat!) —Dicen que han matado a otra persona. — ¡**Virgen Santa**! ('I've been told that they killed another person.' 'Good God!')

Interjection	Meaning/usage	Example
¡(Qué) caramba!, ¡Caray!, ¡Hombre!, ¡Córcholis!, ¡Recórcholis! (*), ¡Híjoles! (Sp.Am.), ¡Mijo/Mija! (Sp.Am.)	Expresses surprise or annoyance.	*¡Caray! No me esperaba eso.* (What the . . . ! I wasn't expecting that.) *¡Qué caramba! Aunque me llamen, no pienso ir.* (The heck with it! Even if they ring me, I don't intend to go.)
*¡Vaya!, ¡Vaya por Dios!, ¡Jo! (*S), ¡Qué vaina! (Sp.Am.), ¡Qué fastidio!, ¡Qué rabia!, ¡(Qué) carajo! (*Sp.Am.)*	Expresses irritation or annoyance.	*¡Vaya! ¡Ahora que por fin me pongo a leer, se despierta el niño!* (For goodness sake! Just as I've fnally started to read, the baby wakes up!) *—¿Raquel? Oye, que tengo una reunión y no puedo ir a recoger al niño al colegio.* *—¡Vaya por Dios! ¿Y ahora qué hacemos?* ('Raquel? Listen, I've got a meeting and I won't be able to pick the boy up from school.' 'Oh, bother! Now what do we do?')
¡Por Dios!, ¡Por favor!, ¡Pero bueno!	Expresses protestation.	*¡Por Dios, dejad ya de discutir!* (For God's sake, stop arguing!)
¡Jesús!	Expresses surprise or shock; also used as 'bless you' when somebody sneezes.	*¡Jesús, qué mal genio tiene ese hombre!* (Blimey, what a bad temper that man's got!) *— ¡Ahhhh . . . chís! — ¡Jesús!* ('Aachoo!' 'Bless you!')
¡Socorro!, ¡Auxilio!	Asks for help.	*¡Socorro, que me ahogo!* (Help, I'm drowning!)
¡Chitón!, ¡Silencio!	Orders to keep silent.	*—Pues yo sigo pensando que . . .* *—¡Chitón! ¡Ni una palabra más!* ('Well, I still think that . . .' 'Silence! Not another word!')
¡Basta!, ¡Basta ya!, ¡Vale ya!	Orders somebody to stop.	*¡Basta ya! ¡A la cama!* (Enough! Get to bed!)
¡Atención!, ¡Mira/Mire!, ¡Oiga/Oye!	Attracts somebody's attention.	*¡Atención, por favor! La comida se servirá en 10 minutos.* (Attention, please! Dinner will be served in 10 minutes.)
¡Y dale!	Shows impatience towards somebody repeating the same thing.	*—¡No, no y no! No pienso ir.* *—¡Y dale! Si nadie te está obligando.* ('No, no and no again! I won't go!' 'Stop going on about it! Nobody's forcing you.')

Ejercicios

1 Read the following mini-dialogues, where you will find a common Spanish interjection in bold. Identify the feeling it expresses from the list.

encouragement • surprise • dismissive reaction • annoyance

a —Juan, estoy preocupada por Mariela. Son ya las 11 y no ha llegado.
   —**Bah**, se habrá entretenido con los amigos.
b —No he podido conseguir entradas para el cine.
   —¡**Vaya, por Dios**! Y ahora, ¿adónde vamos?
c ¡**Ánimo**, muchachos! ¡Ya os queda poco para la meta!
d ¡**Carajo**! Se me quedaron las llaves en casa.
e ¡**Huy**! ¿Tú por aquí? Pensaba que no venías.

2 Now translate the interjections, using expressions that you would use in your own language. Try to think of different possibilities, depending on the context and the intensity of the feeling.

14 The Spanish verb

Level
1/2 A verb is a word that indicates what the action of a sentence is. The verb takes a different form depending on who the subject of the sentence is (the person), the time when the action takes place (the tense) and the attitude of the speaker towards what s/he is saying (the mood).

👁 Note that unlike in English, the subject of a sentence is not always expressed. It is sometimes understood, especially when it appears in a previous sentence. For instance, in the following sentences the subject only appears in the first; it is tacit, or understood, in the second:

> *Los estudiantes vuelven de la playa. Traen la cara morena por el sol y los zapatos llenos de arena.* (The students are coming back from the beach. Their faces are tanned by the sun and their shoes full of sand.) (The subject for both sentences is *Los estudiantes.*)

The three conjugations

The more generic form of the verb is known as the **infinitive** – *el infinitivo* – and it is the form under which verbs appear in the dictionary. Infinitives may have one of three endings - *terminaciones*:

> *-ar* as in *hablar* (to speak)
> *-er* as in *comer* (to eat)
> *-ir* as in *vivir* (to live)

These endings determine the pattern the verb follows when it is conjugated, i.e. the form the verb takes when it is 'I' (*yo*), 'you' (*tú, usted*), 'he' (*él*), etc., as in the following examples:

Person	Verb	Tense	Form	Ending
(tú)	cant**ar**	present	cantas	-as
	vend**er**		vendes	-es
(ella)	sal**ir**	imperfect	salía	-ía
	compr**ar**		compraba	-aba

Person	Verb	Tense	Form	Ending
(nosotros)	com**er**	preterite	comimos	-imos
	habl**ar**		hablamos	-amos

Regular vs irregular verbs

If verbs follow the set endings for a particular tense, like *cantar,* they are said to be 'regular'. If they do not, they are said to be 'irregular'.

Not all verbs are completely regular or completely irregular, but apart from some very irregular verbs like *ser* (to be) and *ir* (to go), even irregularities have some sort of pattern. Most of them occur in the stem of the verb, the part that remains when the ending is removed. For instance in *cantar, -ar* is the ending and *cant-* is the stem. Verbs which are irregular because their stem changes are called 'radical changing verbs'.

Some verbs when conjugated change their spelling for phonetic reasons. For instance, in the past tense, the first person singular of the verb *jugar* is *jugué.* The *g* changes to *gu* to keep the strong /g/ sound.

☞ For the full Spanish verb conjugation see the verb tables in the Appendix.

Transitive vs intransitive verbs

Verbs can also be classified depending on whether or not they imply that the action directly influences an object or person (the direct object). If they do, they are called **transitive verbs (*verbos transitivos*)**. For instance, in the sentence *Luis me escribió una carta* (Luis wrote me a letter), the direct object, or object of the action *escribir,* is *una carta.*

If verbs do not imply a direct influence on a person or object, i.e. they do not take a direct object, they are called **intransitive verbs (*verbos intransitivos*)**, like the verb *morir* in the sentence *Elías murió muy joven* (Elias died when very young).

☞ To learn more about object pronouns go to Sections 5.3 to 5.6.

Most Spanish verbs are transitive. Below is a list of some of the most common intransitive verbs by category:

Verbs of being/existence	*existir, estar, morir, parecer, permanecer, quedar(se), ser, subsistir, vivir*
Verbs of movement	*andar, bajar, caer, caminar, circular, entrar, evolucionar, ir(se), marchar(se), partir, salir, saltar, vacilar, viajar*
Verbs of action	*crujir, estornudar, fracasar, gesticular, gritar, ladrar, llorar, reír, sudar, temblar, toser, volar*

Simple, perfect and continuous tenses

Spanish tenses can be:

Simple	When in one single word the verb expresses person, number, tense and mood	*voy* (present) *será* (future) *compraste* (preterite) *hable* (present subjunctive)
Perfect	Made up by a combination of the auxiliary verb *haber* (to have) + the past participle of the main verb	*he vivido* (perfect) *habías dicho* (pluperfect) *habréis llegado* (future perfect)
Continuous	Made up by a combination of the auxiliary verb *estar* + the gerund (English '-ing' form of the verb)	*están durmiendo* (present continuous) *estaremos llegando* (future continuous)

👁 Perfect and continuous tenses must not be confused with periphrastic constructions, formed by two verbs, one of which is either a gerund or a past participle.

☞ To learn more about periphrastic constructions go to Sections 15.2 and 15.3.

The Spanish mood

Moods indicate whether the speaker is stating facts (**indicative mood** - *modo indicativo*), expressing a command (**imperative mood** - *modo imperativo*), or expressing his/her feelings of uncertainty, hope, anxiety and the like towards the action (**subjunctive mood** - *modo subjuntivo*).

Ejercicios

1 In the following sentences underline the verbs and say whether they are simple, perfect or continuous:

    a Continúan las negociaciones entre el ejército y el gobierno.
    b Se ha descubierto una nueva vacuna contra la hepatitis.
    c La nave espacial está entrando a la atmósfera.
    d Los bosques tropicales sufren la irresponsabilidad de los seres humanos.
    e Cuando salimos del cine ya había oscurecido.

2 Go back to the sentences above and identify whether they have a direct object and therefore whether they are transitive or intransitive.

3 In the following paragraph separate each sentence with a vertical line. In each sentence identify the subject, the verb and the direct object if there is one. Remember that the subject of a sentence is not always expressed in the sentence but this should not be taken to mean that a subject is not present.

    La casa se levanta en la cima del cerro. Los abuelos pintaron la chocita de blanco. Tiene el techo de tejas rojizas. La familia saborea la sopa casera y las arepas de maíz.

15 Impersonal forms of the verb

Most verb forms agree in person and number with the subject of the sentence. However, there are three main verb forms which are impersonal and invariable, i.e. they are not conjugated although some of the verbs they accompany may be. They are: the infinitive (*cantar* – to sing); the gerund, sometimes called the present participle (*lloviendo* – raining); and the past participle (*sido* – been). These non-personal forms often appear after a number of verbs (plus, sometimes, a preposition) in what are called 'periphrastic constructions'. These constructions allow the meaning of the non-personal forms to be extended, e.g. in the sentence *A pesar de muchos intentos, no puede dejar de fumar* (Despite many attempts, she can't stop smoking), *dejar de* adds extra information about the verb that it complements (*fumar*).

15.1 The infinitive

Level
1/2

The infinitive – *el infinitivo* – is the name of the verb. In English it is preceded by 'to', as in 'to sing', 'to speak', 'to learn'. It is the form used to identify verbs in a dictionary.

Form

Infinitives in Spanish end in *-ar*, *-er* or *ir*, as in *hablar, estudiar, comprender, leer, vivir, salir*. These endings set the pattern for verb conjugations in the various tenses.

Use

As a noun. It can be the subject of a sentence and take the definite article.	*(El)* **comer** *es una necesidad y un placer.* (Eating is a necessity and a pleasure.)
To complement the meaning of another verb	*Juan no sabe* **nadar**. (Juan can't swim.)
After many prepositions	*Estoy cansado* **de escuchar** *este tipo de música.* (I am tired of listening to this type of music.) *Nos esforzamos* **por hacer** *las cosas bien.* (We try to do things well.)
As a command in colloquial language*	*¡***Dejar** *de gritar!* (Stop shouting!)

*🌐 This is a use peculiar to Peninsular Spanish and comes from the *vosotros* form of the imperative. The final *d* is substituted by an *r*, probably for ease of pronunciation.

☞ For further information about the imperative go to Unit 19.

Periphrastic constructions with the infinitive

The infinitive appears in a number of periphrastic constructions, e.g. ***Tienen que ir** a la policía.* (They have to go to the police.)

The most common are:

- *comenzar a* + infinitive   (to start to (do))
- *deber* + infinitive   (must – obligation)
- *deber (de)* + infinitive   (must – probability)
- *decidir* + infinitive   (to decide to (do))
- *dejar de* + infinitive   (to stop (do)ing)
- *empezar a* + infinitive   (to start to (do))
- *estar para/por* + infinitive   (to be ready to (do))
- *haber de* + infinitive   (to have to (do)): as *tener que*, but in a formal register
- *hay que* + infinitive   (one has to)
- *ir a* + infinitive   (to be going to (do))
- *llegar a* + infinitive   (to come to (do))
- *poder* + infinitive   (to be able to (do))
- *ponerse a* + infinitive   (to start do(ing))
- *quedar en/de* + infinitive   (to agree to (do))
- *querer* + infinitive   (to want to (do))
- *tener que* + infinitive   (to have to (do))
- *terminar de* + infinitive   (to finish do(ing))
- *volver a* + infinitive   (to (do) again)

Ejercicios

Level 1

1 Complete the following sentences with one of the infinitives in the box.

> reír • cerrar • impedir • nadar • venir

    a ¡ . . . la puerta, que está haciendo mucho frío!
    b Lucila dice que no puede . . . a la fiesta porque tiene mucho trabajo.
    c Si estás deprimido, . . . es una de las mejores terapias.
    d Los ecologistas insisten en . . . la construcción de hoteles en esas playas.
    e Los niños no podrán ir solos en el barco si no saben . . .

Level 1

2 Which use of the infinitive does each sentence in exercise 1 illustrate? Choose from the box.

> verb complement (×2) • imperative • noun subject • following a preposition

3 Complete the following crossword puzzle with the infinitives suggested by the clues.

CRUCIGRAMA

VERTICALES

(1) Servir de modelo a escultores/as o pintores/as.
(2) Partir una cosa en varias partes con un instrumento.
(3) Traspasar la propiedad de una cosa por algún precio.
(6) Levantarse muy temprano.
(8) Adquirir conocimientos de algo.

HORIZONTALES

(4) Hacer que un líquido pase por la boca al estómago.
(5) Sentir un dolor, enfermedad o pena.
(7) Expresar en una lengua lo que originalmente está escrito en otra.
(9) Comenzar algo.
(10) Evitar o impedir una cosa.

Level 1/2

15.2 The gerund

The gerund – *el gerundio* – conveys the idea of progression and continuity, similar to the English ending '**-ing**', but not always.

Form

Regular forms of the gerund

The gerund is formed by adding the endings *-ando* or *-iendo* to the stem of the verb, as follows:

Verbs ending in *-ar* → *-ando*	*Andar* → *and**ando***
Verbs ending in *-er* or *-ir* → *-iendo*	*beber* → *beb**iendo*** *salir* → *sal**iendo***

Irregularities in the gerund

(a) If the last letter of the verb stem is a vowel, *-iendo* becomes *-yendo*, as in the following examples:

Infinitive	Stem	Ending	Gerund
construir	constru-	-ir	construyendo
oír	o-	-ir	oyendo
creer	cre-	-er	creyendo

(b) When a verb is irregular in the third person singular of the preterite owing to changes in its stem, the gerund follows the same pattern of irregularity.

☞ For further information about the preterite go to Section 18.3.

Infinitive	Third person preterite	Gerund
pedir	pidió	pidiendo
venir	vino	viniendo
repetir	repitió	repitiendo

(c) *-iendo* becomes *-endo* after *ñ* or *ll*:

Infinitive	Gerund
gruñir	gruñendo
reñir	riñendo
engullir	engullendo

Use

With the verb *estar* to form the continuous tenses ☞ For further information on the continuous tenses go to Sections 16.2, 17.3, 18.2, 18.6 and 18.8.	*Los estudiantes* **están preparando** *el proyecto final.* (The students are preparing their final project.)
To express how an action is done. In this context it has an adverbial function of manner. ☞ For further information go to Section 26.5 (e).	*Ganó dinero* **invirtiendo** *en la bolsa.* (He earned money investing in the stock exchange.)
To indicate simultaneous actions. In this context it also has an adverbial function. ☞ Section 26.6.	*Llegaron* **cantando**. (They arrived singing.)
With some verbs to reinforce the sense of duration and continuity of an action	*Llevamos mucho tiempo* **esperando** *una respuesta.* (We have been waiting for an answer for a long time.)
To indicate the cause of an action (as an adverbial subordinate clause) ☞ Section 26.5 (a).	**Sabiendo** *que no tenía mucho tiempo se fue en taxi.* (Knowing that there wasn't much time, she took a taxi.)
To indicate a condition for something to happen (as a conditional clause) ☞ Section 26.5 (c).	**Permaneciendo** *unidos venceremos.* (If we remain united we will win.)

Spanish vs English gerund

- The Spanish gerund is sometimes equivalent to the English gerund ending '-**ing**', as in the following example: *Salieron* **gritando**. (They left screaming.)
- However, other uses of the English gerund are not equivalent, especially when in English it functions as a noun or as an adjective. When it is a noun, Spanish uses the infinitive:

    I like **swimming**. *(Me gusta **nadar**.)*

- If it functions as an adjective in English, then a Spanish adjective will be used:

    It's a **worrying** business. *(Es un asunto **preocupante**.)*
    The lecture was very **boring**. *(La conferencia estuvo muy **aburrida**.)*

👁 When the gerund of the auxiliary verb *haber* appears with the past participle of the main verb it is called a **perfect gerund**. It indicates that an action happened prior to the one in the main clause:

    Habiendo terminado *sus tareas, Mariela se marchó a casa.* (Having finished her work, Mariela went home.)

Periphrastic constructions with the gerund

The gerund also appears in a number of periphrastic constructions, e.g. *Juan **terminó llamando** a la policía.* (Juan ended up calling the police.) Some of the more common are:

- *acabar/terminar* + gerund   (to end up (do)ing)
- *andar* + gerund   (to be in the process of (do)ing – colloquial)
- *estar* + gerund   (forms the continuous tenses)
- *ir* + gerund   (to (gradually) become)
- *llevar* + gerund   (to have been (do)ing something over a period of time)
- *seguir/continuar* + gerund   (to continue to (do))

Ejercicios

Level 1

1 Complete the column on the right with the gerund forms corresponding to the infinitives in the left column. Not all the gerunds are regular.

Infinitive	Gerund
(a) jugar	
(b) leer	
(c) ir	
(d) estudiar	
(e) caer	
(f) escribir	

Level 1

2 Complete the following sentences using the correct form of the infinitive or the gerund of one of the following verbs, as appropriate:

ver • bailar • vivir • presentar • sacar

- a   No va a ir a la discoteca porque no le gusta . . .
- b   Empezó su vida profesional . . . las noticias.
- c   Tiene la ilusión de . . . a su familia para su cumpleaños.
- d   Creo que está . . . en Suramérica.
- e   La sorprendieron . . . el dinero de la caja fuerte.

Level 3

3 From the list of periphrastic constructions with the gerund, choose appropriate verbs in the present tense to complete the following sentences. There is more than one possibility, but obviously, depending on the verb you choose, the meaning of the sentence may change.

- a   El Banco del Sur . . . ya diez años invirtiendo en la construcción de hoteles.
- b   Las universidades . . . preparando a los estudiantes para carreras tradicionales.
- c   Es una lástima pero muchos jóvenes . . . trabajando en industrias que los explotan.

d Dicen que García Márquez . . . escribiendo su autobiografía.
e En esta época los automóviles . . . siendo cada vez más veloces.

15.3 The past participle

The Spanish past participle – *el participio* – conveys the idea of finished actions, similar to the English past participle. It is typically found in compound perfect tenses like the perfect (*Ya hemos **comido*** – We have **eaten**), and as adjectives (*Estoy **agotada*** – I am **exhausted**).

☞ To find out about the perfect tenses go to Sections 17.4 (the future perfect), 18.5 (the perfect), 18.7 (the pluperfect) and 21.2 (the perfect subjunctive).

Form

Regular forms of the past participle

The past participle is formed by adding the endings -**ado** or -**ido** to the verb stem:

Verbs ending in -*ar* → -*ado*	*estudiar → estudiado*
Verbs ending in -*er* or -*ir* → -*ido*	*aprender → aprendido* *producir → producido*

Irregular past participles

There are a number of verbs that have irregular past participles and there is no rule to help learn them. However, they can be grouped around certain patterns of irregularity:

Infinitive	Past participle
abrir	abierto
cubrir	cubierto
descubrir	descubierto
escribir	escrito
describir	descrito
freír	frito
imponer	impuesto
poner	puesto
suponer	supuesto
decir	dicho
hacer	hecho
volver	vuelto
soltar	suelto
morir	muerto

Use

With the verb *haber* to form the compound tenses, similar to '**to have**' in English	*La película no* **ha terminado** *todavía.* (The film hasn't finished yet.)
As an adjective after the verbs *estar* or *ser,* and after nouns. Therefore the past participle must agree in gender and number with the noun it refers to.	**Las hijas** *son* **presumidas** *como su padre.* (The daughters are conceited, like their father.)
With the verb *ser* to form the passive voice. The past participle must agree in gender and number with the noun it refers to. ☞ For more information about the passive voice go to Section 23.2.	*Las casas* **serán construidas** *por los vecinos.* (The houses will be built by the community.)
As an adverb, to indicate the manner, aspect or appearance of the subject of the sentence	**La madre** *escuchaba al pequeño* **emocionada**. (The mother listened to her little one, very moved.)
To express an action happening before another action. It is used mostly in formal registers. In this context the past participle often appears at the beginning of the sentence. ☞ For more information go to Section 26.6.	**Hallados** *los cadáveres comenzó la investigación.* (Once the bodies were found the enquiry started.)
To express cause ☞ To see its use in context go to Section 26.5(a).	**Dadas** *las circunstancias, era lo mejor que podía pasar.* (Given the circumstances, this was the best that could have happened.)

Periphrastic constructions with the past participle

The past participle also appears in periphrastic constructions. In these cases, the past participle agrees in gender and number with the noun it refers to, e.g. *Se quedaron aterrados de ver tanta gente.* (They were terrified at seeing so many people.) Some of the more common periphrastic constructions are:

- *andar* + past participle   (to be – colloquial)
  Sofía anda agotada desde que   (Sofía has been exhausted since she ran the
  corrió la maratón.   marathon.)
- *dar por/dejar por* + past participle   (to stop (doing))
  Doy por perdido mi pasaporte   (I consider my passport lost.)
  Dejamos el asunto por terminado.   (We consider the matter finished.)
- *estar* + past participle   (to be in a state of body or mind)
  Está acostumbrado a tomar   (He is used to drinking coffee in the
  café por la mañana.   morning.)
- *quedar* + past participle   (to have arrived at a conclusion/decision/
                                                      outcome)
  El asunto quedó concluido.   (The matter was concluded.)

- *quedarse* + past participle   (to end in a state of body or mind as a result of an action. It often appears in expressions denoting surprise.)

  ¡Se quedaron paralizados!   (They were paralysed!)

- *tener* + past participle   (similar to use of the perfect tense)

  Tienen la boda arreglada para la primavera.   (They have arranged the wedding for the spring.)

Ejercicios

Level 1/2

1 Complete the answers to the questions as in the example:

–¿A qué hora **llega** tu tío?

–Ya ha **llegado**.

a –¿Desde cuándo vives en Madrid?

–Hemos . . . aquí por más de 20 años.

b –¿Han podido descubrir quién se llevó el dinero?

–Todavía no lo han . . .

c –¿Vas a desayunar?

–No, ya he . . .

d –¿Crees que lo van a soltar de la cárcel?

–Me dijeron que ya lo habían . . .

e –¿Ya te escribieron tus padres?

–No, todavía no han . . .

Level 1

2 Use the past participles of the appropriate following verbs to complete the newspaper headlines below:

> bloquear • atrapar • importar • herir • salir

a Los venezolanos han _____ masivamente a votar el plebiscito contra Maduro (*El Tiempo*, Bogotá, 16 de julio de 2017)

b Una generación de jóvenes _____ en España por los salarios bajos (*El País*, Madrid, 16 de julio de 2017)

c Huevo _____ de la UE no cumple con norma mexicana (*La Prensa*, Ciudad de México, 16 de julio de 2017)

d _____ un ciclista en un accidente en Santa Úrsula (*El Día*, Canarias, 16 de julio de 2017)

e EEUU habría _____ planes de Japón para explorar [petróleo] crudo ruso (*La República*, Costa Rica, 16 de julio de 2017)

Level 2/3

3 Complete the following paragraph with the appropriate past participle of the verbs below:

> dejar • morir • abrir • poner • emocionar • comer • asustar • entrecerrar • llegar • encender

Cuando Pulgarcito trató de volver a su casa se dio cuenta de que los pajaritos se habían (a) . . . el pan que él había (b) . . . por el camino. Estaba muy oscuro aunque la noche no había (c) . . . Sentía mucho frío aunque llevaba (d) . . . un abrigo de lana. Pulgarcito estaba (e) . . . de miedo. Miraba (f) . . . las sombras de los árboles en el bosque. De pronto, a lo lejos vio una luz (g) . . . y una puerta (h) . . . Pulgarcito corrió (l) . . . y encontró a su madre esperándolo con los brazos (j) . . .

16 Present tenses of the indicative

The present tenses of the indicative express a wide range of actions, including what is happening in the immediate present (present continuous) and habitual actions (the simple present). They also have other uses, as you will see in this unit.

16.1 The present simple

The present simple – *el presente* – is a very versatile tense. Its use is similar to its English counterpart, and in general it refers to actions that are happening as we speak, to general truths and to habitual actions. The Spanish present simple, however, has other functions that relate to actions in the past or the future, depending on the context.

Form
Regular forms of the present simple

The present tense of the regular verbs changes the infinitive ending (*-ar, -er, -ir*) for a set of endings as shown below:

	-ar	-er	-ir
(yo)	bail**o**	aprend**o**	viv**o**
(tú)	bail**as**	aprend**es**	viv**es**
(él, ella/Ud.)	bail**a**	aprend**e**	viv**e**
(nosotros, -as)	bail**amos**	aprend**emos**	viv**imos**
(vosotros, -as)	bail**áis**	aprend**éis**	viv**ís**
(ellos, -as/Uds.)	bail**an**	aprend**en**	viv**en**

 In Spanish America the form *vosotros* is replaced by *ustedes*.

☞ For further information about personal pronouns go to Unit 5.

Irregularities affecting the stem of the verb

Most irregularities affect the stem of the verb. These types of verbs, commonly referred to as 'radical changing verbs', are grouped into three main categories:

- Verbs that change the *e* in the stem for *ie*
- Verbs that change the *o* in the stem for *ue*
- Verbs that change the *e* in the stem for *i*

e → ie (but not for *nosotros*, -as or *vosotros*, -as forms)	(yo) ci**e**rro, (tú) ci**e**rras, (él, ella/Ud.) ci**e**rra, (nosotros, -as) cerramos, (vosotros, -as) cerráis, (ellos, -as/Uds.) ci**e**rran
Other verbs following this pattern: *acertar, apretar, ascender, atender, atravesar, calentar, comenzar, confesar, convertir(se), defender, despertar(se), digerir, discernir, empezar, entender, enterrar, fregar, gobernar, helar, herir, hervir, invertir, merendar, negar, nevar, pensar, perder, preferir, recomendar, referirse, regar, sembrar, sentar(se), sentir, sugerir, temblar, tropezar*	
o → ue (but not for *nosotros*, -as or *vosotros*, -as forms)	(yo) d**ue**rmo, (tú) d**ue**rmes, (él, ella/Ud.) d**ue**rme, (nosotros, -as) dormimos, (vosotros, -as) dormís, (ellos, -as/Uds.) d**ue**rmen
Other verbs following this pattern: *acostar(se), acordar(se), aprobar, cocer, colgar, comprobar, consolar, contar, costar, demostrar, devolver, doler, encontrar, esforzarse, llover*, mostrar, mover, probar, recordar, renovar, soler, soltar, sonar, soñar, volver, tronar*, volar* *👁 Note that these two verbs are impersonal and are only used in the third person singular: *En abril llueve mucho.* (It rains a lot in April.) *Se oye a lo lejos cómo truena.* (From the distance you can hear how it thunders.) Note that the verb *jugar* (to play) follows the pattern **u → ue** (see page 237 of the verb tables).	
e → i (but not for *nosotros*, -as or *vosotros*, -as)	(yo) p**i**do, (tú) p**i**des, (él, ella/Ud.) p**i**de, (nosotros, -as) pedimos, (vosotros, -as) pedís, (ellos, -as/Uds.) p**i**den
Other verbs following this pattern: *arrepentir(se), competir, concebir, conseguir, consentir, corregir(se), derretir(se), despedir(se), elegir, gemir, impedir, medir, perseguir, repetir, reñir, servir, seguir, vestir(se)*	

Other irregularities in the present simple

Some very common verbs are very irregular in the **first person singular** of the present tense.

☞ Go to the verb tables in the Appendix for the full conjugation of these verbs.

(a) Adding **y** to the first person singular	(yo) do**y**, (tú) das, (él, ella/Ud.) da, (nosotros, -as) damos, (vosotros, -as) dais, (ellos, -as/Uds.) dan
Verbs following this pattern: *dar* and *estar*	

(b) Adding **g** to the first person singular	(yo) ten**g**o, (tú) tienes, (él, ella/Ud.) tiene, (nosotros, -as) tenemos, (vosotros, -as) tenéis, (ellos, -as/Uds.) tienen
Other verbs following this pattern: *hacer, poner, salir, venir, decir, oír* 👁 *decir* also changes the **e** in the stem for **i**: digo, dices, dice, decimos, decís, dicen	
(c) Verbs ending in *-ecer* and *-ducir*, plus *conocer* and its derivatives add **z** to the stem in the first person singular. This also applies to the verbs *nacer, lucir, placer* and their derivatives: *deslucir, complacer*	(yo) cono**z**co, (tú) conoces, (él, ella/ Ud.) conoce, (nosotros, -as) conocemos, (vosotros, -as) conocéis, (ellos, -as/Uds.) conocen
Other verbs following this pattern: *agradecer, aparecer, carecer, compadecer, crecer, conducir, deducir, desaparecer, desconocer, deslucir, envejecer, establecer, merecer, obedecer, parecer, pertenecer, reducir, reproducir, traducir*	
(d) Verbs ending in *-uir* add **y** to their stem in all persons, except in the first and second persons plural	(yo) constru**y**o, (tú) constru**y**es, (él, ella/Ud.) constru**y**e, (nosotros, -as) construimos, (vosotros, -as) construís, (ellos, -as/Uds.) constru**y**en
Other verbs following this pattern: *atribuir, argüir, concluir, constituir, contribuir, destituir, destruir, diluir, disminuir, distribuir, excluir, huir, incluir, instruir, obstruir, prostituir, reconstruir, retribuir, su(b)stituir* 👁 This also applies to the verb *oír*, except for the first person singular, *oigo*.	

Very irregular verbs in the present simple

The verbs *ser* (to be) and *ir* (to go) are totally irregular:

ser 🕮 For more on this verb go to Section 22.1.	(yo) soy, (tú) eres, (él, ella/Ud.) es, (nosotros, -as) somos, (vosotros, -as) sois, (ellos, ellas/ Uds.) son
ir	(yo) voy, (tú) vas, (él, ella/Ud.) va, (nosotros, -as) vamos, (vosotros, -as) vais, (ellos, ellas/ Uds.) van
haber (there is, there are) is only used in the third person singular	*No hay café en la cocina.* (There is no coffee in the kitchen.)

Use

To refer to actions which are happening as we speak. In these cases the present is often interchangeable with the present continuous. 🕮 You can learn about this tense in Section 16.2.	***Oigo*** *ruidos en el jardín.* (I can hear noises in the garden.)
To refer to habitual actions	*Todos los días* ***empezamos*** *las clases a las ocho.* (We start lessons at eight every day.)
To refer to general statements or universal truths not linked to time	*La experiencia* ***es*** *la madre de la ciencia.* (Experience is the mother of knowledge.)

In spoken or written narrative to describe the past, so that it sounds more vivid. It is then called the present historic - *presente histórico*.	*Simón Bolívar* **nace** *en Venezuela y después de liberar cinco repúblicas suramericanas* **muere** *en Colombia triste y desilusionado.* (Simón Bolívar was born in Venezuela, and after liberating five nations died in Colombia, sad and disillusioned.)	
To refer to future events that have been planned. It is often interchangeable with the future tense or with *ir a*. ☞ You can find the future tenses in Unit 17.	*El curso* **termina** *el 12 de julio.* (The course will finish on 12th July.)	
To express a wish for somebody to do something, either as a request or as a command. If the latter, the imperative can also be used. ☞ Go to Unit 19 for information on the imperative.	**Te sientas** *y* **te tomas** *la sopita.* (request) (Sit down and eat your soup.) ¡**Me devuelve** *la cámara inmediatamente!* (command) (Give me the camera back immediately!)	

Ejercicios

Level 1

1 Complete the following table with the corresponding forms of the verbs in the present tense. They are all regular.

	cantar	beber	subir
(yo)	canto		
(tú)			subes
(él, ella/Ud.)		bebe	
(nosotros, -as)		bebemos	
(vosotros, -as)			subís
(ellos, -as/Uds.)	cantan		

Level 1

2 Complete the following dialogue with the correct form of the verbs in brackets.

—¿A qué hora (a) (comenzar, tú) . . . a trabajar mañana?
—A las siete y media. ¡Si no me (b) (despertar, yo) . . . a las seis estaré perdida!
—Pero los niños (c) (dormir, ellos) . . . hasta más tarde, ¿no?
—Sí, porque normalmente no nos (d) (acostar, nosotros) . . . muy temprano.
—Bueno, ya casi es medianoche. ¡Si (e) (seguir, nosotros) . . . hablando de verdad que no te vas a poder levantar!
—Si no (f) (conseguir, yo) . . . levantarme a tiempo, no sé qué va a pasar.
—(g) (poder, yo) . . . llamarte a las seis, si quieres.
—¡Qué me (h) (decir, tú) . . . ! ¡Te (i) (confesar, yo) . . . que no estaba esperando esa sugerencia!

Level 2

3 Complete the following table with the appropriate form of the present tense and say which type of irregularity it is. The first one has been done for you.

(a) conocer	(yo) conozco	Adds 'z' to the stem
(b) oír	(ellos)	
(c) gobernar	(ella)	
(d) salir	(yo)	
(e) encontrar	(tú)	
(f) repetir	(Uds.)	

Level 2

4 Complete the following extract from a weather forecast using the verbs below in the present tense.

ser • preparar • llover • ser • tener • brillar • ver

En Estados Unidos (a) ... mucho mientras que en el Caribe (b) ... el sol. Si observamos qué pasa en Europa Occidental, (c) ... que ese continente (d) ... un clima más uniforme. El 21 de junio (e) ... el solsticio de verano en el hemis-ferio norte y el de invierno en el sur. Todos se (f) ... para el cambio de tiempo.

Level 1

16.2 The present continuous

The present continuous – *el presente continuo* – shows progression of action in the present.

Form

The present continuous is formed using *estar* and the gerund of the main verb.

	estar	-ar → -ando -er *and* -ir → -iendo
(yo)	estoy	
(tú)	estás	pensar → pens**ando**
(él, ella/Ud.)	está	conocer → conoc**iendo**
(nosotros, -as)	estamos	escribir → escrib**iendo**
(vosotros, -as)	estáis	
(ellos, -as/Uds.)	están	

☞ You can revise the gerund in Section 15.2.

Use

To emphasise that actions are taking place as we speak	*Mamá **está lavando** el coche.* (Mum is washing the car.)
To refer to actions perceived as ongoing or in progress. In this case the present continuous is often interchangeable with the present	*Manuel ahora **está viviendo** en Argentina.* (Manuel is now living in Argentina.)

👁 The use of the present continuous is similar in many instances to the use of its equivalent in English, for instance when referring to actions happening as we speak: *Estoy leyendo* (I am reading). However, when in English this tense is used to refer to actions happening in the future, Spanish does not use the present continuous but the simple present or a future form, e.g.

*Nos **vamos** el viernes.* (We are leaving on Friday.)

Ejercicios

Level 1

1 Complete the following sentences with the correct form of the present continuous.

    a   Juan (cambiar) . . . unos dólares en el banco.
    b   Mis padres (viajar) . . . por Centroamérica.
    c   Los ciclistas (correr) . . . en la Vuelta a Colombia.
    d   Gloria y yo (leer) . . . *La casa de los espíritus*.
    e   Me contaron que tú y María (vender) . . . la casa.

Level 1

2 Look at the following pictures and spot the differences between the two using the present continuous of one of the verbs below, as in the example.

leer • correr • sonreír • llorar • dormir • beber • consultar • comer

A la izquierda:

(a) la mujer **está leyendo**; (b) el niño . . .; (c) el perro . . .; (d) y los muchachos . . . un mapa.

A la derecha:
(i) la mujer . . . agua; (ii) el niño . . .; (iii) el perro . . .; (iv) y los muchachos . . . un bocadillo.

17 Future tenses of the indicative

The Spanish future tenses – *los tiempos del futuro* – are used to refer to actions that will take place after the speaker has spoken. They are very similar to the English tenses used to talk about the future:

- the future simple (*Lo **compraré** mañana.* – I shall buy it tomorrow.)
- the future continuous (*Mañana a estas horas **estaremos llegando**.* – Tomorrow at about this time we will be arriving.)
- the future perfect (*Cuando te despiertes ya **habrá llegado** Papá Noel.* – When you wake up Father Christmas will have been.)
- and the most common way to refer to the future in Spanish, the future with *ir a* + infinitive (going to) (***Voy a decirle** a Luisa lo que pienso.* – I am going to tell Luisa what I think.)

17.1 The future with *ir a*

This is similar to the future with 'going to' in English.

Form

It is formed by the present tense of *ir a* + the infinitive of the verb.

(yo) voy	a buscar
(tú) vas	a ganar
(él, ella/Ud.) va	a salir
(nosotros, -as) vamos	a perder
(vosotros, -as) vais	a construir
(ellos, -as/Uds.) van	a comer

Use

The future with *ir a* + infinitive refers to a near future or a not so immediate, but planned future	***Vamos a empezar** el viaje en Semana Santa.* (We are going to start the journey at Easter.)

Ejercicios

Level 1

1 Write sentences with *ir a* + infinitive, as in the example:

Ejemplo

(tú, salir tarde) **Vas a salir tarde.**

a (yo, hablar con el gerente)   **c** (Luis y Mariela, visitar el museo de arte)
b (Carlos, confirmar el viaje)   **d** (vosotros, no encontrar las llaves)

Level 1

2 Complete the following postcard using the future with *ir a*.

Bogotá, 6 de julio

Querida Marina:

Estamos disfrutando mucho de nuestras vacaciones. Esta tarde Juan y yo (a) (visitar) . . . el Museo del Oro, el cual parece magnífico. Mientras tanto los niños (b) (jugar) . . . con los hijos de nuestros amigos en el parque de diversiones Jaime Duque. ¡Estupendo para ellos! Mañana yo sola (c) (conocer) . . . el Museo de Arte Moderno. Juan tiene otros planes y (d) (subir) . . . al cerro de Monserrate. ¿Y tú, qué (e) (hacer) . . . el resto del verano?

Recuerdos a todos,

Carmen, Juan y los chicos

Level 2

17.2 The future simple

The future simple – *el futuro* – is similar to the English future with 'will' or 'shall':

Compraremos la casa este año. (We shall buy the house this year.)

Form
Regular forms of the future

The future tense is formed by adding the corresponding endings to the **infinitive** of the verb. They are the same for all verbs, regardless of whether they end in -*ar, -er,* or -*ir*.

	-ar	-er	-ir
(yo)	comprar**é**	comprender**é**	añadir**é**
(tú)	comprar**ás**	comprender**ás**	añadir**ás**

	-ar	-er	-ir
(él, ella/Ud.)	comprar**á**	comprender**á**	añadir**á**
(nosotros, -as)	comprar**emos**	comprender**emos**	añadir**emos**
(vosotros, -as)	comprar**éis**	comprender**éis**	añadir**éis**
(ellos, -as/Uds.)	comprar**án**	comprender**án**	añadir**án**

Irregular verbs in the future

There are 12 basic irregular verbs in the future. All other irregular verbs are compounds of those listed below, e.g. *componer* follows the same pattern as *poner*.

Infinitive	Future
caber	cabré, cabrás, cabrá, cabremos, cabréis, cabrán
decir	diré, dirás, dirá, diremos, diréis, dirán
haber	habré, habrás, habrá, habremos, habréis, habrán
hacer	haré, harás, hará, haremos, haréis, harán
poder	podré, podrás, podrá, podremos, podréis, podrán
poner	pondré, pondrás, pondrá, pondremos, pondréis, pondrán
querer	querré, querrás, querrá, querremos, querréis, querrán
saber	sabré, sabrás, sabrá, sabremos, sabréis, sabrán
salir	saldré, saldrás, saldrá, saldremos, saldréis, saldrán
tener	tendré, tendrás, tendrá, tendremos, tendréis, tendrán
valer	valdré, valdrás, valdrá, valdremos, valdréis, valdrán
venir	vendré, vendrás, vendrá, vendremos, vendréis, vendrán

👁 Verbs that are irregular in the future are also irregular in the conditional tense.

☞ For more information about the conditional tenses go to Unit 20.

Use

To refer to events that will take place after the speaker has spoken	*El sector agrícola pronto* **recibirá** *apoyo del gobierno.* (The agricultural sector will soon receive government support.)
To emphasise that an action will take place	*La* **llamaré** *y le* **pediré** *perdón.* (I will call her and ask her to forgive me.)
To indicate probability as we speak. Sometimes called the 'hypothetical future'.	**Será** *ya la medianoche.* (It must be midnight.)
To make predictions about future events	*Un día* **se quedará** *sin familia y sin fortuna.* (One day he will be left without family or fortune.)
To convey uncertainty; often expressed in the form of questions	¿**Será** *cierto?* (Could it be true?)

Ejercicios

Level 1

1 After checking the key for exercise 1 of Section 17.1, change the sentences to the future tense, as in the example.

Ejemplo

Vas a salir tarde. Saldrás tarde.

Level 1

2 Answer the following questions using the future tense as in the example.

Ejemplo

–¿Ya preparaste las maletas?
– Las prepararé esta noche.

    a   –¿Marta y Carolina vienen esta tarde?
        –No, . . . el martes.
    b   –¿Le vas a dar el libro a Inés?
        –Se lo . . . pronto.
    c   –¿Luisa se va a poner las botas?
        –No, se . . . los zapatos negros.
    d   –¿Sabéis cuándo llegan?
        –Lo . . . mañana.

Level 2

3 Complete the horoscope below using the verbs in brackets in the future tense.

> ### HORÓSCOPO
>
> *TAURO*
>
> Este mes (a) (Ud., sentirse) . . . un poco presionado en su vida de trabajo, pero (b) (mantener) . . . el buen humor y estado de ánimo que le (c) (ayudar) . . . a tomar decisiones importantes. En el plano doméstico, la familia le (d) (dar) . . . todo el apoyo que necesita. Sin embargo, algunos familiares lejanos no (e) (poder) . . . visitarlo como estaba planeado y no le (f) (ellos, avisar) . . . hasta el último momento. Pero en general todo (g) (ir) . . . muy bien y (h) (ser) . . . un mes muy interesante.

Level 1

4 Complete the following paragraph with the correct form of the future tense of the verbs in brackets.

> ### Lanzan la primera plataforma digital para aprender música en Colombia
>
> Esta semana, el Ministerio de Cultura, la Fundación Nacional Batuta y la Organización de Estados Iberoamericanos lanzaron "Viajeros del Pentagrama", una plataforma digital gratuita que (a) (buscar) _____ fomentar la enseñanza de la música.
>
> Cualquier padre de familia, docente y niño de básica primaria (b) (poder) _____ acceder a los contenidos pedagógicos que ofrece esta herramienta

accesible a través de la siguiente página web www.viajerosdelpentagrama.gov.
co. El objetivo de esta plataforma (c) (ser) _____ apoyar a los profesores en
el proceso de formación musical de sus estudiantes e involucrar a sus familias
en este aprendizaje.

Los contenidos se (d) (presentar) _____ en diferentes formatos, desde
videos, imágenes y videojuegos hasta textos y audios. La aplicación
(e) (estar) _____ disponible también en celulares y tabletas con
sistemas operativos Android.

(Adaptado de *Semana 35 años*, Colombia, 13 de julio de 2017)

17.3 The future continuous

Level 2

The future continuous – *el futuro continuo* – refers to actions which may be happening
in the present, or which are likely to take place in the near future.

Form

The future continuous is formed with the future of *estar* plus the gerund.

☞ You can revise the gerund in Section 15.2.

	estar	-ar → -ando -er and -ir → iendo
(yo)	estaré	
(tú)	estarás	acabando
(él, ella/Ud.)	estará	bebiendo
(nosotros, -as)	estaremos	recibiendo
(vosotros, -as)	estaréis	
(ellos, -as/Uds.)	estarán	

Use

To speculate about an event that may be happening now (hypothetical future)	*Estarán durmiendo ya.* (They may already be asleep.)
To refer to actions or events that are likely to happen in the near future. This is similar to English.	*Mañana a estas horas estaremos saludando a tu madre.* (Tomorrow at this time we will be saying hello to your mother.)

Ejercicio

Level
2

1 Answer the following questions as in the example.

Ejemplo

—¿Crees que ya llegaron?
—Sí, ya (desempacar las maletas) **estarán desempacando las maletas.**

a   —¿Sabes si ya empezó la película?
     —Sí, ya (terminar) . . .

b   —¿Crees que ya terminó la operación?
     —Sí, ya (el, despertarse) . . .

c   —¿Sabes cuándo comenzaron el examen?
     —No sé, pero me imagino que ya (ellos, acabar) . . .

d   —¿Crees que el avión de Juana ya aterrizó?
     —Seguro, ya (ella, salir) . . . del aeropuerto.

Level
3

17.4 The future perfect

The future perfect – *el futuro perfecto* – refers to a finished action that will have taken place before another action in the future.

Form

The future perfect is formed by the future of *haber* + the past participle of the main verb, similar to **will have** + **past participle** in English.

	haber	+ past participle
(yo)	habré	
(tú)	habrás	aprobado
(él, ella/Ud.)	habrá	celebrado
(nosotros, -as)	habremos	aprendido
(vosotros, -as)	habréis	puesto
(ellos, -as/Uds.)	habrán	

👁 Remember that not all past participles are regular.

☞ To revise the past participle go to Section 15.3.

Use

To refer to a future, finished action that will take place before another event in the future	*Cuando vuelvas ya* **habrán terminado** *el puente*. (When you come back they will have finished the bridge.)
To show that an event may have happened by the time we speak	*Ya* **habrán llegado**. (They may have arrived already.)
To express sceptical acceptance of actions that may have happened in the past and have some relationship with events in the present	*Luisa* **habrá sido** *muy rica, pero hoy no tiene un peso*. (Luisa may have been very wealthy, but she hasn't got a penny nowadays.)

Ejercicios

Level 3

1 Write sentences using the future perfect as in the example.

Ejemplo

—Llamé a mi hermana pero no contesta. (salir)
—Habrá salido.

  a —Es raro que no haya escrito. (estar enferma)
  b —No sé por qué no ha venido. (tener mucho trabajo)
  c —No los he visto trabajar. (terminar)
  d —No la vi en la estación con el resto de la familia. (tomar el tren antes que ellos)

Level 3

2 Make questions using the future perfect, as in the example.

Ejemplo

—Creo que llegaron ayer. (a qué hora)
—¿A qué hora habrán llegado?

  a —Me contaron que Jorge y Lola ya se fueron para Caracas. (cuándo)
  b —Javier llamó a alguien para reparar la lavadora. (a quién)
  c —Creo que Herminia sí encontró el libro que se le había perdido. (dónde)
  d —Dicen que ganó el festival una de las películas cubanas. (cuál)

Level 3

3 Complete the following paragraph with the verbs below in the future perfect.

subir • contaminar • perder • desaparecer • terminar

Nuestro planeta se enfrenta a un futuro muy triste. Dentro de poco tiempo (a) (nosotros) . . . con los bosques tropicales. La temperatura de los océanos (b) . . . peligrosamente. Muchas especies de peces (c) . . . El hombre (d) . . . el ambiente irremediablemente. Nuestros hijos (e) . . . su herencia más valiosa.

18 Past tenses of the indicative

Past tenses express actions that took place in the past. There are several tenses in Spanish, the imperfect, the preterite, the perfect and the pluperfect, which express different nuances of meaning in relation to the past. Each is explained in a different section. Tenses in the indicative mood refer to actions as facts which have really happened. The perfect has been included in this section because it is used to bridge time spans between the past and the present.

Level 1

18.1 The imperfect

The Spanish imperfect – *el pretérito imperfecto* – expresses meanings corresponding to the English past continuous (was/were (do)ing), the structure 'used to (do)' and the simple past when used to show continuity of action, e.g. 'We used to live in Leeds' and 'We were working in Canada at the time'.

Form
Regular forms of the imperfect

The regular conjugation is formed by adding the endings to the stem of the verb.

	caminar	beber	salir
(yo)	camin**aba**	beb**ía**	sal**ía**
(tú)	camin**abas**	beb**ías**	sal**ías**
(él, ella/Ud.)	camin**aba**	beb**ía**	sal**ía**
(nosotros, -as)	camin**ábamos**	beb**íamos**	sal**íamos**
(vosotros, -as)	camin**abais**	beb**íais**	sal**íais**
(ellos, -as/Uds.)	camin**aban**	beb**ían**	sal**ían**

Irregular verbs in the imperfect

Only three Spanish verbs are irregular in the imperfect:

	ser	ver	ir
(yo)	era	veía	iba
(tú)	eras	veías	ibas
(él, ella/Ud.)	era	veía	iba
(nosotros, -as)	éramos	veíamos	íbamos
(vosotros, -as)	erais	veíais	ibais
(ellos, -as/Uds.)	eran	veían	iban

Use

To refer to an ongoing action or state in the past with an unspecified time frame	*En aquella época yo **vivía** en una casa a la orilla del río.* (In those days I lived in a house by the river.)
To refer to habitual actions in the past	*Todos los días **me levantaba** a las 5 de la mañana y **solía** ir a entrenar.* (Every day I woke up at 5 in the morning and used to go training.)
To describe people, places and objects in the past	*La casa **era** oscura y siniestra. **Tenía** un jardín que **parecía** una jungla.* (The house was dark and sinister. It had a garden which looked like a jungle.)
To set the scene in a narrative in the past (the actions would normally be in the preterite) ☞ Go to Section 18.4 for the contrast between preterite and imperfect.	*Aquel día **hacía** mucho viento. Cogí el abrigo y salí. No se **veía** un alma.* (It was very windy that day. I grabbed my coat and went out. There was not a soul in sight.)
To express politeness	*—Buenos días, ¿qué **deseaba**?* *—**Quería** un kilo de fresas.* ('Good morning, what would you like?' 'I'd like a kilo of strawberries.')

☞ For information on the use of the imperfect in reported speech, go to Unit 27.

trabajaba
IMPERFECT

PAST TIME   (now)   PRESENT TIME

En aquella época trabajaba en la fábrica de Ford-Valenci.

☞ The verbs *soler* and *acostumbrar (a)* can also be used in the imperfect to express habitual actions in the past. Go to Section 22.4 if you need to revise these verbs.

Ejercicios

Level 1

1 Put the following infinitives into the imperfect. Do as many as you can in one minute.

jugar (nosotras)	estudiar (yo)	aprender (tú)	leer (vosotros)
crecer (él)	trabajar (Uds.)	beber (ellas)	escribir (Ud.)
ayudar (Ud.)	vivir (ellos)	caminar (ella)	construir (yo)

Level
1

2 In the previous exercise, were there any verbs whose imperfect you found particularly difficult to remember? Can you explain why? Make a note of them and revise them frequently.

Level
1

3 Prepare four questions, using the imperfect, that you would like to ask a friend about his or her past.

Level
1

4 Say two things about these people from your past: one to describe what they were like and another one about what they used to do.

> mi madre o mi padre • mi profesor/a de matemáticas • mi primer/a novio/a

Ejemplo

Mi primer novio era bajito y tenía barba. Era muy simpático y comprensivo. Le gustaba la música clásica y jugaba al baloncesto en el equipo del barrio.

Level
1/2

5 Do you remember what your bedroom looked like when you were a teenager or a child? Describe it orally for 1 to 2 minutes. Make some notes about the things you want to mention, before you start.

Level
2

6 Complete the gaps in this description of an old house, using the imperfect tense of the most appropriate verbs from the list below.

> crecer • entrar • estar • defender • parecer • quedar • ser • haber

La casa de la abuela se murió con ella. Cuando después de unos años fui a verla de nuevo comprendí que las casas viven o mueren igual que las personas. No (a) . . . nada de la alegría y la hospitalidad que yo recordaba. En aquella casa no (b) . . . un rayo de luz. El camino que atravesaba el jardincito de entrada (c) . . . totalmente cubierto de hierba y zarzas. Enfrente, el gran portalón (d) . . . la entrada con aire amenazador, totalmente impenetrable. La hiedra (e) . . . por todas las paredes de la casa, y muchas de las ventanas (f) . . . totalmente cubiertas. El jardín (g) . . . una auténtica jungla. (h) . . . basura por todas partes. Todo en la casa (i) . . . decir: "He muerto. Sólo me queda desaparecer. ¿Por qué vienes aquí?"

Level
2

18.2 The imperfect continuous

The imperfect continuous – *el pretérito imperfecto continuo* – expresses an ongoing action in the past, i.e. an action which was taking place when another action was happening or happened, e.g. *La banda **estaba tocando** cuando llegó el alcalde* (The band **was playing** when the mayor arrived.).

Form

Imperfect of *estar* + gerund of verb	*En el momento en que cayó el rayo **estábamos jugando a las cartas**.* (At the moment when the lightning struck we were playing cards.) *El precio de las casas **estaba subiendo** tanto que el mercado colapsó.* (House prices were going up so much that the market crashed.)

Ejercicio

1 Complete the following sentences using the imperfect continuous to show what was going on when something else happened.

   a (nosotros, pasear por el campo) . . . cuando comenzó a llover torrencialmente.
   b (niños, hacer tanto ruido) . . . que no oímos el timbre de la puerta.
   c (nosotras, ver la televisión) . . . y de repente, se fue la luz y nos quedamos a oscuras.
   d (viento, soplar tan fuerte) . . . que arrancó un árbol del parque.

18.3 The preterite

The Spanish preterite – *el pretérito perfecto simple o pretérito indefinido* – expresses single, complete actions in the past, e.g. *Murió en 1551* (She died in 1551); *Me lo encontré ayer* (I bumped into him yesterday).

Form

Regular forms of the preterite

	-ar	-er	-ir
(yo)	camin**é**	beb**í**	sal**í**
(tú)	camin**aste**	beb**iste**	sal**iste**
(él, ella/Ud.)	camin**ó**	beb**ió**	sal**ió**
(nosotros, -as)	camin**amos**	beb**imos**	sal**imos**
(vosotros, -as)	camin**asteis**	beb**isteis**	sal**isteis**
(ellos, -as/Uds.)	camin**aron**	beb**ieron**	sal**ieron**

Irregular forms of the preterite

There are a number of irregularities in the preterite tense: those affecting the stem of the verb, those involving spelling changes, and the 'strong preterite' forms.

(a) Radical changing verbs (changes only affect the third person singular and plural)

-e- → -i-	sentir → s**e**ntí, s**e**ntiste, s**i**ntió, s**e**ntimos, s**e**ntisteis, s**i**ntieron
Other verbs following this pattern include: *advertir, arrepentirse, competir, concebir, consentir, convertir, corregir, derretirse, despedir, divertir(se), elegir, freír, gemir, herir, impedir, interferir, invertir, medir, mentir, pedir, perseguir, preferir, referirse (a), reír, rendirse, repetir, reñir, seguir, servir, sonreír, sugerir, vestirse*	
-o- → -u-	dormir → d**o**rmí, d**o**rmiste, d**u**rmió, d**o**rmimos, d**o**rmisteis, d**u**rmieron morir → m**o**rí, m**o**riste, m**u**rió, m**o**rimos, m**o**risteis, m**u**rieron

(b) Verbs ending in -ducir

-ducir → -duj-	introducir → introduje, introdujiste, introdujo, introdujimos, introdujisteis, Introdujeron
Other verbs following this pattern include: *aducir, conducir, deducir, inducir, producir, reducir, reproducir, seducir, traducir*	

(c) Verbs which undergo a spelling change in the first person singular

This is to preserve the sound of the consonant in the infinitive.

-car → -qué	aparcar → aparqué (but aparcaste, aparcó, etc.)
Other verbs following this pattern include: *arrancar, atacar, roncar*	
-gar → -gué	jugar → jugué (but jugaste, jugó, etc.)
Other verbs following this pattern include: *ahogar, colgar, pagar, pegar, regar*	
-zar → -cé	cruzar → crucé (but cruzaste, cruzó, etc.)
Other verbs following this pattern include: *abrazar, almorzar, empezar, rezar*	
-guar → -güé	averiguar → averigüé (but averiguaste, averiguó, etc.)
Other verbs following this pattern include: *amortiguar, apaciguar*	

(d) Verbs that undergo a spelling change -i- → -y-

This only affects the third persons, singular and plural.

Vowel -er/-ir (mostly -uir pattern) → -yó, -yeron	concluir → concluí, concluiste, concluyó, concluimos, concluisteis, concluyeron
Other verbs following this pattern include: verbs ending in -**uir**: *afluir, constituir, construir, contribuir, destituir, destruir, diluir, distribuir, excluir, fluir, huir, incluir, influir, instituir, instruir*; but also others: *leer, oír, caer, decaer, recaer*	

(e) The 'strong preterites'

'Strong preterites' – *pretéritos fuertes* – differ from the general rule but nevertheless share a pattern: in all of them the stress falls on the stem of the verb, not on the verb ending. They have been grouped according to similarities.

Verbs that change the root vowel for **u**	
caber	cupe, cupiste, cupo, cupimos, cupisteis, cupieron
haber	hubo, hubieron
poder	pude, pudiste, pudo, pudimos, pudisteis, pudieron
poner	puse, pusiste, puso, pusimos, pusisteis, pusieron
saber	supe, supiste, supo, supimos, supisteis, supieron
Verbs that change the vowel root for **i**	
decir	dije, dijiste, dijo, dijimos, dijisteis, dijeron

hacer	hice, hiciste, hizo, hicimos, hicisteis, hicieron
querer	quise, quisiste, quiso, quisimos, quisisteis, quisieron
venir	vine, viniste, vino, vinimos, vinisteis, vinieron
Verbs that add **uv** at the end of the root	
andar	anduve, anduviste, anduvo, anduvimos, anduvisteis, anduvieron ( But also commonly conjugated as a regular verb: *andé,* etc., especially in parts of Spanish America.)
estar	estuve, estuviste, estuvo, estuvimos, estuvisteis, estuvieron
tener	tuve, tuviste, tuvo, tuvimos, tuvisteis, tuvieron
One-syllable verbs *dar* and *ver* also change their vowel to *i*	
dar	di, diste, dio, dimos, disteis, dieron
ver	vi, viste, vio, vimos, visteis, vieron
Verbs that add a *j*	
decir	dije, dijiste, dijo, dijimos, dijisteis, dijeron
traer	traje, trajiste, trajo, trajimos, trajisteis, trajeron
ir and *ser* both have the same preterite form	
ir/ser	fui, fuiste, fue, fuimos, fuisteis, fueron

Note that verbs belonging to the family of any of the above share the same pattern:

e.g. *superponer* (like *poner*) → *superpuse,* etc.; *contener* (like *tener*) → *contuve,* etc.

Use

To refer to single, complete actions in the past	**Se cayó** *por las escaleras y* **se rompió** *la pierna.* (He fell down the stairs and broke his leg.)
To locate an event in the past	*Cervantes* **murió** *en 1616.* (Cervantes died in 1616.)
To refer to a period of time that is considered finished	**Viví** *en Veracruz durante 10 años.* (I lived in Veracruz for 10 years.)
To refer to the events in a narrative in the past	**Llegó** *a la casa,* **sacó** *la llave e* **intentó** *abrir la puerta.* **Se abrió** *al momento con un chirrido.* (She got to the house, took out her key and tried to open the door. It creaked open immediately.)
To refer to a past event completed before a second one	**Oyó** *un ruido y* **se puso** *a correr.* (He heard a noise and started running.)

aterrizó
PRETERITE

←——————————————————|————————×——————→

(las 17 horas)   (now)
PAST TIME   PRESENT TIME

El avión aterrizó a las 17 horas.

☞ You can look at the contrast between the imperfect and the preterite in Section 18.4.

☞ The preterite is used extensively in combination with other tenses to express time relations between actions that took place in the past. Go to Section 26.6 to see how it is used.

🌍 Note that in Spanish America and some regions of Spain (Galicia, Asturias and Castilla-León) the preterite and the perfect are not used in exactly the same way. (☞ Section 18.5.)

Ejercicios

Level 1

1 Put the following infinitives into the appropriate person of the preterite tense. All of them are regular.

saltar (nosotras)	estudiar (yo)	aprender (tú)	leer (vosotros)
crecer (él)	trabajar (Uds.)	beber (ellas)	escribir (Ud.)
ayudar (Ud.)	vivir (ellos)	caminar (ella)	volar (yo)

Level 1/2

2 The following verbs all have *pretéritos fuertes*. Put the infinitives into the appropriate person of the preterite tense.

poder (yo)	decir (ellos)	venir (tú)	estar (vosotros)
poner (yo)	hacer (ellos)	decir (tú)	tener (vosotros)
saber (yo)	querer (ellos)	querer (tú)	hacer (vosotros)

Level 1/2

3 In the previous exercise, were there any verbs that you found particularly difficult? Practise them with different persons. And were there any particular persons (e.g. *vosotros*) that were especially difficult? Practise them with different verbs.

Level 2

4 The following preterite forms are not totally regular. Write down the infinitive in front of each verb in the preterite and then match the verb with the type of irregularity that has occurred.

Ejemplo

(a) pedir (pidió) . . .

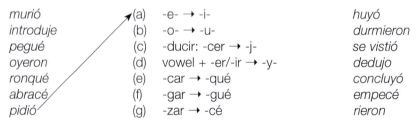

murió	(a) -e- → -i-		*huyó*
introduje	(b) -o- → -u-		*durmieron*
pegué	(c) -ducir: -cer → -j-		*se vistió*
oyeron	(d) vowel + -er/-ir → -y-		*dedujo*
ronqué	(e) -car → -qué		*concluyó*
abracé	(f) -gar → -gué		*empecé*
pidió	(g) -zar → -cé		*rieron*

Level 2

5 Write seven sentences, each with a verb that exemplifies one of the types of irregularities from the last exercise.

Level 2

6 Here is a short biography of La Malinche, an Aztec princess who lived at the time of the conquest of Mexico, in the sixteenth century. Complete the gaps to find out about her. Use the verbs from the list, putting them in the preterite.

> nacer • llegar • contribuir • morir • permanecer • ser • tener • vender •
> casar • convertirse

La Malinche (a) . . . a principios del siglo XVI. Tras la muerte de su padre la
(b) . . . como esclava y así (c) . . . al servicio de Hernán Cortés. (d) . . . su
traductora, consejera y amante, y con él (e) . . . un hijo, Martín. (f) . . . con Cortés
desde 1519 hasta 1522. En 1524 Cortés la (g) . . . con uno de sus capitanes.
(h) . . . al poco de nacer su hija, en 1529. Esta mujer (i) . . . enormemente a la
causa de los españoles e incluso (j) . . . al cristianismo.

18.4 Choosing between the preterite and the imperfect

Learners of Spanish often find it difficult to choose between the imperfect and the
preterite when referring to actions which took place in the past. Use the following
guidelines to help you.

The preterite is used to express **single actions in the past**, while the imperfect is used to refer to **actions which happened habitually** or **repeatedly.**	*Ayer me **dormí** y **llegué** tarde al colegio.* (Yesterday I slept in and was late for school.) ***Llegaba** tarde al colegio a menudo, sobre todo si era lunes.* (I was often late for school, especially on a Monday.)
The preterite is used when the action is **complete** and **finished.** The imperfect is used when an action is **in progress,** without specifying a beginning or an end.	*Aquella profesora **enseñó** Matemáticas el trimestre que el profesor titular **estuvo** enfermo.* (That teacher taught mathematics during the term our normal teacher was ill.) (The limits of the period when she taught mathematics are specified.) *Aquella profesora **enseñaba** Matemáticas.* (That teacher taught mathematics.) (It is not specified if she has stopped teaching mathematics.)
In a narrative the preterite is used to **relate events,** while the imperfect is used for the **framework** and for **descriptions of characters and scenes**.	***Era** una noche terrible. **Caían** los rayos sobre las frágiles casuchas de la aldea. Pedro y su abuela no **podían** dormir . . . En esto, se **oyeron** unos golpes en la puerta y una voz desesperada **gritó**: "¡Por el amor de Dios! Abran, por favor." Pedro se **acercó** temblando a la puerta. Afuera el viento **seguía** aullando.* (It was a terrible night. Lightning crashed over the flimsy houses in the hamlet. Pedro and his grandmother could not sleep. Suddenly, there was a knock on the door and an anguished voice shouted: 'For the love of God! Open the door, please.' Pedro went to the door, trembling. Outside the wind roared.)
The preterite is used to express **the exception** or **the uniqueness** of an action, where the imperfect expresses **the norm.**	*Yo **amaba** a mi Leonor pero aquella noche la **odié** con todas mis fuerzas.* (I loved my Leonor but that evening I hated her with all my heart.)

When two actions are simultaneous, **the main action** takes the preterite, while **the ongoing action** takes the imperfect or imperfect continuous. ☞ To learn more about time relations, go to Section 26.6.	*Iba por la calle cuando oí mi nombre.* (I was walking down the street when I heard my name.) *Cuando sonó la alarma estábamos jugando al parchís.* (When the alarm went off we were playing Ludo.)

Ejercicios

Level 2/3

1 Read the following extract and decide which of the past tenses (in bold) would take the imperfect and which would take the preterite if the extract were translated into Spanish.

> The face in the photo **was** lean and tanned and smiling lightly with lips closed. The white shirt under the red store jacket **had** a buttonless collar and a tasteful striped tie. He **appeared** neat, in shape, and the man who **took** the photo actually **spoke** with Nicholas as he pretended to shop for an obsolete gadget; said he was articulate, helpful, knowledgeable, a nice young man. His name badge **labelled** Easter as Co-Manager, but two others with the same title **were spotted** in the store at the same day.
>
> (John Grisham (1996), *The Runaway Jury* (London: Arrow Books), p. 2)

Level 2

2 Put the following sentences into the past, choosing the preterite or imperfect, as appropriate.

  a Pedro no viene a comer hoy. (Change *hoy* to *ayer*.)
  b Todos los días da un paseo de media hora.
  c La vista desde la cima es magnífica.
  d Le ha fastidiado mucho la actitud de sus compañeros.
  e Es una chica muy equilibrada pero hoy se ha enfadado muchísimo. (Change *hoy* to *ese día*.)

Level 2

3 Complete the following extract with the appropriate verb. The meaning and tense of the verbs will help you.

vio • encontraba • preguntó • había • era • sacó • replicó • iba • puso

> (a) . . . una vez una mujer cuyo oficio (b) . . . contar cuentos. (c) . . . por todas partes ofreciendo su mercadería, relatos de aventuras, de suspenso, de horror o de lujuria, todo a precio justo. Un mediodía de agosto se (d) . . . en el centro de una plaza cuando (e) . . . avanzar hacia ella un hombre soberbio, delgado y duro como un sable. [. . .] ¿Tú eres la que cuenta cuentos?, (f) . . . el extranjero. Para servirte, (g) . . . ella. El hombre (h) . . . cinco monedas de oro y se las (i) . . . en la mano.
>
> (Isabel Allende (1988), *Eva Luna*, 6th edn (Barcelona: Plaza & Janés), p. 258)

Level 2

4 Decide which part of the text in the exercise above gives background information, which part sets the scene for what is to happen and which actually relates what happened. Can you see the part played by the verb tenses?

5 In this extract from the novel *Como agua para chocolate* by the Mexican author Laura Esquivel, complete the gaps with the imperfect or preterite, as appropriate. The extract starts with Pedro eating a piece of watermelon and thinking of Tita.

> Pedro, sentado en su hamaca, (a) (comer) . . . la sandía y (b) (pensar) . . . en Tita. Su cercanía le (c) (producir) . . . una gran agitación. No (d) (poder) . . . dormir imaginándola ahí a unos pasos de él . . . y de Mamá Elena, por supuesto. Su respiración se (e) (detener) . . . unos instantes al escuchar el sonido de unos pasos en las tinieblas. (f) (Tener) . . . que tratarse de Tita, la fragancia peculiar que se esparció por el aire, entre jazmín y olores de la cocina sólo (g) (poder) . . . pertenecer a ella. Por un momento (h) (pensar) . . . que Tita se había levantado para buscarlo.
>
> (Laura Esquivel (1995), *Como agua para chocolate* (Barcelona: Grijalbo Mondadori), p. 88)

18.5 The perfect

In the sentences 'I have asked him to come' and 'She has not said a word yet' the verbs are in the perfect tense – *el pretérito perfecto*. Spanish also has this tense and its use is similar to English, although there are some differences.

The *pretérito perfecto* refers to actions which stretch from the past to the present. In many cases it is clear that the action started in the past and it is still going on, e.g. *Siempre ha sido un soñador* (He has always been a dreamer). This use of the perfect tense is shared by all speakers of Spanish.

In other cases the action has finished but its relation with the present depends on the speaker's perception of the present, e.g. *Me he comprado un coche nuevo* (I have bought a new car). In this example the action is finished but the speaker situates it in a 'present time' framework since the effect of the action is ongoing. Although this use is not shared by all speakers of Spanish, there are nevertheless examples of its use from across the Spanish-speaking world that illustrate the link between the past and the present in relation to the speaker's own time frame, e.g. *El rey ha muerto* (The king has died). This sentence suggests that the death is very recent and possibly that the funeral hasn't yet taken place.

In this unit the meaning and uses of the perfect are explained in terms of a 'retrospective' present, this is, a tense that refers to actions which may stretch from those that have already taken place to those which are still ongoing, but always in a time frame related to the present, to the speaker's 'now'. The main dialectal differences are also reviewed.

Form

The perfect is formed with the present tense of *haber*, plus the past participle of the verb.

☞ You can revise the past participle forms in Section 15.3.

	haber	+ past participle
(yo)	he	
(tú)	has	tom**ado**
(él, ella/Ud.)	ha	com**ido**
(nosotros, -as)	hemos	ped**ido**
(vosotros, -as)	habéis	or irregular form (e.g. *sido, vuelto* . . .)
(ellos, -as/Uds.)	han	

Remarks

- The past participle is invariable in the compound tenses formed with *haber,* as shown in these examples:

  *Lo hemos **visto**. Los hemos **visto**. La hemos **visto**. Las hemos **visto**.*

- Reflexive and object pronouns precede the auxiliary *haber,* e.g.

  ***Se** ha acostado tarde.* (She has gone to bed late.)

  ***Me** han mentido.* (They have lied to me.)

  ☞ If you need to revise the reflexive pronouns, go to Section 22.5.

- In Spanish, contrary to English, no word may stand between the auxiliary *haber* and the past participle, e.g.

  ¿Has encontrado los cuadernos ya? (Have you found your notebooks yet?)

  No las he probado nunca/Nunca las he probado. (I have never tried them.)

Use

There are some differences in how speakers of Spanish use the perfect tense. It is more widely used in Spain (but less so in Galicia, Asturias and Castilla-León). The various uses of this tense across the Spanish-speaking world are explained below.

(a)   Universal use of the perfect

To refer to an action or event that takes place over a period of time, including the present	*No lo **he terminado**.* (I haven't finished it yet.) *Julián siempre **ha sido** un miedoso.* (Julián has always been a scaredy cat.)

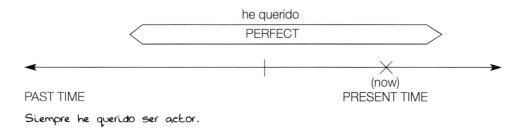

Siempre he querido ser actor.

The perfect is often found accompanied by adverbs of time or phrases (☞ Unit 10) such as:

todavía, siempre, nunca, jamás, muchas veces, a menudo, alguna vez, etc.	*Nunca* me *he emborrachado*. (I have never got drunk.) ¿No *has llamado* a la abuela *todavía*? (Haven't you called Grandma yet?) ¿*Has ido* a Acapulco *alguna vez*? Sí, he ido *muchas veces*. (Have you ever been to Acapulco? Yes, I have been many times.)

(b)   Peninsular Spanish use of the perfect

As well as the universal use above, Peninsular Spanish (except Galicia and Asturias) also uses the perfect:

To refer to an action or event which happened in the past but is considered to be in a time frame which is still in the present	¿A qué hora *has llegado* esta mañana? (What time did you arrive this morning?) Compare with: ¿A qué hora llegaste ayer? (What time did you arrive yesterday?)
To refer to a past action or event which has a result in the present or is linked to the present in some other way	*Ha tomado* demasiado alcohol. (She has had too much to drink.) (Therefore she is drunk.) *Han vuelto* a casa. (They are back home.) (Therefore they are at home.)

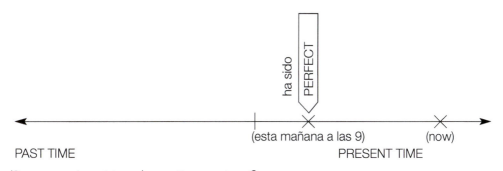

El examen ha sido esta mañana a las 9.

When used like this the perfect is often accompanied by adverbs of time or phrases such as:

hoy, hoy por hoy, esta mañana, estos días, esta semana, este mes, este año, en el presente siglo, etc.	No la **he visto hoy** en todo el día. (I have not seen her at all today.) **Me he encontrado** con ella dos veces **esta semana**. (I have bumped into her twice this week.)
recién, recientemente, últimamente, en los últimos tiempos, ya, etc.	**Últimamente** no **nos hemos visto**. (We have not seen each other lately.) **Ya han vuelto** de sus vacaciones. (They have now come back from their holidays.)

Preterite vs perfect in Peninsular Spanish

The perfect is used to refer to an action that took place in the speaker's time frame, as if the action had taken place in some sort of 'extended present time'; when this is not the case, the preterite is used. Compare the following sentences.

*Hoy me **he levantado** a las 8. **Ayer** me **levanté** a las 6.* (Today I got up at 8. Yesterday I got up at 6.)

In both sentences the actions (getting up in the morning) are past actions but in the first sentence the speaker considers himself or herself to be in the same time frame as the action, i.e. today. In the second sentence, however, the action is placed in a time frame (yesterday) which is different from the speaker's (today).

Note, though, that the choice of tense depends on what the speaker considers 'the present', and therefore depends on how the speaker views an action. Look at the following two answers:

(Today is Saturday. Juan saw María on Wednesday.)

–¿Has visto a María últimamente, Juan?

(a)   –Sí, la he visto este miércoles pasado.
(b)   –Sí, la vi el miércoles.

In (a) the speaker considers the action as part of a period of time not finished yet (*esta semana*) while in (b) the speaker considers the action as part of a period of time different from the one he is in. Note that the choice of one tense or the other has implications for the hearer as to how close or remote the action is perceived.

Time adverbs or phrases often used with the perfect are: *esta mañana, este mes, este año, en el siglo actual*, etc.

Time adverbs or phrases often used with the preterite are: *ayer, antes de ayer, aquel día, la semana pasada, el año pasado, en aquel tiempo*, etc.

(c) American Spanish use of the perfect

The most generalised use of the perfect in Spanish America is what we have called the 'Universal use of the perfect' in (a) above. However, different uses may be found in some areas:

To refer to an action or event which happened in the past but is considered to be in a time frame which is still in the present (Peru and Argentina) (i.e. a similar use to that more associated with Peninsular Spanish)	*Los niños hoy* **han llegado** *muy temprano.* (The children arrived very early today.) *Esta mañana* **he visto** *a Juan en la panadería.* (I saw Juan at the baker's this morning.)
For added impact and emotion when telling a story (spoken or written) (various regions)	*¡De repente llegó la policía, cogió a los ladrones y les* **ha dado** *una paliza de miedo!* (Suddenly the police arrived, caught the thieves and gave them a good beating.) *¡El hombre lo gritó, lo insultó y lo* **ha amenazado** *de muerte!* (The man shouted, insulted him and threatened to kill him!)
In greetings when there is a tacit reference to a period of time that has passed since the speakers were last in touch (widespread throughout Spanish America)	*¿Cómo* **has estado**? (How are you? Literally, 'How have you been (since we last met)?') *¿Cómo te* **ha ido**? (How are things? Literally, 'How have (things) been (since we last met)?')

 Level 3 **Comparison of Peninsular and American Spanish usage**

The following examples illustrate the contexts in which American Spanish prefers the preterite to the perfect:

American Spanish	Peninsular Spanish	
*¿***Leíste** *el email que te mandé esta mañana?*	*¿***Has leído** *el email que te* **he mandado** *esta mañana?*	(Did you read the email I sent you this morning?)
Ya **llegaron**.	*Ya* **han llegado**.	(They have already arrived.)
Llamaron *apenas hace unos minutos.*	**Han llamado** *apenas hace unos minutos.*	(They called just a few minutes ago.)

Other tips for selecting the perfect or the preterite

Despite the above guidelines, it is not always clear to students of Spanish when the perfect or the preterite should be used. Sometimes the perfect is used because choosing the preterite would give a different nuance to the sentence. Here are some examples:

- (a) *¿Has visto la última película de Almodóvar?*
- (b) *¿Viste la última película de Almodóvar?*

(a) would be used when the film is showing at the cinema (Have you been to see it yet?) or as a general question (Have you ever seen this film?), whereas (b) would be used to refer to the time when the film was on (Did you see it when it was on last month?).

- (a) *Siempre le ha gustado el teatro.* (He/She has always liked theatre.)
- (b) *Siempre le gustó el teatro.* (He/She always liked theatre.)

   (a) would be used to refer to an ongoing hobby of a person still living, whereas (b) would be used when the person is dead.

Ejercicios

1 Change the words in brackets so that the sentences are in the perfect tense.

   a (nosotros, estar) . . . en casa todo el día.
   b ¿(tú, oír) . . . las últimas noticias?
   c Todavía no (ella, llegar) . . . Estamos esperándola.
   d —¿(tú, tener) . . . noticias de Juan? —Sí, (él, volver) . . . a Londres.

2 Read the following letter and decide whether the perfect or the present simple should be used in each case.

> Querida Marta
>
> ¿Cómo estás? No (a) (poder) . . . contestar tu carta antes porque (b) (estar) . . . enferma. Ya (c) (estar) . . . mejor, aunque no completamente recuperada. Estos días no (d) (ir) . . . a trabajar y (e) (quedarse) . . . en casa descansando. Te (f) (escribir) . . . desde la cama. Son las 10 de la mañana y todavía no me (g) (levantar) . . . ¡Me (h) (hacer) . . . una perezosa!

3 Explain the differences in meaning between the following pairs:

   a (i) A Juana toda la vida le gustó hacer grandes viajes.
      (ii) A Juana toda la vida le ha gustado hacer grandes viajes.
   b (i) He soñado con ser periodista toda mi vida.
      (ii) En aquel tiempo soñaba con ser periodista.
   c (i) ¿Has leído *Cien años de soledad*?
      (ii) ¿Leíste *Cien años de soledad* cuando te lo dejé?

18.6 The perfect continuous
Form

Perfect of *estar* + gerund of verb	—Apenas hemos visto a Lourdes estas vacaciones. —Es que **ha estado estudiando** para los exámenes de fin de curso. ('We have hardly seen Lourdes during the holidays.' 'She has been studying for her final exams.')

This tense is often accompanied by time phrases such as: *todo el día, toda la noche, durante todo el fin de semana, desde las* (time), *hasta las* (time), etc.

Use

This tense – *el pretérito perfecto continuo* – is used to add a sense of progressive or continuous action to the perfect. In the example *Últimamente ha estado estudiando mucho* (She has been studying a lot recently) the perfect continuous is used to stress that the action of studying has been going on for a period of time (*últimamente* – recently).

Ejercicio

Level 2

1 Give answers to the following questions, using the perfect continuous.

    a ¿Por qué no me has llamado últimamente? (salir con otra chica)

    b ¿Ya has encontrado la respuesta al problema? (no, pensar, toda la noche)

    c ¿Vienes de Veracruz? ¿Has estado visitando a tu hermana? (no, trabajar, ayer y hoy)

    d ¿Alguien ha visto al señor Benítez últimamente? (yo, preguntar, nadie sabe nada)

Level 2

18.7 The pluperfect

The pluperfect – *el pretérito pluscuamperfecto* – indicates that an action took place before another past action, very much like the English sentence 'I went to pick her up but she **had** already **left** for the party.'

Form

The pluperfect is a compound tense formed by the imperfect of *haber* and the past participle of the verb.

	haber	past participle
(yo)	había	
(tú)	habías	cant**ado**
(él, ella/Ud.)	había	vend**ido**
(nosotros, -as)	habíamos	sal**ido**
(vosotros, -as)	habíais	or irregular form (e.g. *ido, hecho* . . .)
(ellos, -as/Uds.)	habían	

☞ To revise the past participles go to Section 15.3.

Use

To express actions in the past which had already taken place before other past actions occurred	*Los vikingos ya **habían alcanzado** el norte de América antes de que Colón llegara al Caribe en 1492.* (The Vikings had already reached North America before Columbus arrived in the Caribbean in 1492.)

Note: the adverb *ya* often accompanies the pluperfect tense to reinforce the idea that the event had **already** taken place when something else happened. Similarly, *todavía no* and *aún no* are used to show that the action had not **yet** taken place.

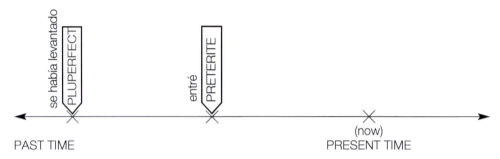

Ya se había levantado cuando entré en su alcoba.

Time relations using the pluperfect

With the perfect and the preterite it indicates the action that took place first.	**He llegado/Llegué** *a la tienda cinco minutos tarde y* **había cerrado**. (I got to the shop five minutes late and it had already closed.)
With the imperfect, it expresses an action which habitually took place before another habitual action.	*En aquella época, cuando* **llegaba** *a casa del trabajo los niños* **se habían ido** *a la cama.* (At that time when I got home from work the children had already gone to bed.)
The pluperfect can also relate to adverbs or adverbial phrases of time, such as *antes de, para entonces,* etc.	**Para** *los 40 años ya* **se había hecho** *rico.* (He had become rich by the age of 40.) **Antes de** *(cumplir) los 20 años* **se había casado** *y* **había tenido** *dos niños.* (Before the age of 20 he had married and had two children.)

☞ For the use of the pluperfect in reported speech, see Unit 27.

Ejercicios

Level 2

1 Put the following infinitives in the correct form of the pluperfect.

   a   Nunca (yo, pasar) . . . tanto miedo.
   b   Él ya (abrir) . . . la carta cuando llegué y la estaba leyendo.
   c   Antes de aquella discusión, mi marido y yo jamás (reñir) . . .
   d   El director comunicó a los obreros que la empresa (quebrar) . . .

Level 2

2 Make sentences with the following elements (and any others that you may want to add), showing that the second set happened **before** the first one.

   a   (i) yo, correr con todas mis fuerzas. (ii) los bomberos, llegar unos minutos antes.
   b   (i) Luis, a los 13 años, dar su primer concierto. (ii) empezar a tocar, con su padre.

    c (i) el país, estar destrozado. (ii) la guerra, terminar, el año anterior.
    d (i) ir a detenerlo. (ii) él, escaparse.

Level 2

3 Complete the gaps with the most appropriate verb to complete this extract from the novel *Noticia de un secuestro*, by Gabriel García Márquez.

> habían hecho • habían empezado • rebasó • tuvo • siguieron • cerró • giraron

> El taxi y el Mercedes (a) . . . al automóvil de Maruja, siempre a la distancia mínima, tal como lo (b) . . . desde el lunes anterior para establecer las rutas usuales. Al cabo de unos veinte minutos todos (c) . . . a la derecha en la calle 82, a menos de doscientos metros del edificio de ladrillos sin cubrir donde vivía Maruja con su esposo y uno de sus hijos. (d) . . . apenas a subir la cuesta empinada de la calle, cuando el taxi amarillo (e) . . . el automóvil de Maruja, lo (f) . . . contra la acera izquierda, y el chofer (g) . . . que frenar en seco para no chocar.
>
> (Gabriel García Márquez (1996), *Noticia de un secuestro* (Barcelona: Nueva Narrativa), p. 8)

Level 3

18.8 The pluperfect continuous

The pluperfect continuous – *el pretérito pluscuamperfecto continuo* – is used to refer to an action which had been going on before another action, as in English 'Peter came in at that moment. He **had been playing** tennis with Margaret and looked exhausted'.

Form

Pluperfect of *estar* + gerund of the verb	*Lucía miró a su marido.* **Había estado preparándose** *para este momento todo el día, así que se armó de valor y habló.* (Lucía looked at her husband. She had been preparing for this moment all day, so she plucked up courage and spoke.)

Use

The pluperfect continuous emphasises the progressive or ongoing nature of an action before the subsequent action took place.

Ejercicio

Level 2

1 Complete the following sentences, saying what had been going on before the action took place, using the pluperfect continuous.

    a Finalmente llegamos a la cima de la montaña. (caminar) . . . durante toda la mañana y nos encontrábamos agotados.

    b El médico se enfadó mucho cuando se enteró de que Teresa no (tomar) . . . la medicina que le había mandado.

    c Al final del día llegaron los recolectores de aceitunas. (trabajar) . . . desde las 5 de la mañana pero se lavaron, se cambiaron de ropa y se fueron a las fiestas del pueblo a bailar.

19 Imperatives

Level
2 The imperative – *el imperativo* – is a mood used to give commands, and is similar to the imperative in English (*¡Lávate las manos!* – Wash your hands!).

Form
Regular affirmative commands

(a) The imperative in the *tú* form corresponds to the third person singular form of the present indicative tense:

-ar → -a	acab**a**, aparc**a**, and**a**, copi**a**, piens**a** (tú)
-er, -ir → -e	cog**e**, corr**e**, escog**e**, le**e** (tú) decid**e**, pid**e**, recib**e** (tú)

(b) The imperative for *vosotros* is formed by taking away the *r* of the infinitive and adding *d:*

Infinitive	Imperative
pag**ar**	paga**d** (vosotros)
ped**ir**	pedi**d** (vosotros)
suger**ir**	sugeri**d** (vosotros)
volv**er**	volve**d** (vosotros)

(c) The imperative for *usted* and *ustedes* follows the form of the third persons singular and plural of the present subjunctive.

☞ To learn about the conjugation of the present subjunctive go to Section 21.1.

-ar → -e	acab**e** (Ud.), aparqu**e** (Ud.), and**en** (Uds.), copi**en** (Uds.)
-er, -ir → -a	escoj**a** (Ud.), le**a** (Ud.), decid**an** (Uds.), recib**an** (Uds.)

Irregular affirmative commands

(a) There are a few irregular imperatives in the second person singular *tú*. The most important ones are listed below:

decir	di (tú), decid (vosotros, -as), diga (Ud.), digan (Uds.)
hacer	haz (tú), haced (vosotros, -as), haga (Ud.), hagan (Uds.)
ir	ve (tú), id (vosotros, -as), vaya (Ud.), vayan (Uds.)
poner	pon (tú), poned (vosotros, -as), ponga (Ud.), pongan (Uds.)
salir	sal (tú), salid (vosotros, -as), salga (Ud.), salgan (Uds.)
ser	sé (tú), sed (vosotros, -as), sea (Ud.), sean (Uds.)
tener	ten (tú), tened (vosotros, -as), tenga (Ud.), tengan (Uds.)
venir	ven (tú), venid (vosotros, -as), venga (Ud.), vengan (Uds.)

(b) Verbs with any irregularities in the present tense (e.g. with radical changes) keep the same irregularity in the imperative, except in the *vosotros/vosotras* form.

☞ To revise the radical changing verbs in the present tense go to Unit 16.

Present tense	Imperative
aprietas	aprieta (tú), apretad (vosotros, -as), apriete (Ud.), aprieten (Uds.)
pides	pide (tú), pedid (vosotros, -as), pida (Ud.), pidan (Uds.)
cuelgas	cuelga (tú), colgad (vosotros, -as), cuelgue (Ud.), cuelguen (Uds.)

Negative commands

The negative imperative is formed by placing *no* before the present subjunctive form. This applies to all negative forms, singular and plural, *tú* or *usted*. Verbs ending in *-ar* take endings with *-e* in the subjunctive, verbs ending in *-er* or *-ir* take endings with *-a*.

☞ For further information on the present subjunctive go to Section 21.1.

-ar → *-e*	no termines (tú), no olvide (Ud.), no cantéis (vosotros -as), no hablen (Uds.)
-er, *-ir* → *-a*	no corras (tú), no lea (Ud.), no subáis (vosotros, -as), no sufran (Uds.)

🌐 Remember that the pronoun *vosotros/vosotras* is not used in Spanish America and therefore the corresponding imperative form is not used either.

In Spain, in colloquial contexts, the imperative form for *vosotros* loses the final *-d* and it is often replaced by *-r*. As a result, *pagad, sugerid, volved, comprad* become *pagar, sugerir, volver* and *comprar*, e.g. *¡Volver aquí!* (Come back here!)

Enclitic object pronouns with the imperative

Object pronouns are appended to the imperative form when it is affirmative.

☞ To revise the object pronouns go to Sections 5.3 and 5.4.

👁 Note that in some cases the form takes a written accent to maintain the stress on the same syllable.

Compra **el coche azul**	→	Cómpralo
Vendan **la casa**	→	Véndanla
Llamen **a los niños**	→	Llámenlos
Abra **las ventanas**	→	Ábralas

Imperative constructions equivalent to the English forms 'Let's . . .', 'Let him/her/them . . .'

In sentences with the first person plural ('Let's . . .'), the construction follows the same form as the first person plural of the present subjunctive	***Compremos*** *las entradas para el cine*. (Let's buy the tickets for the cinema.) ***¡Bebamos*** *a la salud de los novios!* (Let's drink to the bride and bridegroom's health!)
In sentences with the other persons of the conjugation ('Let him/her/them . . .'), the subjunctive is also used, but in these cases it is preceded by *que*	*¡**Que se vayan**!* (Let them go!) *¡**Que** lo **castigue** la ley!* (Let the law punish him!)

Pronominal verbs in the imperative

The reflexive pronouns that are part of pronominal verbs are also appended to the imperative form when it is affirmative.

☞ For further information about pronominal verbs go to Section 22.5.

(tú)	*levánta**te**, acuésta**te**, báña**te***
(Ud.)	*levánte**se**, acuéste**se**, báñe**se***
(vosotros) 👁 Note that these forms lose the *-d* at the end of the imperative form for *vosotros*, and that in colloquial contexts it is often replaced by an *r*, e.g. *bañaros*.	*levanta**os**, acosta**os**, baña**os***
(Uds.)	*levánten**se**, acuésten**se**, báñen**se***
(nosotros) 👁 Note that in this case, the imperative form for the first person plural loses the **s** that precedes the object pronoun.	*levanté**monos**, acosté**monos**, bañé**monos***

Use

To give orders	¡**Salgan** del edificio inmediatamente! (Leave the building immediately!)
To give instructions	**Ponga** la tapa y luego **gíre**la hacia la derecha. (Put the cap on and then turn it to the right.)
To give advice	**Habla** con el médico a ver él qué piensa. (Talk to the doctor to see what he thinks.)

👁 Note that commands can also be expressed by using the present or the future tenses. ☞ For further information about these tenses go to Units 16 and 17 respectively.

Ejercicios

Level 1

1 Complete the sentences in the following table with the corresponding forms of the imperative. Some of them have been completed for you. Remember that not all verbs are regular in all persons.

(tú)	(Ud.)	(vosotros, -as)	(Uds.)	(nosotros, -as)
Compra el pan.				
	Lea la nota.			
		Acostaos pronto.		
			Apaguen la luz.	
				Empecemos ya.

Level 2

2 Take all the sentences with the verb *leer* in the previous exercise and put them in the negative form.

Level 2

3 Complete the following sentences with the correct form of the imperative, as in the example.

Ejemplo

(cerrar, tú) la ventana. **Cierra** la ventana.

a (tener, Ud.) . . . paciencia, que todo se arreglará.

b (escuchar, Uds.) . . . con atención, pues esto es muy importante.

c ¡(decir, tú) . . . la verdad!

d ¡No (hablar, vosotros) . . . tan alto!

Level 2

4 Advertisements are full of expressions using the imperative. Read the following advertisements and complete them with the correct imperative form of one of the verbs from the box.

pensar • olvidar • aplicarse • usar • perder • ir

(a)   ¿Está perdiendo el pelo? ¡No . . . la cabeza!, . . . Pelusán.

(b)   Si quiere comprar a crédito ¡ . . . con cuidado la materia gris! . . . al Banco del Llano.

(c)   ¿Tiene ganas de unas vacaciones? ¡No lo . . . dos veces! Ecotur se lo arreglará todo a la mayor brevedad.

(d)   ¿Se siente deprimido o falta de ánimo? No . . . tomar Vitadón todos los días.

20 Conditional tenses

Conditionals express hypotheses and refer to events which are dependent on a condition that needs to be fulfilled for the events to take place.

Level 2

20.1 The conditional

The simple form of the conditional – *el condicional simple* – is equivalent to 'would' + infinitive in English. (*Si tuviera tiempo, iría al teatro contigo.* – If I had time I would go to the theatre with you.)

Form

Regular forms of the conditional

The form of the conditional has some similarities with the form of the future tense. Like the future tense, the conditional adds the relevant endings to the infinitive. Endings are the same for *-ar*, *-er* or *-ir* verbs:

	-ar	-er	-ir
(yo)	compraría	comprendería	añadiría
(tú)	comprarías	comprenderías	añadirías
(él, ella/Ud.)	compraría	comprendería	añadiría
(nosotros, -as)	compraríamos	comprenderíamos	añadiríamos
(vosotros, -as)	compraríais	comprenderíais	añadiríais
(ellos, -as/Uds.)	comprarían	comprenderían	añadirían

Irregular verbs in the conditional

👁 There are 12 verbs that are irregular in the conditional. They are the same verbs that are irregular in the future. ☞ Section 17.2.

Infinitive	Conditional
caber	cabría, cabrías, cabría, cabríamos, cabríais, cabrían
decir	diría, dirías, diría, diríamos, diríais, dirían
haber	habría, habrías, habría, habríamos, habríais, habrían
hacer	haría, harías, haría, haríamos, haríais, harían
poder	podría, podrías, podría, podríamos, podríais, podrían
poner	pondría, pondrías, pondría, pondríamos, pondríais, pondrían
querer	querría, querrías, querría, querríamos, querríais, querrían
saber	sabría, sabrías, sabría, sabríamos, sabríais, sabrían
salir	saldría, saldrías, saldría, saldríamos, saldríais, saldrían
tener	tendría, tendrías, tendría, tendríamos, tendríais, tendrían
valer	valdría, valdrías, valdría, valdríamos, valdríais, valdrían
venir	vendría, vendrías, vendría, vendríamos, vendríais, vendrían

Use

To express what could or should happen	*Mario **debería** cambiar su modo de vida.* (Mario should change his lifestyle.) *Yo **podría** venir mañana.* (I could come tomorrow.)
To express a present or future hypothesis. It is similar to 'would'. It is common after conditional sentences with *si*, equivalent to 'if clauses' in English. (☞ Refer to Section 26.7 for types and meanings of conditional sentences.)	*¿Qué **contestarías** tú?* (What would you reply?) *Si tuviéramos dinero **nos iríamos** enseguida.* (If we had money we would leave straightaway.)
To give advice	*Yo en tu lugar **hablaría** con un abogado.* (If I were you I would talk to a solicitor.)
To make polite requests	*¿**Podría** decirme qué hora es?* (Could you tell me what time it is?)
To express probability or hypothesis in relation to events in the past	*En esa época **habría** una gran mortalidad infantil.* (In those times there must have been a high child mortality rate.)
In indirect speech to refer to future events (☞ For further information about direct and indirect speech go to Unit 27.)	*Isabel dijo que **vendrían** el domingo.* (Isabel said that they would come on Sunday.)

Ejercicios

Level 2

1 Complete the following sentences with the conditional form of the verbs in brackets.

   a Entonces (tener, nosotros) . . . unos quince años.

   b Si supieran la verdad no te (volver, ellos) . . . a hablar.

    c   Yo pienso que María (deber) . . . buscar otro empleo.

    d   Dijeron que las tiendas (cerrar) . . . durante el carnaval.

    e   ¿(poder, tú) . . . pedirme un taxi?

Level 2

2 Give advice according to the situation, as in the example.

Ejemplo

–No sé si alquilar una casa o un apartamento. (casa)

–Yo alquilaría una casa.

    a   No sé si reservar habitación en un hotel o en una pensión. (pensión)

    b   Pienso dibujar un paisaje o un autorretrato. (paisaje)

    c   Me gustaría llevar unos chocolates o unas flores. (chocolates)

    d   Quisiera abrir un restaurante o una cafetería. (cafetería)

Level 2

3 Julián is preparing a birthday party for Graciela. He needs to sort out the house, buy food and drink, and get some music. He asked for help from his friends. The following are extracts from Julián's phone conversations with his friends. Read them and then change the sentences below into indirect speech, using the conditional, as in the example.

Ejemplo

Julián: Hola, Paco, ¿en qué puedes ayudar tú?

Paco: Pues si quieres yo puedo arreglar la casa.

Paco dijo que (él) podría arreglar la casa.

    a   Julián: Irene, ¿me puedes echar una mano con lo de la fiesta?

        Irene: Claro, ya hago yo la tortilla.

    b   Julián: Manolo, ¿puedes traer algo para la fiesta de Graciela?

        Manolo: Seguro, llevaré tres botellas de vino.

    c   Julián: Elena, ¿quieres preparar algo para esta noche?

        Elena: Lo siento, no puedo, pero puedo comprar los platos y las servilletas de papel.

    d   Julián: Santiago, Irene va a traer una tortilla y Manolo vino. ¿Juana y tú tenéis tiempo de preparar algo?

        Santiago: No hay problema. Nosotros preparamos una ensaladilla rusa.

Level 3

20.2 The conditional perfect

The conditional perfect – *el condicional compuesto* – expresses hypothesis and probability in relation to past actions.

Form

The conditional perfect is formed by the conditional of *haber* + the past participle of the verb. It is equivalent to the English construction '**would have**' + **past participle**.

	haber	past participle
(yo)	habría	
(tú)	habrías	aprobado
(él, ella/Ud.)	habría	puesto
(nosotros, -as)	habríamos	escrito
(vosotros, -as)	habríais	or irregular form (e.g. *sido, vuelto* . . .)
(ellos, -as/Uds.)	habrían	

☞ Remember that not all past participles are regular. For more information about the past participle go to Section 15.3.

Use

To express probability in the past. (In this context the conditional perfect is sometimes interchangeable with the pluperfect.) ☞ For more on the pluperfect go to Section 18.7.	*No la vi durante la manifestación. A lo mejor **se habría marchado** antes de llegar nosotros.* (I didn't see her during the demonstration. She may have left before we arrived. Literally: It is likely that she would have left before we arrived.)
In conditional sentences, to refer to an outcome that did not materialise, since the condition was not met. It normally follows *si* + imperfect subjunctive ☞ For more information about conditional clauses go to Section 26.7.	*Si hubiera sabido que estabas enferma no **habría venido**.* (If I had known you were ill I wouldn't have come.)
In indirect speech, to report actions that in direct speech would be expressed in the future perfect. ☞ For further information about indirect speech go to Unit 27.	*Dijeron que para el lunes ya **habrían firmado** el contrato.* (They said that by Monday they would have signed the contract.)

Ejercicios

Level 2

1 Complete the following sentences using the conditional perfect as in the example.

Ejemplo

Si hubieras venido, (ver) **habrías visto** al bebé de Cristina.

a Me preguntó si para el próximo verano ya me (regresar) . . . para Quito.
b Contesté que para las próximas Navidades (concluir) . . . el proyecto.
c Si hubiéramos telefoneado (poder) . . . excusarnos.
d Me advirtió que para dentro de una semana el comité ya (publicar) . . . los resultados.
e Si me hubierais llamado os (dar) . . . la noticia.

Level 3

2 Write sentences to say what you think may have happened, as in the example.

Ejemplo

–Llamé a mi hermana pero no contestó. (salir)
–Habría salido.

a Pasé por su casa pero no vi su coche. (ponerlo en el garaje)
b Dijo que no habían podido entrar. (perder la llave)
c Noté a Inés muy cansada esta mañana. (volver muy tarde de la fiesta anoche)
d No vinieron a la oficina por la tarde. (venir por la mañana)
e Rosa sacó una calificación muy alta. (estudiar mucho)

Level 3

3 Complete the following sentences saying what you think somebody would have done if the following had or had not happened, as in the example.

Ejemplo

Si el partido de fútbol no hubiera sido hoy habríamos ido a la playa.

a Si los trabajadores no hubieran terminado la obra el viernes . . .
b Si Alicia no hubiera perdido las llaves de su apartamento . . .
c Si a Jaime se le hubiera olvidado el cumpleaños de su esposa . . .
d Si Anita hubiera hecho lo que le ordenó el médico . . .
e Si los niños no hubieran tenido un resfriado . . .

21 Subjunctive tenses

The subjunctive – *el subjuntivo* – is one of the verb moods (*modos*) used to express uncertainty, possibility, emotions and wishes. (☞ For further information on what a mood is, go to Unit 14.) There are four tenses in the subjunctive mood: the present, the perfect, the imperfect and the pluperfect.

21.1 The present subjunctive
Form
Regular forms of the present subjunctive

The form of the present subjunctive – *el presente de subjuntivo* – is based on the present indicative forms, but *-ar* verbs take *-er/-ir* endings and vice versa. ☞ To revise the present tense go to Section 16.1.

Verbs ending in *-ar* form the present subjunctive with *-e, -es*, etc.	acab**e**, acab**es**, acab**e**, acab**emos**, acab**éis**, acab**en**
Verbs ending in *-er* or *-ir* form the present subjunctive with *-a, -as*, etc.	corr**a**, corr**as**, corr**a**, corr**amos**, corr**áis**, corr**an** sub**a**, sub**as**, sub**a**, sub**amos**, sub**áis**, sub**an**

Irregularities in the present subjunctive

All irregularities in the present indicative (☞ see Section 16.1) are mirrored in the present subjunctive.

(a)	Radical changing verbs: e → ie (e.g. *cerrar*) o → ue (e.g. *volver*) (but **not** in the first and second persons in the plural) e → i (e.g. *medir*)	c**ie**rre, c**ie**rres, c**ie**rre, c**e**rremos, c**e**rréis, c**ie**rren v**ue**lva, v**ue**lvas, v**ue**lva, v**o**lvamos, v**o**lváis, v**ue**lvan m**i**da, m**i**das, m**i**da, m**i**damos, m**i**dáis, m**i**dan
(b)	Adding *g* (e.g. *salir, decir*)	sal**g**a, sal**g**as, sal**g**a, sal**g**amos, sal**g**áis, sal**g**an di**g**a, di**g**as, di**g**a, di**g**amos, di**g**áis, di**g**an
(c)	*c → zc* in verbs ending in *-ecer, -ducir* and others such as *nacer, lucir, placer* (and their derivatives)	tradu**zc**a, tradu**zc**as, tradu**zc**a, tradu**zc**amos, tradu**zc**áis, tradu**zc**an

(d) *i* → *y* in verbs ending in -*uir* (e.g. *destruir*)	destru**y**a, destru**y**as, destru**y**a, destru**y**amos, destru**y**áis, destru**y**an

Some verbs are irregular and do not follow a pattern:

ser	sea, seas, sea, seamos, seáis, sean
estar	esté, estés, esté, estemos, estéis, estén (form seems regular but notice the stress on the ending)
caber	quepa, quepas, quepa, quepamos, quepáis, quepan
dar	dé, des, dé, demos, deis, den (the verb *dar* is irregular in that it takes a written accent on the first and third persons singular to distinguish them from the preposition *de*)
haber	haya, hayas, haya, hayamos, hayáis, hayan
saber	sepa, sepas, sepa, sepamos, sepáis, sepan
ir	vaya, vayas, vaya, vayamos, vayáis, vayan

Spelling changes

Some spelling changes are needed in some verbs to reflect consistency in pronunciation:

-*ger*/-*gir* → *j* (to preserve the sound /x/ or /h/)	co**g**er → co**j**a, co**j**as, etc. corre**g**ir → corri**j**a, corri**j**as, etc.
-*gar* → *gu* (to preserve the sound /g/)	car**g**ar → car**gu**e, car**gu**es, etc.
-*guir* → *g* (to preserve the sound /g/)	se**gu**ir → si**g**a, si**g**as, etc.
-*guar* → *gü* (to preserve the vowel /u/)	averi**gu**ar → averi**gü**e, averi**gü**es, etc.
-*car* → *qu* (to preserve the sound /k/)	sa**c**ar → sa**qu**e, sa**qu**es, etc.
-*zar* → *c* (not for pronunciation reasons, but because it is not usual in Spanish to have the letter *z* before -*e* or -*i*.)	ca**z**ar → ca**c**e, ca**c**es, etc.

Use
(a) In independent sentences

After *ojalá*, and in idiomatic expressions of desire starting with *que*	*Ojalá* **llegue** *a tiempo*. (I hope he arrives on time.) *Que Dios te* **bendiga**. (God bless you.) *¡Que lo* **pases** *bien!* (Have a good time!)
After adverbs expressing uncertainty and possibility, like *quizá(s)*, *tal vez* and *posiblemente*	*Quizá Amelia* **se anime** *a probar el vuelo sin motor con nosotros*. (Perhaps Amelia will have a go at gliding with us.)
To form some **imperatives** ☞ To revise the imperative go to Unit 19.	*¡Que se* **calle**! (Literally, May he/she/you (sing. frml.) shut up!) *No me* **llames** *al móvil, estaré en una reunión*. (Don't call me on my mobile, I'll be in a meeting.)

👁 Some of the above adverbs of possibility or probability can be followed by the indicative or the subjunctive. The choice depends on the level of certainty as perceived by the speaker. Look at these examples:

> *Posiblemente no sabe nada todavía.*
> *Posiblemente no sepa nada todavía.*

In the first, the sentence is almost like *Seguramente no sabe nada todavía*, whereas in the second there is a greater degree of uncertainty as to whether the person knows anything about it by now or not.

👁 The present subjunctive is also used to form some imperatives.

☞ To revise the imperative go to Unit 19.

(b) In subordinate clauses

In general the present subjunctive is used when the action in the subordinate clause is considered **possible** or refers clearly to **the present** or **the future**. The main verb is in a present or future tense.

(i) In noun clauses starting with *que* (where the subject of the subordinate verb is different from that in the main verb). (☞ See below for further uses of the subjunctive in noun clauses.)	*Lamento que no **puedas** venir a Praga con nosotros.* (I'm sorry you can't come to Prague with us.)
(ii) In relative clauses when the event, action, or outcome is unknown or hasn't yet happened	*No te será fácil encontrar un amigo que te **comprenda** como Luis.* (It won't be easy for you to find a friend who understands you as well as Luis does.)
(iii) In adverbial clauses the subjunctive is **always** used in clauses expressing **purpose** and can be used in clauses expressing **cause**, **concession**, **condition**, **manner**, **place** and **time**. The main verb is in a present or future tense or the imperative. Most commonly, the subjunctive is used after the following connectors.	
Expressing purpose, such as *para que, de modo que, de manera que, de forma que*	*Llámala **para que sepa** que estamos aquí.* (Call her so that she knows we are here.)
Expressing condition, such as *con tal de que, siempre y cuando, a menos que, a no ser que, con tal de que, a condición de que*, etc. (but not *si*, which does not take the present subjunctive)	*Puedes irte **con tal de que llegues** temprano mañana.* (You can leave, provided you arrive early tomorrow.)
Expressing concession, such as *aunque, aun cuando, por más que, por mucho que*	*Iremos **aunque tengamos** poco dinero.* (We will go even if we haven't got much money.)

☞ For more information on the indicative and the subjunctive in relative and adverbial clauses, see Sections 26.4 and 26.5 respectively.

Types of noun clauses where the subjunctive is needed

The subjunctive is used in a variety of noun clauses and expresses different meanings according to the main verb in the sentence.

In **negative sentences** after expressions that deny truth, opinion or knowledge	*No creo que **sea** verdad.* (I don't believe it is true.)
With verbs that express **wish**, **request**, **preference**, **order**, **prohibition**, **advice** and **suggestion**, such as: *querer, desear, preferir, ordenar, pedir, prohibir, aconsejar, sugerir, recomendar*	*¿Me permite que la **tutee**?* (May I use *tú*?)
With verbs of **liking** and **disliking** and verbs which show an emotional reaction, e.g. **pleasure**, **surprise**, **sorrow**, **hope**, **expectation**, **fear** and **doubt**, such as *gustar, fascinar, encantar, odiar, irritar, agradar, sentir, lamentar, molestar, sorprender, emocionar, extrañarse de, esperar, temer, tener miedo de, dudar*, etc.	*Siento que no te **encuentres** bien.* (I'm sorry you are not feeling well.)
With verbs and impersonal phrases expressing **need**, **possibility** and **probability**, such as *necesitar, hacer falta, es preciso/necesario/ imprescindible, es posible, es probable*, etc.	*Es probable que **vuelva** a subir la tasa de interés.* (Interest rates will probably go up again. Literally: It's probable that . . .)
With verbs and phrases expressing **aims for the future**, such as *intentar, pretender, querer, conseguir, el objetivo es . . .*, etc.	*Lo que intentamos es que los niveles de seguridad ciudadana **crezcan**.* (What we are trying to do is improve levels of public safety.)
With impersonal verb phrases which express a **value statement**, such as es *una pena*, es *una gran cosa*, es *justo*, es *natural*, es *mejor*, es *preferible*, es *lógico*, lo *lógico es . . .*, etc.	*Lo correcto es que **llamen** primero por teléfono.* (The proper thing is to phone first.)
With verbs of **agreement/disagreement** such as *estar de acuerdo* and *estar en desacuerdo*	*La asamblea de vecinos está en desacuerdo con que se **construya** el nuevo puente.* (The local residents' association disagrees with the plans to build a new bridge.)
In **indirect speech** to report an order expressed in the imperative when the reporting verb is in the present ☞ You can revise the rules of indirect speech in Unit 27.	*¡Bájate inmediatemente de esa valla!* → *Papá dice que te **bajes** inmediatamente de esa valla.* (Come down off that fence this minute! → Dad says to come down off that fence this minute.)

◉ Note that verbs of opinion and belief in affirmative sentences are followed by the indicative, e.g. *Creo que es una idea fenomenal* (I think it's an excellent idea).

◉ Impersonal verb phrases starting with *es* can take the infinitive, but note that the sentence is completely impersonal. Compare *Es mejor madrugar* (It's better to get up early) with *Es mejor que madrugues* (It's better for you to get up early). The exception to this rule is *es probable*, which must always be followed by a *que* clause: *Es probable que llueva*. (It'll probably rain.)

Ejercicios

Level 2

1 Put the infinitive in brackets into the correct form of the present subjunctive.

    a   Grítale para que te (escuchar) . . .
    b   Nos encanta que los niños (divertirse) . . .
    c   Es posible que la fiesta (ser) . . . el sábado.
    d   No habrá partido de fútbol por más que (hacer) . . . sol.
    e   Ojalá no (caer) . . . la Bolsa.

Level 2

2 Read the following extract taken from an article published in the magazine *Tierramérica* and underline all the verbs that are in the present subjunctive.

> ### ¿Qué América quiero?
>
> Quizá si lo supiera se lo diría . . . Pensemos . . .
>
> Quizá una donde no exista la pobreza . . . ¿Se puede?
>
> O tal vez donde no hayan problemas sociales . . .
>
> ¡Ya sé! Se me ocurre que quiero una América donde las madres no tengan que preguntar por sus hijos desaparecidos, donde los niños no sean forzados a renunciar a su infancia para tener que alimentarse.
>
> (Ariana Fernández Muñoz, *Tierramérica*, December 1996)

Level 3

3 Answer the following questions using *ojalá*, as in the example.

Ejemplo
—¿Van a venir tus padres?
—¡Ojalá vengan!

    a   ¿Crees que hay sitio para todos?
    b   ¿Sabes si van a salir a cenar con nosotros?
    c   ¿Crees que acabaremos pronto?
    d   ¿No te importa si nos oyen quejarnos tanto?

Level 3

21.2 The perfect subjunctive
Form

The perfect subjunctive – *el pretérito perfecto de subjuntivo* – is formed by the present subjunctive of *haber* and the past participle of the verb.

☞ To revise the past participle see Section 15.3.

	haber	past participle
(yo)	haya	terminado
(tú)	hayas	salido
(él, ella/Ud.)	haya	sido
(nosotros, -as)	hayamos	or irregular form (e.g. *sido, vuelto . . .*)
(vosotros, -as)	hayáis	
(ellos, -as/Uds.)	hayan	

Use

The perfect subjunctive shares the same general uses as the present subjunctive. (☞ See Section 21.1.) Like the present subjunctive, its time frame is the present. Its specific uses are as follows:

(a) In independent sentences: the perfect subjunctive expresses a wish that something had happened or alludes to the possibility that something may have happened	*Quizá **hayan telefoneado** mientras estábamos fuera.* (They may have phoned while we were out.)
(b) In subordinate clauses: the perfect subjunctive is used where the main verb is in the present, future or present perfect, and refers to an action that may have taken place	*¡Cómo tardan! Espero que no **hayan tenido** algún accidente.* (Look how late they are! I hope they haven't had an accident.)

The perfect subjunctive differs from the present in that it conveys the meaning of an action which would, or might, have taken place, i.e. a finished action. Compare:

> *Espero que lleguen a tiempo para coger el avión.* (I hope they arrive on time to catch the plane.)

with

> *Espero que hayan llegado a tiempo para coger el avión.* (I hope they arrived on time so that they could catch the plane.)

Ejercicios

Level 3

1 Complete the following sentences with the correct form of the perfect subjunctive.

    a Los alumnos que (cumplir) . . . con los requisitos podrán graduarse.
    b No podremos comprar el coche hasta que (nosotros, obtener) . . . el préstamo.
    c No he conocido a nadie que no (sufrir) . . . de jaquecas en algún momento de su vida.
    d No me interesa lo que (pasar) . . . entre vosotros.

Level 3

2 Complete the following sentences by joining each part of the sentence on the left with its corresponding half on the right.

(a) Saldremos a pasear otra vez	(i) tan pronto haya recibido nuestra carta.
(b) No saldrán de la oficina	(ii) hasta que hayan terminado el trabajo.
(c) Inés nos escribirá	(iii) después de que haya acabado los antibióticos.
(d) El médico quiere ver a Alfonso	(iv) cuando hayamos descansado.

Level 3

3 Answer the questions below using *ojalá*, *quizá(s)*, *tal vez* or *posiblemente* and the perfect subjunctive, as in the example.

Ejemplo

—¿Habrán aterrizado ya tus hermanos?

—Ojalá hayan aterrizado.

a   ¿Crees que ya lo han publicado?
b   ¿Habrá salido el anuncio también en el periódico?
c   ¿Crees que terminaremos antes de Semana Santa?
d   ¿Alguien sabe si le han dado el premio a Loreto?

Level 3

21.3 The imperfect subjunctive

Form

Regular forms of the imperfect subjunctive

The imperfect subjunctive – *el pretérito imperfecto de subjuntivo* – has two forms. They are interchangeable and using one or the other is a matter of choice.

🌐 Both the -*ra* and -*se* forms are widely used in Spain, although the -*se* form tends to be more restricted to the written language; in Spanish America the -*ra* form is generally preferred.

The imperfect subjunctive is based on the third person plural of the preterite tense				
	-ar → -aron → -ara/-ase		*-er* or *-ir → -ieron → -iera/-iese*	
(yo)	cant**ara**	cant**ase**	conoc**iera**	conoc**iese**
(tú)	cant**aras**	cant**ases**	conoc**ieras**	conoc**ieses**
(él, ella/Ud.)	cant**ara**	cant**ase**	conoc**iera**	conoc**iese**
(nosotros, -as)	cant**áramos**	cant**ásemos**	conoc**iéramos**	conoc**iésemos**
(vosotros, -as)	cant**arais**	cant**aseis**	conoc**ierais**	conoc**ieseis**
(ellos, -as/Ud.)	cant**aran**	cant**asen**	conoc**ieran**	conoc**iesen**

Irregularities in the imperfect subjunctive

Irregularities affecting the third person forms of the preterite are reflected in the imperfect subjunctive.

-*e*- becomes -*i*- in the 3rd person sing./pl.	p**i**diera/p**i**diese, etc.
-*o*- becomes -*u*-	d**u**rmiera/d**u**rmiese, etc.
-*ducir* becomes -*duj*-	condu**j**era/condu**j**ese, etc.
-*i*- becomes -*y*-	instru**y**era/instru**y**ese, etc.
Note that irregularities in strong preterites will also show in the imperfect subjunctive and that *ir* and *ser* share the same form:	
anduviera*/anduviese*	pudiera/pudiese
cupiera/cupiese	pusiera/pusiese

dijera/dijese	quisiera/quisiese
diera/diese	supiera/supiese
estuviera/estuviese	tuviera/tuviese
fuera/fuese	trajera/trajese
hubiera/hubiese	viera/viese
hiciera/hiciese	

*⊕ The verb *andar* is also conjugated as a regular verb in many regions of the Spanish-speaking world.

☞ For more information about irregularities in the preterite and the verbs affected by them go to Section 18.3.

Use

The perfect and imperfect subjunctives share the general uses listed in Section 21.1. The imperfect subjunctive, however, refers to the past or expresses hypothetical meanings. Some of the specific meanings when using the imperfect subjunctive are explained below.

(a) After *ojalá* to express a wish for something which is difficult or unlikely to materialise	*¡Ojalá **ganáramos** esta vez!* (I wish we could win this time!)
Note that the emphasis is different from *¡Ojalá ganemos esta vez!* The imperfect subjunctive expresses a more remote possibility of winning than the present subjunctive.	
(b) In subordinate clauses where the time frame is the past and therefore the main verb is in a past tense	*El profesor nos pidió que le **entregáramos** el trabajo al día siguiente.* (The teacher asked us to hand our work in the next day.)
Compare with *El profesor nos ha pedido que le entreguemos el trabajo mañana.* (The teacher has asked us to hand our work in tomorrow.)	
(c) In conditional sentences when the condition is not met ☞ To revise conditional sentences and conditional connectors, refer to Sections 26.7 and 26.5(c) respectively.	*Si **tuviese** dinero iría contigo al cine.* (If I had any money I would go to the cinema with you.)
(d) In indirect speech the imperfect subjunctive is used in some cases when the reporting verb is in the past. ☞ To revise indirect speech rules see Unit 27.	*Preséntate a las 4 de la tarde. → Me ordenó que me **presentara** a las 4 de la tarde.* (Be there at 4 pm. → He ordered me to be there at 4 pm.)

Ejercicios

Level 3

1 Complete the following sentences with the correct form of the imperfect subjunctive of the verb in brackets.

    a No era verdad que la familia (vivir) . . . en la pobreza.
    b La patronal no aceptó que los empleados (salir) . . . a la huelga.
    c Las fuerzas del gobierno desearían que los terroristas (firmar) . . . el alto el fuego antes del domingo.
    d No hubo ningún participante que (responder) . . . correctamente.
    e Temía que su hermano (saber) . . . la verdad.

Level 3

2 Change the following sentences as in the example. Note that you will have to make changes both to the main verb and the present subjunctive in the '*que*' clause.

Ejemplo

Te aconsejo que estudies. Te aconsejé que estudiaras.

    a Ha sugerido que avisen a la policía cuanto antes.
    b Nos extraña que tenga tanto dinero de repente.
    c Te prohíbo que hables con esa persona.
    d Nos tememos que venga sin avisar.

Level 3

3 Complete the clauses with *Si* . . . in the following sentences with one of the verbs in the box below.

> ser • haber • saber • costar

    a Si . . . tres puestos más en el bus, cabríamos todos.
    b Si la conferencia . . . gratis, seguro que vendrían muchísimos estudiantes.
    c Si los billetes no . . . tanto, podrías visitarnos con más frecuencia.
    d Si nosotros . . . cuánto vale el apartamento, ahorraríamos para comprarlo.

Level 3

21.4 The pluperfect subjunctive

Form

The pluperfect subjunctive – *el pretérito pluscuamperfecto de subjuntivo* – is formed using the imperfect subjunctive of *haber* and the past participle.

	haber	past participle
(yo)	hubiera/hubiese	
(tú)	hubieras/hubieses	cerrado
(él, ella/Ud.)	hubiera/hubiese	conocido
(nosotros, -as)	hubiéramos/hubiésemos	decidido
(vosotros, -as)	hubierais/hubieseis	or irregular form (e.g. *sido, vuelto* . . .)
(ellos, -as/Uds.)	hubieran/hubiesen	

☞ See Section 15.3 to revise the past participles.

Use

The imperfect and pluperfect subjunctives share the general uses listed in Section 21.1. Like the imperfect subjunctive, the time frame of the pluperfect subjunctive is clearly the past. Its specific uses are as follows:

(a) After *ojalá, quizá, tal vez*, to express an unfulfilled wish or possibility	*¡Ojalá **hubiera aceptado** ese trabajo!* (I wished I had accepted that job offer!)
(b) In subordinate clauses where the subordinate verb refers clearly to an action in the past. It often refers to finished actions in the past or to a hypothetical event which did not materialise (the main verb is normally in a past tense or the conditional but it can also be in the present)	*Es probable que **hubieran salido** ya.* (It is likely that they would have left already.) *Se lo dijo para que **supiera** la verdad.* (She told him so he'd know the truth.)
(c) In conditional sentences when the condition was not met ☞ You can revise conditional sentences in Section 26.7 and the conditional connectors in Section 26.5(c).	*Si no **hubiéramos cogido** los billetes con antelación no habríamos tenido sitio.* (If we had not bought the tickets beforehand we would not have had seats.)
(d) In indirect speech, in some cases when the reporting verb is in the past ☞ Revise indirect speech rules in Unit 27.	*Me extraña que la niña haya dicho semejante mentira.* → *Dijo que le extrañaba que la niña **hubiera dicho** semejante mentira.* (I am surprised the child has lied like that. → He said he was surprised that the child had lied like that.)

It is not always easy for the learner of Spanish to understand the nuances in meaning between the pluperfect subjunctive and the perfect subjunctive. Compare *Es extraño que Luz no haya llamado, ¿verdad?* (It is strange Luz hasn't called, isn't it?) with *Es extraño que Luz no hubiera llamado, ¿verdad?* (It is strange Luz didn't call, isn't it?). The second sentence refers to a past situation when Luz did not call, although this was expected of her. The first sentence refers to a present situation, in which the speakers are still expecting a call from Luz.

Ejercicios

Level 3

1 Complete the following sentences with the correct form of the pluperfect subjunctive of the verbs in brackets.

    a   Habrían dejado entrar a cualquier persona que (aparecerse) . . . por allí.

    b   No habríamos roto la carta si (nosotros, saber) . . . que era tuya.

    c   No comprenderías la situación a menos que (tú, pasar) . . . por una experiencia similar.

    d   Es posible que (ellos, oír) . . . las noticias y por eso se escaparon.

Level 3

2 Change the following sentences as in the example.

Ejemplo

Los niños no habían llegado y me pareció raro. Me pareció raro que los niños no hubieran llegado.

a Le habían dado un buen trabajo y estaba orgulloso de ello.
b Nos habían dado el premio y estábamos muy contentos de eso.
c Me había gritado y eso me enfureció.
d Sus padres se habían divorciado y esto le afectó mucho.

Level 3

3 Complete the first part of the sentences below using S. . . , as in the example:

Ejemplo

Llegamos tarde y perdimos el avión.
Si no hubiéramos llegado tarde, no habríamos perdido el avión.

a No terminamos el trabajo y no salimos a tiempo.
. . . , habríamos salido a tiempo.
b Perdí las llaves y mi madre se enojó.
. . . , mi madre no se habría enojado.
c No llegasteis temprano y no visteis a la tía.
. . . , habríamos visto a la tía.
d Hablaron con el profesor y entendieron el problema.
. . . , no habrían entendido el problema.

22 Special verbs

Level 1/2

22.1 To be: *ser* and *estar*

In Spanish there are two main ways of translating the verb 'to be': *ser* and *estar*.

Uses of *ser*

Ser is used in the following cases:

As a main verb	
To indicate origin, profession, family relationship, religion or political affiliation	*Es argentino.* (He is Argentinian.) *Es de Buenos Aires.* (He is from Buenos Aires.) *Es ingeniera.* (She is an engineer.) *Es mi primo.* (He is my cousin.) *Es ateo.* (He is an atheist.)
To talk about the material something is made of, and about who the author is	*Es de madera.* (It's made of wood.) *Este cuadro es de Frida Kahlo.* (This painting is by Frida Kahlo.)
To talk about possession	*Es mío.* (It's mine.) *Es de mi hermana.* (It is my sister's.)
To identify something or somebody	*Este es mi novio.* (This is my boyfriend.)
Followed by an adjective, it is used to talk about the habitual aspect of things or people, or their inherent properties	*Es redondo, es verde por fuera y naranja por dentro.* (It's round, it's green on the outside and orange in the inside.)
To tell the time	*Son las cuatro y media.* (It's half past four.)
To say where/when something is taking place	*La cena es a las diez.* (Dinner is at ten.)
To express how much something costs	*¿Cuánto es?* (How much is it?) *Son mil doscientos pesos.* (It's one thousand two hundred pesos.)
Ser + para is used to indicate purpose or recipient	*El cuchillo es para cortar el pan.* (The knife is to cut the bread with.) *Este regalo es para ti.* (This present is for you.)
Followed by an adjective, it is used to express subjective opinions or reactions to events	*Es extraño que no abra la puerta.* (It's strange that he won't open the door.)
As an auxiliary	
To form the passive. ☞ For more on the passive see Section 23.2.	*La noticia fue retransmitida por la radio.* (The news was broadcast on the radio.)

Uses of *estar*

Estar is used in the following cases:

As a main verb	
To indicate location, the place where something is	*¿Dónde **están** las llaves?* (Where are the keys?) *Cali **está** en Colombia.* (Cali is in Colombia.)
Followed by an adjective, it is used to express that the condition is the result of a change	***Está** morena.* (She is tanned – i.e. because she has been sunbathing.)
Followed by an adjective, it is used to express a temporary state, which might therefore change	***Está** enferma.* (She is ill.) ***Está** asustada.* (She is frightened.)
With adjectives to denote a subjective impression	*El pollo **está** muy rico.* (The chicken tastes very good.)
Used with the adverbs *bien* and *mal*	*—¿Cómo **está** tu madre?* *—**Está** muy bien.* ('How's your mother?' 'She's fine.')
To talk about temporary occupations (i.e. *estar* + *de* + occupation)	*Pablo **está** de camarero en un restaurante.* (Pablo is working as a waiter in a restaurant.) The emphasis here is that it is a temporary job, or that it is not his real profession. Compare with: *Pablo es camarero* (Pablo is a waiter).
As an auxiliary	
To form the present and past continuous tenses	***Está** hablando por teléfono.* (She's talking on the phone.)
To form the passive with *estar* and express a state of affairs which is a consequence of something. ☞ For more on the passive see Section 23.2.	*La ventana **está** abierta.* (The window is open.)

<hr>

Level 2

Choice of *ser* and *estar*

Many adjectives can take both ser and *estar*, but the meaning is slightly different. Compare the following pairs of sentences:

ser/estar limpio, -a	*Juan **es** una persona muy limpia.* (Juan is a very clean person.) He is inherently clean.	*La cocina **está** limpia.* (The kitchen is clean.) This is a temporary state – until it's dirty again.
ser/estar caro, -a	*El caviar **es** caro.* (Caviar is expensive.) This is an inherent quality of caviar; it is always an expensive item.	*El caviar **está** caro.* (Caviar is (particularly) expensive (at the moment).) This is a temporary state – maybe it's particularly expensive because there is too much demand at the moment.
ser/estar guapo, -a	*Alicia **es** guapa.* (Alicia is good-looking.) This is an inherent quality; she is a good-looking woman.	*Tomás **está** guapo.* (Tomás looks handsome.) This could express a subjective impression (I think he looks handsome). It could also be the result of a change (he's had a haircut and therefore he looks handsome).

Other examples are: *ser/estar desordenado, -a; ser/estar dulce; ser/estar duro, -a.*

Adjectives that change their meaning with ser and estar

The meaning of some adjectives changes depending on whether they are used with *ser* or with *estar*. You should learn the two elements in each pair as different vocabulary items.

estar abierto, -a (to be open)	*ser abierto, -a* (to be open – in character)
estar atento, -a (to pay attention)	*ser atento, -a* (to be attentive)
estar bueno, -a (to taste good)	*ser bueno, -a* (to be kind, good natured or good by nature)
estar delicado, -a (to suffer from ill health)	*ser delicado, -a* (to be delicate)
estar despierto, -a (to be awake)	*ser despierto, -a* (to be bright, clever)
estar interesado, -a (to be interested)	*ser interesado, -a* (to be selfish, self-centred)
estar listo, -a (to be ready)	*ser listo, -a* (to be clever)
estar nuevo, -a (to look/feel new)	*ser nuevo, -a* (to be new)
estar orgulloso, -a (to be proud of something)	*ser orgulloso, -a* (to be haughty)
estar verde (to be green – i.e. not mature)	*ser verde* (to be green – colour)
estar viejo, -a (to look/feel old)	*ser viejo, -a* (to be old)
estar vivo, -a (to be alive)	*ser vivo, -a* (to be lively, intelligent)

◉ Other ways of translating 'to be'

Note that the verb 'to be' can also be translated by other verbs apart from *ser* and *estar*. Here are some of the most common:

To be tired/sleepy, hungry, thirsty	**tener** *sueño, sed, hambre*	**Tengo** *sueño*. (I'm tired/sleepy.)
To be sunny, hot, cold	**hacer** *sol, calor, frío*	*Ayer* **hacía** *sol, pero hoy* **hace** *mucho frío.* (Yesterday was sunny, but today it's very cold.)
To be XX years old	**tener** *XX años*	*Ana* **tiene** *36 años.* (Ana is 36.)

Ejercicios

Level 1

1 Explain why *ser* is used in the following sentences:

    a   Este **es** Enrique. **Es** el marido de Laura. **Es** ingeniero.
    b   Esta caja **es** de plata. **Era** de mi abuela. **Es** para guardar las sortijas.
    c   La conferencia **es** a las dos. **Será** en el salón de actos.

Level 1

2 Now explain why *estar* is used in the following sentences.

a   Mar **está** en Londres. **Está** de *au pair* con una familia inglesa.
b   Después de las vacaciones Violeta **está** muy morena. La verdad es que **está** muy guapa.
c   Su habitación **estaba** muy desordenada, así que la **está** ordenando.

Level 2

3 Read the following sentences and decide which of the two verbs, *ser* or *estar*, is the correct one for each gap.

a   Necesito ir a comprar leche, pero creo que la tienda . . . (es/está) cerrada.
b   Aunque sólo lo tengo desde hace cuatro años el coche ya . . . (es/está) bastante viejo.
c   Ya . . . (es/está) todo listo para la fiesta.
d   Carlitos ya está en la cama pero todavía . . . (es/está) despierto.
e   Como persona, Carlos . . . (es/está) bastante cerrado.
f   . . . (es/está) evidente que la niña . . . (es/está) muy lista porque a los tres años ya sabe leer.
g   La abuela de María tiene 92 años y . . . (es/está) bastante delicada.
h   Mi hija ha sacado muy buenas notas y . . . (soy/estoy) muy orgullosa de ella.

Level 1

4 Translate the following sentences into Spanish, paying attention to the translation of the verb 'to be'.

a   I am 46 years old.
b   The baby is hungry.
c   Are you sleepy, Laura?
d   It's hot today, but yesterday it was quite cold.

Level 1/2

22.2   The verb *haber*

The verb *haber* has two very different uses: on its own it expresses the idea 'there is'/'there are' (*Hay mucha gente en la calle.* (There are a lot of people in the street.)); as an auxiliary it forms compound verb tenses.

Uses of *haber*

As an impersonal verb	
It can be used to denote existence ('there is', there are'). As such, it is always used in the third person **singular** of the present.	*Hay un bar en la esquina, y después **hay** dos zapaterías.* (There is a bar in the corner, and then there are two shoe shops.)
To denote existence. It can also be used in the past or the future. In Peninsular Spanish it is invariable in form, but in Spanish America, it can be used in the third person plural.	*En casa de mi abuela **había** muchos libros de mi bisabuelo.* (Spain)/***habían** muchos libros de mi bisabuelo.* (Spanish America) (In my grandmother's home there were many of my great grandfather's books.)
As an auxiliary	
It is used to form the compound tenses.	***He** terminado.* (I have finished.)

☞ See Appendix: verb tables, section The Spanish verb conjugation: especially complex irregular verbs (p. 240).

Ejercicios

Translate the following sentences into Spanish.

a There are some oranges in the fridge.
b Is there a bank near here?
c There is no sugar. Is there any honey?
d There were lots of people in the concert, weren't there?
e There is nothing here.
f In grandma's garden there were lots and lots of flowers.

22.3 *Gustar* and similar verbs

Spanish does not have a direct equivalent of the verb 'to like' when referring to things or actions. Instead it uses the verb 'to please' (*gustar*) in an inverted construction. So, for example, you cannot literally say 'I like chocolate' or 'He likes Italian cars'. You must say 'Chocolate pleases me' (*Me gusta el chocolate*) or 'Italian cars please him' (*Le gustan los coches italianos*).

Form and use

Object pronoun + *gusta/gustan* + infinitive/noun phrase/clause			
Gustar always uses the indirect object to show the person or people who are the subjects of the action, i.e. those people who are doing the liking. The indirect object pronouns are as follows. ☞ See also Section 5.4 for more on indirect object pronouns.			
me **te** **le** **nos** **os** **les**	*gusta +*	singular noun infinitive *que* clause	***Me gusta** la cerveza/nadar/que seas sincero.* (I like beer/swimming/you to be sincere.)
	gustan +	plural noun	***Le gustan** las ostras.* (She likes oysters.)

👁 The plural form of *gustar* (*gustan*) is used when the thing that is liked is in the plural.

Notice, too, how *gustar* can be followed by both a noun (*las ostras*), a verb in the infinitive (*nadar*) or a *que* clause (*que seas sincero*).

Object pronouns are always used, even when the indirect object or objects are specifically mentioned.	***A Concha le** gusta bucear.* (Concha likes scuba diving.) ***A los chicos les** gusta el acuaplano.* (The boys like surfing.)

Use of pronouns with prepositions

Object pronouns can be used with what is called the prepositional form. In these cases, the preposition *a* ('to') is used with the appropriate noun or pronoun.

a mí me gusta(n) **a ti** te gusta(n) **a el/ella/Ud**. le gusta(n) **a nosotros/nosotras** nos gusta(n) **a vosotros/vosotras** os gusta(n) **a ellos/ellas/Uds**. les gusta(n)	*A él le gusta hacer 'puenting'*. (He likes bungee jumping.) *A vosotras os gusta la ópera, ¿verdad?* (You like opera, don't you?)

Gustar in questions and negatives

Questions and negatives follow the same pattern as affirmative sentences.	*¿Te gusta el ajedrez?* (Do you like chess?) *A Miguel no le gusta mucho el fútbol*. (Miguel doesn't like football much.)

Verbs similar to *gustar*

The following verbs use structures similar to *gustar*: *agradar* (to please), *apasionar* (to fill with passion), *apetecer* (to fancy) (Spain), *chiflar* (to be crazy about) (colloquial), *complacer* (to please), *concernir* (to affect), *disgustar* (to upset), *encantar* (to love (something)), *fascinar* (to love (something)) (Spanish America), (to captivate) (Spain), *hacer ilusión* (to look forward to) (Spain), *importar* (to matter), *interesar* (to interest), *parecer* (to seem), *placer* (to please) (formal), *preocupar* (to worry), *tocar* (to affect)	*Le apasiona todo lo relacionado con las civilizaciones precolombinas*. (He loves everything to do with pre-Columbian civilisations.) *Me preocupa que no haya llamado en las últimas dos semanas*. (I'm worried that she hasn't called in the last two weeks.)

Ejercicios

Level 1

1 Complete the following sentences with the correct indirect object pronoun.

> me • te • le • nos • os • les

a A Sandra y a sus tres hermanos . . . gustaba jugar al tenis.
b Os voy a llevar a esquiar, seguro que . . . gusta mucho.
c ¿Qué . . . gustaría hacer cuando crezcas?
d A mí y a mis amigos no . . . gustaban nada las matemáticas.
e ¿Qué . . . gusta hacer a tu hijo en su tiempo libre?

2 Complete the following sentences with *gusta* or *gustan*, as appropriate.
  a Le . . . jugar al rugby.
  b Nos . . . mucho la poesía de Lorca.
  c Les . . . todos los deportes acuáticos.
  d ¿Te . . . las almejas, o prefieres los mejillones?
  e No me . . . que sea tan arrogante.

3 Write five sentences about your personal likes and dislikes, or those of your family and friends.

22.4 *Soler* and *acostumbrar*

Soler

Spanish has a special verb, *soler*, which conveys the idea of actions as usual or habitual occurrences. In the present tense it is radical-changing. It is normally expressed in English by the word 'usually', and by the verb form 'used to' in the past.

Form

(yo)	suelo	(nosotros, -as)	solemos
(tú)	sueles	(vosotros, -as)	soléis
(él, ella/Ud.)	suele	(ellos, -as/Uds.)	suelen

Use

Soler expresses habitual actions in the present and imperfect tenses. Remember that the imperfect tense (☞ see Section 18.1) can also be used when talking about habits in the past.	**Suele** *llegar a la oficina a eso de las ocho y media.* (She usually arrives at the office around eight thirty.) **Solíamos** *ir de vacaciones a las Baleares.* (We used to go to the Balearics for our holidays.)

🌎 *Soler* is used commonly throughout Spain, but rarely in Spanish America, where the verb *acostumbrar (a)* is more usual.

Acostumbrar (a)

Acostumbrar (a) functions in exactly the same way as *soler*, except that, in Peninsular Spanish, it sounds slightly more formal and is particularly associated with the written language.	*En aquella época se* **acostumbraba a** *bendecir los campos.* (At that time they used to bless the fields.)
As noted, *acostumbrar (a)* is a normal alternative to *soler* in Spanish America. Note that in certain parts of the continent it is used with the preposition *a*.	**Acostumbra a** *leer los periódicos mientras se desayuna.* (He usually reads the newspapers while he's having breakfast.)

Ejercicios

1 Read the following passage, written in the imperfect tense, about a prisoner called Rodolfo. Rewrite it using *soler* or *acostumbrar (a)* to say what Rodolfo usually did each day. Remember that you will not necessarily need to repeat adverbial expressions meaning 'generally' or 'normally'.

> Rodolfo Suárez era prisionero. Para él todos los días eran iguales. El despertador normalmente sonaba a las seis de la mañana. Se levantaba en seguida e iba al comedor a desayunar. A las siete empezaba a trabajar en el taller de hamacas. Por lo general terminaba a la una y, después de almorzar, pasaba una hora haciendo ejercicio en el corral de la cárcel. Luego tenía dos horas de tiempo libre: jugaba a las damas o al ajedrez. Por regla general volvía a su celda a las siete y se apagaban las luces a las nueve.

2 Think about the things that you normally do during an average day. Make notes. How would you tell someone else about your habits and routines, using *soler* and *acostumbrar (a)*?

22.5   Pronominal verbs

Pronominal verbs – *los verbos pronominales* – are always conjugated with reflexive pronouns, which change according to the person of the verb. Pronominal verbs have *se* as part of their infinitive, e.g. *levantarse*, which is how they are listed in the dictionary. If the pronoun *se* appears in brackets it means that the verb exists in both a pronominal and a non-pronominal form.

Form

The reflexive pronouns are *me*, *te*, *se*, *nos* and *os*. Below are examples of how pronominal verbs are conjugated in the present tense.

(yo)	me	lavo, acuesto, despierto
(tú)	te	ríes, aburres, afeitas
(él, ella/Ud.)	se	cansa, va, asusta
(nosotros, -as)	nos	comprendemos, hablamos, acordamos
(vosotros, -as)	os	llamáis, bañáis, dormís
(ellos, -as/Uds.)	se	odian, arreglan, visten

Use

Many Spanish verbs take a pronominal form. This allows a number of meanings to be expressed. The most common are shown on the following pages:

(a) Verbs whose meanings change depending on whether or not they take a pronominal form

(i) **Reflexive verbs**, i.e. which express actions done by the subject for/to himself/ herself. For instance, *lavar* means 'to wash', and its pronominal form *lavarse* means 'to wash oneself'	*Durante el verano **me ducho** más de una vez al día.* (During the summer I 'shower myself' (i.e. take a shower) more than once a day.)

Other reflexive verbs include: *acostarse, afeitarse, arreglarse, bañarse, conocerse (a sí mismo), cortarse (el pelo), ducharse, peinarse, ponerse (ropa), quitarse (ropa), vestirse*

(ii) Pronominal verbs that look reflexive but express non-voluntary actions or metaphorical meanings	*Él siempre **se consideró** culpable de la muerte de su hermana.* (He always considered himself guilty for his sister's death.) ***Se ha golpeado** en la cabeza al salir.* (He's hit his head going out.) ***Se ha roto** el espejo.* (The mirror has broken.) ***Se ha roto** la pierna.* (She has broken her leg.)

Other verbs of this type include: *abrirse* (e.g. *una puerta*), hacerse (e.g. *una herida*), *levantarse, llamarse* (+ name), *moverse* (e.g. *la cortina*), *sentarse*; verbs expressing an incipient emotion: *alegrarse, asustarse, emocionarse, entristecerse, inquietarse, ponerse* (e.g. *nervioso, contento*), *preocuparse*; periphrasis with infinitive, such as: *echarse a llorar, decidirse a (hacer algo,* e.g. *a hablar), negarse a (hacer algo,* e.g. *a pedir perdón)*

(iii) **Reciprocal verbs** (only in the plural forms) indicate that the subjects do the action of the verb to each other, e.g. *ayudarse*, 'to help each other'	***Se quieren** como si fueran hermanas.* (They love each other as if they were sisters.) ***Se pegaron** una paliza.* (They had a brawl.)

Other verbs with reciprocal meaning include: *amarse, comunicarse, conocerse, escribirse, gritarse, hablarse, mirarse, odiarse, pelearse, quererse, verse*
👁 Note that some of these verbs can also be reflexive, e.g. *Alicia sonrió cuando se miró en el espejo.* (Alicia smiled when she looked at herself in the mirror.) The category will become clear in the context.

iv) Verbs that exist both in pronominal and non-pronominal forms, where the pronominal form adds a special emphasis	***Nos comimos** un pollo entero.* (We ate a whole chicken.) Compare this with: ***Comimos** pollo al almuerzo.* (We ate chicken for lunch.)

Many verbs fall into this category:
Verbs of consumption: *beberse/tomarse (una cerveza), comerse*;
Verbs of movement: *bajarse, escaparse, irse, marcharse, subirse, volverse*;
Verbs that denote perception or knowledge: *aprenderse, conocerse, creerse (algo), estudiarse, imaginarse, leerse* (e.g. *el libro en una sola noche), olvidarse* (e.g. *la cartera en el coche), saberse* (e.g. *los verbos irregulares*);
Other verbs: *morirse (de repente, de un susto, sin darse cuenta...).*

(v) Verbs that exist both in pronominal and non-pronominal forms, with totally different meanings	*Al fin **no acordamos** nada.* (In the end we didn't agree anything.) *Laura **no se acordó** de traer el libro.* (Laura didn't remember to bring the book.)

Other examples of verbs with completely different meanings in the pronominal and non-pronominal forms are:
dormir (to sleep) – *dormirse* (to fall asleep); *marchar* (to march) – *marcharse* (to go away); *negar* (to deny) – *negarse (a)* (to refuse); *ocupar* (to occupy a space) – *ocuparse de* (to make something one's business/to look after); *saltar* (to jump) – *saltarse* (to jump over, to skip something) (metaphorical)

(b) Verbs which can be either pronominal or non-pronominal without a basic change of meaning

These are verbs with a slightly different grammatical structure, like those which can take the preposition *de*	***Admiro*** *el valor de las unidades de rescate de la Cruz Roja*. (I admire the courage of Red Cross rescue units.) ***Me admiro de*** *su coraje*. (I admire his courage.)
Other examples of this category of verbs are: *confesar/confesarse de*; *entrenar/entrenarse*; *olvidar/olvidarse de*; *reír/reírse*	

(c) Verbs which do not have a non-pronominal form

Verbs that exist only in the pronominal form	*Ella* ***se queja*** *de todo*. (She complains about everything.)
The most common verbs that exist only in the pronominal form are: *abstenerse (de)*, *aferrarse (a)*, *arrepentirse (de)*, *atragantarse*, *atreverse (a)*, *dignarse (a)*, *enterarse (de)*, *esforzarse (en)*, *fugarse*, *jactarse (de)*, *portarse (bien/mal)*, *quejarse (de)*, *rebelarse*, *reconciliarse (con)*, *resignarse (a)*, *suicidarse*, *vanagloriarse (de)*.	

👁 Use of the reflexive when the action is performed on the subject (rather than by the subject)

Note that, in Spanish, actions such as *cortarse el pelo*, *hacerse un traje*, *hacerse la manicura* and *depilarse* (literally, 'to cut oneself's hair', 'to make oneself a suit', 'to do oneself the manicure' and 'to wax oneself') use a reflexive form. They are, however, not true reflexives, as it is understood that these actions are performed on the subject by somebody else, as is made clear by the English translations ('to have one's hair cut', 'to have a suit made', 'to have a manicure' and 'to have one's legs waxed').

Some examples are:

Estoy pensando teñirme el pelo y hacerme una permanente. (I'm thinking of getting my hair dyed and having a perm. / I'm intending to get my hair dyed and have a perm.)

Es tan alto que tiene que hacerse los trajes a medida. (He's so tall that he has to have his suits made to measure.)

🌎 Although the majority of pronominal verbs are common to both sides of the Atlantic, there are some verbs which are pronominal in Spanish America but not in most of Spain. Some examples are:

devolverse, regresarse (to return) – *regresar* in Spain
desayunarse (to have breakfast) – *desayunar* in Spain

enfermarse (to fall ill) – *enfermar* in Spain

soñarse (to dream) – *soñar* in Spain

robarse (to steal) – *robar* in Spain

verse (to look) as in *Se ve muy bien* – in Spain, *Queda muy bien*

vomitarse (to vomit) – *vomitar* in Spain

Ejercicios

1 Fill in the gaps in the following sentences, which all use pronominal verbs, with the correct pronoun.

    a Siempre . . . despertamos a las seis de la mañana.
    b ¿Cuándo . . . cortaste el pelo?
    c Alicia y Dora . . . encontraron en el teatro.
    d Tú y Antonio . . . entendéis muy bien.
    e Yo no . . . acuerdo nunca de su nombre.

2 Complete the captions under each picture using one of the verbs from the list below.

comunicarse a señas • peinarse • reírse • gritarse • lavarse las manos

¿Qué están haciendo?

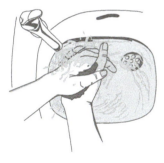

a *Carmen . . .*   **b** *Los niños . . .*   **c** *Luisa y Ana . . .*

d *Fernando y Óscar . . .*   **e** *Pedro y Raquel . . .*

3 Read the following extracts from a play and underline all the pronominal verbs. Then note down the infinitive for each.

El drama ocurre en una ciudad del Caribe con treinta y cinco grados a la sombra. [. . .] Graciela y su marido regresan de una cena informal [. . .]. Ella lleva un traje sencillo de tierra caliente con joyas cotidianas. [. . .] Tira el bolso de mano en un sillón [. . .]. Se quita las joyas y las pone sobre la mesa de centro. [. . .] Se sienta a fumar, se quita los zapatos, se sumerge en una reflexión profunda en un tono bajo y tenso [. . .] y reanuda el sartal de reproches interminables:

¿Qué te creías: que íbamos a cancelar a última hora la fiesta más hablada del año, para que yo quedara como la mala del cuento y tú bañándote en agua de rosas? Pero mientras tanto te niegas a contestarme, te niegas a discutir los problemas como la gente bien, te niegas a mirarme a la cara.

(Gabriel García Márquez (1994), *Diatriba de amor contra un hombre sentado*, Bogotá: Arango Editores, pp. 11 and 12)

23 Special verb constructions

Level 1/2

23.1 Impersonal sentences

Impersonal sentences – *las frases impersonales* – are those where the agent or 'doer' of the action is absent, unknown or irrelevant. Spanish has a number of structures which are impersonal. Many of them also exist in English, where 'one', 'you' and 'they' (among others) can also be used in impersonal sentences, e.g. 'One should think twice before crossing him' and 'They say she was a witch'.

Note that in some cases an impersonal sentence will have a grammatical subject, even if it does not refer to an identifiable 'doer' (as in the English examples above, where 'one' and 'they' are grammatical subjects even if they do not refer to anyone in particular), but in other cases the impersonal construction does not admit a grammatical subject (e.g. *Está lloviendo* – It's raining).

Level 1

Impersonal constructions

Verbs with no grammatical subject	***Conviene*** *lavarse los dientes todos los días*. (It is advisable to brush one's teeth every day.) *Hoy* **llueve** *y* **hace frío**. (Today it's raining and cold.) ***Es posible*** *que mañana* **haga** *bueno*. (It may be nice tomorrow.) **Hay** *leche en la nevera*. (There is milk in the fridge.)
Verb in the third person plural: impersonal *ellos*	***Cuentan*** *que emigró a America*. (They say that she emigrated to America.) (Note that the grammatical subject must **not** be present. The *ellos* in *Ellos cuentan que emigró a América* would be understood to refer to an element mentioned before, for instance, *mis abuelos*.)
Verb in the second person singular: impersonal *tú*	*Aquí, incluso en verano* **tienes** *que dormir con manta*. (Here, even in summer you need a blanket during the night.)
Use of *uno* or *una* as subject of the verb	*En este país* **uno** *no puede decir lo que piensa*. (In this country one cannot say what one thinks.)
Sentences with 'impersonal *se*' (See below)	***Se llega*** *a la cima en unas dos horas*. (One reaches the summit in about two hours.)

Level 2

Impersonal *se*

Note that this construction is impersonal in all senses, i.e. there is not even a grammatical subject to the verb.

Form

se + third person singular verb form

Types

(a) With copulative verbs (*ser* and *estar*)	*En esta vida* **se es** *completamente feliz muy pocas veces.* (In this life one is only rarely completely happy.)
(b) With intransitive verbs	**Se sube** *por un sendero estrecho.* (The way up is by a narrow path.)
(c) With transitive verbs	*En estas reuniones* **se bebe** *muchísimo.* (People drink a lot at these gatherings.) *En España no* **se toma** *té,* **se toma** *café.* (In Spain people do not drink tea, they drink coffee.) (This type of impersonal construction looks similar to the passive reflexive with *se* (e.g. *Los langostinos se comen con las manos.* (King prawns are eaten with the hands.) ☞ See Section 23.2). However, the impersonal construction would be the type translated into English by 'people + verb' (or similar), and not with a passive.)
(d) With transitive verb + personal object with *a*	*En Colombia* **se respeta** *mucho* **a** *los ancianos.* (In Colombia elderly people are very much respected.) (This structure avoids the ambiguity of *En Colombia los ancianos se respetan mucho*, which could mean that they respect each other very much.)

👁 *Se* cannot be used in sentences which already have *se* (i.e. those with pronominal verbs); instead, *uno/una* must be used to achieve the impersonal effect: *ducharse* → *En aquellos tiempos* **uno** *no se duchaba todos los días, como hoy.* (At that time you didn't shower every day, like today.)

☞ The impersonal *se* structure is very similar to the passive with *se* (in Section 23.2). To clarify the different uses of *se*, refer to Section 23.3.

Ejercicios

Level 1/2

1 Put the verbs in brackets into a form that makes the sentence impersonal.

  a En las Filipinas casi no (hablar) . . . español.
  b Te (llamar) . . . de la oficina hace un ratito.
  c Mañana (anunciar) . . . una nueva subida en el precio de la gasolina.
  d (Intentar) . . . hacer las cosas lo mejor posible, y ¡nadie te lo agradece!

Level 1/2

2 Make four impersonal sentences with *se* using the following words:

  Ejemplo

  trabajar • domingo: El domingo no se trabaja

  a necesitar • harina • pastel
  b España • parar • trabajar • hora de comer
  c avisar • ganadores del concurso • teléfono (use the future tense)
  d Argentina • hablar • fútbol

23.2 The passive

The passive and active voices

Voice – *la voz* – is a grammatical term which shows the relationship between the subject of the verb and the action of the verb. The choice between the **active** and the **passive voice** may be determined by whether the speaker wishes to emphasise the subject or the object. In the active voice the subject of the verb is presented as the 'active doer' of the action, e.g. *Picasso pintó el* Guernica (**Picasso painted** *Guernica*). In the passive voice the object of the verb is given prominence and the subject takes a secondary or 'passive' place, e.g. *El* Guernica *fue pintado por Picasso* (*Guernica* **was painted** by Picasso). Indeed the 'doer' is often not mentioned at all, as in *El* Guernica *fue pintado en 1937* (*Guernica* **was painted** in 1937).

In Spanish the passive voice is expressed by two grammatical constructions: the passive with *ser* and the passive with *se.*

Active construction	Passive with *ser*
Mi abuelo construyó la casa en 1912. (My grandfather built the house in 1912.)	*La casa* **fue construida** *(por mi abuelo) en 1912.* (The house was built (by my grandfather) in 1912.)
	Passive with *se*
	La casa **se construyó** *en 1912.* (The house was built in 1912.)

(a) The passive with *ser*

Form

Object + *ser* + past participle (masc./fem.) (+ *por* . . .)	*Los premios* **serán anunciados** *por la directora del colegio.* (The prizes will be announced by the head teacher of the school.)

If the subject of the action (passive subject) is included, it is preceded by the preposition *por* (as in English 'by'): *por la directora del colegio.*

◉   The past participle of the verb agrees in number and gender with the passive subject, e.g. *Estas casas han sido restauradas recientemente* (These houses have been recently restored.).

Use

The passive construction with *ser* is similar to English, but less common in Spanish. It is widely used in written Spanish but much more limited in oral and informal language.

◉   English speakers typically overuse the passive with *ser.* A tip: make the passive with *se* your first option (see (b)) or just use an active construction: instead of *Ha sido financiado con dinero público*, you can use *Lo han financiado con dinero público* or *Se ha financiado con dinero público* (It has been financed with public funds).

Conjugation of the most common tenses in the passive

Indicative tenses	
Present	(yo) soy amado (por . . .), etc.
Imperfect	(nosotras) éramos vigiladas (por . . .), etc.
Preterite	(ellos) fueron criados (por . . .), etc.
Present perfect	(Uds.) han sido engañados (por . . .), etc.
Pluperfect	(yo) había sido avisada (por . . .), etc.
Future	(tú) serás alabada (por . . .), etc.
Conditional tenses	
Conditional	(nosotros) seríamos alabados (por . . .), etc.
Conditional perfect	(ellos) habrían sido trasladados (por . . .), etc.
Subjunctive tenses	
Present	(que yo) sea educada (por . . .), etc.
Imperfect	(que vosotras) fuerais contratadas (por . . .), etc.
Present perfect	(que usted) haya sido engañado (por . . .), etc.
Pluperfect	(que ellos) hubieran sido castigados (por . . .), etc.

(b)   The passive with *se* (reflexive passive)

Form

This construction is formed only with transitive verbs.

Se + third person verb form (singular/plural)	***Se anunciaron*** *los premios a los postres. (= Los premios fueron anunciados a los postres.)* (The prizes were announced over dessert.)

Verb agreement rules for the passive with *se*

(a) If the passive subject does not refer to human beings, the verb agrees in number with it.	*Se compr**an** terreno**s**.* (Plots bought.) ***El*** *libro se public**ó** hace dos años.* (The book was published two years ago.)
(b) If the passive subject refers to human beings, the verb is in the singular and the personal *a* must be used.	***Se avisó a*** *los familiares.* (His relatives were notified.) (Technically, this structure is considered an impersonal with *se* ☞ 23.1.)

(c) When the verb is followed by a *que* clause, an infinitive, or an interrogative such as *qué*, *cuánto(-a, -os, -as)* or *cuál(-es)*, it takes the singular.	***Se dice*** *que va a subir la gasolina otra vez.* (Petrol is said to be going up again.) ***Se espera*** *saldar la deuda nacional para 2025.* (The national debt is expected to be paid by 2025.) ***Se desconoce*** *qué repercusiones tendrá la dimisión del director general.* (It is not known what repercussions the managing director's resignation will have.)
(d) Some modal verbs require the verb to go in the plural if the object of the infinitive is a plural noun. This happens with *querer, tener que, poder, deber* and *acabar de*.	***Se tienen*** *que buscar soluciones.* (Solutions must be found.)

Use

Because Spanish tends to favour active constructions, the passive with *se* is more common than the passive with *ser*, especially in informal spoken language.

Note that the passive with *se* does not allow for information about the 'doer' of the action and therefore does not take *por*. For this reason it is often used as an impersonal sentence.

See Section 23.1 for impersonal sentences and Section 23.3 for the distinction between impersonal *se* and passive *se*.

(c) The passive with *estar*

Form

Object + *estar* + past participle (masc./fem.) + *por* + passive subject

Este asunto está ya zanjado. (The matter is closed.)

Use

The passive with *ser* denotes an action as a process: *La carta **fue abierta*** (The letter was opened), whereas the passive with *estar* shows the result of an action: *La carta **estaba abierta*** (The letter was open).

Note that the possibility of making this contrast is confined to verbs denoting action rather than description. Compare *Fue detenido* (He was arrested) with *Estaba detenido* (He was under arrest).

Some tricky sentences

Here are a few structures which you may find difficult to translate into Spanish:

- I have been told to be careful. → *Me han dicho que tenga cuidado.*
- John was told to be careful. → *Le dijeron a John que tuviera cuidado.*
- He was thought to be a spy. → *Se creía que era un espía./Creían que era un espía./Le creían un espía.*

Ejercicios

Level 2

1 Match the two columns to form coherent sentences.

a	Este secreto	(i)	están siendo explotados.
b	Estos trabajadores	(ii)	ha sido traducido a decenas de idiomas.
c	Todos los familiares de la víctima	(iii)	no será revelado a nadie.
d	*Cien años de soledad*	(iv)	fueron interrogados por la policía.

Level 2

2 Put the following passive sentences into the active voice.

a El Museo Guggenheim-Bilbao fue diseñado por el arquitecto Frank Ghery.
b Han sido descubiertos los autores del fraude de Tabacos Serguiya.
c La nueva colección primavera-verano será presentada por los grandes modistos europeos en Mónaco.

Level 2

3 Rewrite the following sentences using the passive with *ser*.

a Han creado mil puestos de trabajo en Veracruz.
b Arrestaron al presunto ladrón y lo pusieron a disposición judicial.
c Se clasifican las cartas en la Oficina Central de Correos; a continuación se reparten a sus destinatarios.

Level 2

4 The following passage explains the correct way to sow seeds. Substitute the verbs in bold with passives with *se*.

> A partir de abril-mayo (a) **podemos** ya plantar directamente varios tipos de hortalizas, especialmente ensaladas. Es importante que la zona dedicada a plantar esté enriquecida; para conseguirlo (b) **puede añadir** turba o tierra rica en humus. Una vez enriquecida la tierra, (c) **siga** los siguientes pasos para la siembra: en primer lugar (d) **deberá nivelar** la tierra con un rastrillo ancho; después, (e) **espolvoree** las semillas de una forma regular y espaciada; a continuación (f) **entierre** las semillas a una profundidad aproximada de un centímetro. Por último (g) **riegue** bien el terreno.
>
> (Adapted from Martin Stangl (1981), *Manual práctico del jardinero*, Barcelona: Omega, p. 26)

Level 3

5 Complete the gaps in the following text, choosing the most appropriate verb from the box and putting it in the tense of the passive voice indicated.

> arrancar • administrar • denegar • probar • elaborar

> Yo le cuento la historia de la vacuna GO-16. El problema de esta medicina es que su eficacia no (a) (present perfect) . . . suficientemente. (b) (preterite) . . . por un grupo de farmacéuticos cubanos en 1987 y, después de algunas pruebas, (c) (preterite) . . . a los enfermos más graves, como último recurso. Y los enfermos sanaron, sí señor, se puede decir que aquellos enfermos (d) (preterite) . . . de las garras de la muerte por la GO-16. El problema es que hoy día el uso de uno de los ingredientes de la GO-16 está prohibido por la OMS, de modo que la petición de investigar más sobre esta medicina (e) (present perfect) . . . indefinidamente.

Level 1/2

23.3 Uses of *se*

A potentially confusing point for the student of Spanish is the various uses of *se*. This section attempts to clarify them by listing them and explaining their meanings.

(a) *Se* as a third person personal pronoun

As third person reflexive pronoun	**Se lava** *el pelo todos los días.* (He washes his hair every day.)
As third person reciprocal pronoun	**Se quieren** *muchísimo.* (They love each other very much.)
In other pronominal verbs, where *se* is compulsory (e.g. *arrepentirse*, *atreverse*, *suicidarse*, etc.)	**Se cayó** *de la escalera.* (She fell off the steps.)
In pronominal uses of some verbs (a) with change of meaning or (b) for emphatic or expressive effect	(a) *No* **se acordaba** *de mi nombre.* (She did not remember my name.) (b) **Se bebió** *la cerveza de un trago.* (She drank the beer in one gulp.)
To substitute *le* or *les* when accompanying *lo, la, los, las* ☞ Section 5.6.	*Ya* **se lo** *he contado.* (I have told him.) *¡Dá**selas**!* (Give them to her!)

☞ You can revise the pronoun *se* and other personal pronouns in Unit 5. You can revise pronominal verbs in Section 22.5.

👁 Remember that in the case of the pronominal verbs (including reflexive and reciprocal), *se* is only used when the verb is in the third person singular or plural. With other verb forms the appropriate personal pronoun must be used, as in the following examples: **Se comió** *el bocadillo en dos segundos* (He gobbled up his sandwich in two seconds) and **Me comí** *el bocadillo en dos segundos* (I gobbled up my sandwich in two seconds).

(b) *Se* in impersonal sentences

se + third person singular verb form	*En Navidades **se gasta** mucho.* (At Christmas people spend a lot of money.) ***Se sufre** mucho cuando **se está** solo.* (People suffer a lot when they are alone.)

☞ See Section 23.1 for more on impersonal sentences.

(c) Passive *se*

se + third person verb form (singular/plural, transitive verb) (☞ Section 23.2)	***Se estudiarán** todos los casos minuciosamente.* (All the cases will be carefully studied.) ***Se analizará** cuántos bebés nacieron completamente sanos aquel año.* (The number of completely healthy babies born that year will be analysed.)

Impersonal *se* or passive *se?*

In a number of cases involving transitive verbs it is not always easy to establish whether a sentence is impersonal or whether it is a reflexive passive. In practice this should not be a huge problem for the learner of Spanish, who will be able to interpret the meaning correctly from the context. Here is a summary of the rules of agreement, to ensure you produce correct sentences every time:

• Remember that *se* (whether impersonal or passive) must always be followed by a **third person** verb form;

• The verb goes in the singular in the following cases:

se + copulative verb	***Se está** muy bien al sol.* (It is very pleasant in the sun.)
se + intransitive verb	***Se ascendía** por una ladera suave.* (The way was up a gentle hill.)
se + transitive verb + singular object	***Se busca** piso.* (Apartment sought.) ***Se necesita** carpintero.* (Carpenter required.) *En España **se fuma** bastante.* (In Spain people smoke quite a bit.)
se + transitive verb + personal *a*	*En este colegio **se quiere** mucho **a** los profesores.* (In this school teachers are very much loved.)
se + transitive verb + *que* clause	***Se dice que** está embarazada.* (They say she's pregnant.)
se + transitive verb + infinitive	*En general **se prefiere comprar** en lugar de alquilar.* (People generally prefer to buy rather than rent.)
se + transitive verb + clause introduced by an interrogative	*Así **se aclarará a qué** hora exactamente murió la víctima.* (That way the exact time that the victim died will become clear.)

- The verb goes in the plural in the following case:

se + transitive verb + plural object	*Se compran* y *venden* joy**as** de segunda mano. (Second-hand jewellery bought and sold.)
se + some modal verbs (*querer, tener que, poder, deber, acabar de . . .*) + infinitive when the object of the infinitive is a plural noun	*Se deben estudiar* bien **las** distint**as** opcion**es** antes de *decidir.* (The different options must be properly studied before making a decision.) *Se acaban de terminar* **las** cervez**as**. (We have just run out of beer.)

Ejercicios

Level 2

1 Look at the following sentences and say which category the phrase with *se* belongs to.

> reflexive verb • reciprocal verb • other type of pronominal verb •
> *se* instead of *le* • impersonal or passive

    a **Se** miraron durante unos segundos y luego **se** abrazaron.
    b **Se** sospecha que cruzó la frontera a Perú.
    c **Se** lo he dicho mil veces pero no me hace caso.
    d El pobre anciano **se** murió aquella misma tarde.
    e María **se** parece a su madre físicamente pero es muy distinta de carácter.
    f —Dale a tu hermano las llaves del coche.
        —Ya **se** las he dado.
    g **Se** castigará a los culpables.
    h ¡Míre**se**, señor Benítez! Está usted todito cubierto de barro.
    i Niños, vengan aquí, pídan**se** perdón y den**se** la mano.

Level 2

2 Translate the following English sentences using a construction with *se*. To do this, think of the sense of the English sentence, look for a verb form with *se* which translates the action, and adapt the rest of the elements of the sentence to it.

    a They will say it was an accident.
    b The palace was entered through a magnificent door.
    c This is the way to dance the polka.
    d In my opinion, the best twentieth-century Spanish poetry was written in the period before the Civil War.
    e He was suspected of being a spy.

Level 2

3 The following dialogue illustrates many of the uses of *se*. You can identify the different uses if you want to.

24 Sentence organisation: the simple sentence

A sentence is a combination of words which is able to stand alone and express a coherent thought. From the most basic to the most complex, the way sentences are put together follows certain rules of grammar called syntactical rules. In the following units you will become familiar with these.

A simple sentence – *la oración simple* – consists of only one clause and expresses a complete, independent and coherent thought. The basic components of a clause are a verb and a subject, although it can also have objects and complements.

<u>*Sara*</u>   <u>*lee*</u>   <u>*el periódico*</u>   <u>*todas las mañanas*</u>. (Sara reads the paper every morning.)
subject   verb   direct object   time complement

Types of simple sentences

Affirmative *versus* negative sentences	
An *affirmative* sentence has a verb that conveys a positive meaning.	*La capital de Paraguay es Asunción*. (The capital of Paraguay is Asunción.)
A *negative* sentence has a particle that inverts the positive meaning of the verb.	*No tengo hambre*. (I am not hungry.) *¡Jamás nos vencerán!* (We shall never be defeated!)

☞ See Unit 25 to revise the negative construction.

Declarative and interrogative sentences	
A **declarative** sentence is a sentence that makes a statement. The word order is generally: subject + verb + object.	*Va a llover*. (It's going to rain.) *Neruda nació en 1904*. (Neruda was born in 1904.)
An **interrogative** sentence is a sentence that asks a question. They have their special intonation in the spoken language and are marked by question marks in the written language (¿?) There are 3 types:	

(a) A **closed question** seeks verification or negation and therefore requires a 'yes' or 'no' answer. The most common word order is verb + subject.	*¿No vives en Veracruz?* (Don't you live in Veracruz?) *¿Compró mamá las flores para la abuela?* (Did Mum buy the flowers for Grandma?)
(b) An **open question** starts with an interrogative (*qué, quién(es), cómo, cuánto(-a, -os, -as), dónde, cuándo*) and requires new information in the answer. The word order is usually: interrogative + verb + subject.	*¿Cómo te llamas?* (What's your name?) *¿Cuándo es tu cumpleaños?* (When is your birthday?)
(c) A **tag question** is formed by a declarative sentence to which a tag is added for confirmation or negation of the statement. In Spanish the most common tags are *¿verdad?, ¿no?* and *¿cierto?*	*Llegaste ayer, ¿no?* (You arrived yesterday, didn't you?) *Eres argentina, ¿cierto?* (You are from Argentina, aren't you?)

☞ You can revise the interrogatives in Unit 11.

◉ Note that Spanish word order is quite free in comparison with English. The comments on word order are broad generalisations and the learner should be prepared for numerous exceptions to them, especially in spoken Spanish.

◉ **Word order in open interrogative sentences**

Where the question word is preceded by a preposition (e.g. *para quién, desde dónde*, etc.), these two items should never be separated, contrary to English usage, e.g. *¿De dónde eres?* (**Where** do you come **from**?).

Exclamatory sentences	
Exclamatory sentences express feelings. They are marked in the spoken language by a special intonation and in the written language by exclamation marks.	*¡Viva la vida!* (Hurray for life!) *¡Qué chico más listo!* (What a clever boy!)

◉ Remember that in written Spanish you must use both the opening and closing question and exclamation marks: '¿'/ '?' and '¡'/ '!'

Ejercicios

Level
1

1 Say which of these sentences are negative, interrogative, exclamative or declarative/affirmative and mark the element(s) that give you the clue for your answer.

    a ¡Estamos salvados!
    b Nunca más se supo de aquel hombre.
    c ¿Seguro que te encuentras bien?
    d Parece que va a hacer bueno.

2 Write an appropriate question for each of the following answers and say if it is an open or closed question.

    a   Sí, me llamo Rosa Mari Bermúdez.

    b   Rosa Mari Bermúdez.

    c   En 1904. Neruda nació en 1904.

3 Make the following statements interrogative by adding a question tag.

    a   Estás invitado a la boda.

    b   No has visto a Juani en todo el día.

    c   El año pasado fuisteis de vacaciones a Miami.

25 Negatives

Like English, Spanish has a range of negative words to show the different nuances of meaning in non-affirmative sentences. Examples in English include: 'no', 'not', 'nothing'/'not . . . anything', 'none'/'not . . . one', 'nobody/'not . . . anybody' and 'never'/'not . . . ever'.

No

No means 'no' and 'not', and is the most common negative word in Spanish, e.g. *–¿Conoces a Alberto? –No, no lo conozco.* ('Do you know Alberto?' 'No, I don't.')

When it means 'not', *no* precedes the verb (+ any direct or indirect object pronouns).	**No** *se lo dije.* (I didn't say it to her.)
After verbs of reporting, belief, desire, assurance, hope, etc., *que no* is used in short answers where the speaker does not want to repeat a clause.	*Creo* **que no**. (I don't think so.)
¿No? is used as a tag question, i.e. it can be appended to a statement to elicit a yes/ no answer. However, *¿no?* always seeks agreement with the speaker, and implies that he or she already knows the answer.	*Eres de Sevilla,* **¿no?** (You're from Seville, aren't you?) *Mírate los ojos, ¡hombre! Has tomado mucho,* **¿no?** (Look at your eyes, good lord! You've had a lot to drink, haven't you?)

Double negation

In Spanish, unlike in English, all negative indicators in a negative sentence must be negative, e.g.

> *No ha visto a **nadie** desde hace cinco años.* (He hasn't seen **anyone** for five years.)

Nada

Nada means 'nothing'. It is used with *no* in a double negative construction.	**No** *oímos* **nada**. (We didn't hear anything.)

Nada can be used without no. In these cases it precedes the verb. (Note this is formal or literary style, and is not common in speech.)	**Nada** oímos. (We heard nothing.)
Nada can reinforce an adjective or adverb in a sentence.	A Champollion no le fue **nada fácil** descifrar el significado de la Piedra de Rosetta. (It wasn't at all easy for Champollion to decipher the meaning of the Rosetta Stone.)

☞ See Unit 9 on *algo* vs *nada* in indefinites.

Nadie

Nadie means 'no one'/'nobody'. It is used in double negative constructions as well as on its own before the verb.	**No** vino **nadie**./**Nadie vino**. (Nobody came.) (where *nadie* is the subject of the sentence) **Nadie** preguntó por él. (Nobody asked after him.)
It takes personal a if it is the object, rather than the subject, of a verb.	**No** conocíamos **a nadie**. (We didn't know anybody.) (where *nadie* is the object of the sentence)

☞ See Unit 9 on *alguien* vs *nadie* in indefinites.

Ninguno

Ninguno, -a can be used as both a pronoun and an adjective.

As a pronoun, *ninguno* means 'none' or 'not one'. It can refer to objects or people, and it agrees in gender with the nouns that it replaces.	**Ninguna** de mis tres hermanas me reconoció cuando salí disfrazado al escenario. (None of my three sisters recognised me when I walked onto the stage in disguise.)
As an adjective it means 'no (+ noun)'/'not . . . any (+ noun)'.	Parece que **ningún diccionario** define ese término. (That term doesn't appear to be defined in any dictionary.)

👁 Notice how the masculine singular form *(ninguno)* apocopates (i.e. drops the '-o') in front of a noun (to give *ningún*).

Notice, too, that the usage in the plural is limited. It can be found in noun phrases that would not normally be used in the singular form (e.g. *ningunas ganas)*.

☞ See Unit 9 on *alguno* vs *ninguno* in indefinites.

Nunca and jamás

Nunca means 'never'. It is used in double negative constructions as well as on its own before the verb: both constructions are equally acceptable to most native speakers.	**No** he visitado **nunca** el Museo del Prado (I have never visited the Prado.) **Nunca** he estado en Bilbao. (I have never been to Bilbao.)

Nunca can combine with other negatives in a range of constructions.	**Nunca** ocurre **nada** en las obras de Samuel Beckett. (Nothing ever happens in Samuel Beckett's plays.) ¡**Nadie** nos dice **nunca nada**! (No one ever tells us anything!)
más que nunca, menos que nunca, comparative + que nunca	Aquel día los niños se portaron **peor que nunca**. (The children behaved worse than ever that day.)
Jamás is a near synonym of nunca. However, it is used less frequently and its register is slightly more formal. It cannot be used with comparisons to mean 'ever'.	**Jamás** habían visto un accidente de carretera tan horroroso. (They had never seen such a horrific road accident.)
Note the emphatic expression nunca jamás ('never ever').	No quiero volver a verla **nunca jamás**. (I never want to see her ever again.)

Nunca is also used with comparisons as a word on its own to mean 'ever':

Nos divertimos como nunca. (We had the best time ever.)

☞ See Section 4.3 and 4.5 for more on comparatives.

Ni

Ni means 'neither' or 'nor', and is used with no in double negative constructions, often in the form of ni . . . ni, corresponding to the English 'neither . . . (n)or'.	No nos han invitado a la fiesta **ni** a ti **ni** a mí. (They haven't invited either you or me to the party.)
However, if ni appears before the verb, no is omitted in most varieties of modern Spanish.	**Ni** tú **ni** yo estamos invitados a la fiesta. (Neither you nor I are invited to the party.)
Combined with the word siquiera, ni has the emphatic meaning 'not even'.	**Ni siquiera** mi esposa sabía que me había tocado la lotería. (Not even my wife knew that I had won the lottery.)

Ni in idiomatic expressions

Ni is used in a range of common and colloquial expressions, with the meaning 'no . . .' or 'not a . . .': ¡Ni idea! ¡Ni un centavo! ¡Ni hablar! ¡Ni madres! (Mexicanism)	–¿Quién rompió el florero este? –¡**Ni idea!** ('Who broke this vase?' 'No idea!')

Apenas

Apenas means 'scarcely' or 'hardly'. It can be used on its own before the verb, or alternatively after it with no in a double negative construction.	Estaba tan resfriada que **apenas** podía hablar/ . . . que **no** podía hablar **apenas**. (She was so cold-ridden that she could hardly talk.)
It can also combine with other negatives.	**No** había **apenas nadie**. (There was hardly anybody there.)

Nunca ocurre nada en las obras de Samuel Beckett.

Tampoco

Tampoco means 'neither'. It can be used on its own before the verb, or after the verb with *no* in a double negative construction ('not . . . either')	*Mi mujer me dijo que no le gustaba cocinar. Le respondí que a mí **no** me gustaba **tampoco**/ . . . que a mí **tampoco**.* (My wife told me she didn't like cooking. I told her I didn't (like it) either.)
Tampoco without *no* tends to be used with subject pronouns or prepositional forms for emphasis	*–Los niños no quieren ir a la piscina hoy por el frío que hace. –¡Hombre, **tampoco** queremos ir nosotros!* ('The children don't want to go to the pool today because of the cold.' 'Too right, we don't want to go either!')
Tampoco can stand on its own as a word meaning 'Me/you/he/she, etc. neither'	*–Desgraciadamente no hablo alemán. ¿Y tú? –**Tampoco**.* ('Unfortunately I don't speak German. What about you?' 'Me neither'.) (*Yo tampoco* is also correct.)

Ejercicios

Level 2

1 Challenge the following assertions about Christopher Columbus, using the prompts.

a Cristóbal Colón descubrió las Américas, ¿no es verdad?
(Say no, <u>he</u> didn't discover anything. There were people there already.)

b Sí, pero desde la perspectiva europea fue el primero en llegar al continente, ¿no es cierto?
(Say no, you can hardly say that. The Vikings arrived earlier.)

c Bueno, sí, pero él fue el primer explorador europeo que lo reconoció como un continente hasta entonces desconocido, ¿verdad que sí? (Say no, he didn't even recognise it as such. He thought he'd reached the Far East.)

d Vale, de acuerdo. Pero pronto se dio cuenta de su error, ¿verdad?
(Say no, I don't think so. He never realised his mistake.)

e Ah . . . pues, al menos consiguió fama y riqueza, ¿no es así? (Say no, not even that. He died in poverty.)

Level 2

2 Read the following short description of a factory.

Había mucha gente en la fábrica. Todas las máquinas funcionaban, se oía mucho ruido, y también había mucha actividad fuera en el área de carga-descarga.

Now describe the scene in the factory in the middle of the night, when the night-watchman (*vigilante nocturno*) checked everything. Use appropriate negative forms.

Level 2

3 Think about some of the things that you have not done in your life, but which you would still like to do. Then write a paragraph listing five of these things. Finish the paragraph with the sentence *Sin embargo, aún me gustaría hacer estas cosas.* Try to use a variety of negative forms such as *ni . . . ni, tampoco* or *ni siquiera*.

26 Sentence organisation: compound and complex sentences

Level
1/2

26.1 The compound sentence

Compound sentences – *las oraciones compuestas* – are formed by joining simple sentences. (☞ Simple sentences in Unit 24.) This can be done using one of two devices: by juxtaposition, that is, by linking simple sentences without using a specific connector – *conector* – or link word (e.g. *No me gusta, te lo regalo* (I don't like it, I am giving it to you)); and by using what are called **co-ordinating conjunctions** or **connectors** (e.g. *No ha terminado todavía **pero** terminará pronto* (She has not finished yet **but** she will soon)).

Juxtaposed	
Separated by a comma, a semi-colon or a colon	*Me voy a casa; estoy agotada.* (I'm going home; I'm exhausted.) *El policía gritó: "¡Alto ahí!"* (The policeman shouted: 'Stop there!')
Co-ordinated	
To express added information (copulative) Joined by *y* (or *e*) in affirmative sentences or *ni* in negative sentences	*El edificio es muy bonito **y** tiene buenas vistas.* (The building is lovely and has good views.) *Juan **no** ha llegado **ni** ha llamado por teléfono.* (Juan hasn't arrived or phoned.)
To express an alternative (disjunctive) Joined by *o* (or *u*)	*¿Vienes con nosotros **o** te vas con tus amigos?* (Are you coming with us or are you going with your friends?)
To express a restriction or contrast (adversative) Joined by *pero* or *sino*, *aunque*, *sin embargo* or *no obstante*	*No ganaron el partido **pero** lucharon hasta el final.* (They did not win the match but they fought till the end.)
To express a consequence or cause and effect (consecutive) Joined by *así*, *así que*, *luego*, *conque*, *por (lo) tanto*, *por consiguiente* or *de forma/modo/manera que*	*No entiendo nada de lo que tengo que hacer, **así que** voy a ir a preguntarle al profesor.* (I don't understand what I have to do so I'm going to ask the teacher.)

Co-ordinated	
To express a distribution of ideas (distributive) Joined by: *ya . . . ya* *bien . . . bien* *sea . . . sea*	*Bien por la mañana, bien por la tarde, siempre pasaba a ver a su madre.* (Whether it was morning or afternoon, he always popped in to see his mother. Literally: Either in the morning or in the afternoon . . .)

Co-ordinating connectors

Co-ordinating conjunctions or connectors join together elements that have the same value, e.g. *Juan y Pedro son mis hermanos* (Juan and Pedro are my brothers) or *Fue al kiosko y compró el periódico* (She went to the newsagent's and bought the paper).

Connector	Function and remarks	Examples
Copulative	Joins together copulative sentences so that sentence A information is added to sentence B information. Similar to English 'and', 'neither/nor . . . nor'.	
y (or *e* before words starting with *i-, hi-* or *y-*)	Join affirmative statements. Note: when enumerating elements, commas are used and the conjunction is used to join the last two elements.	*Madre e hijo están bien.* (Mother and child are well.) *La casa estaba muy descuidada, no tenía jardín y era muy pequeña.* (The house was in bad shape, didn't have a garden and was very small.)
no . . . ni/ni . . . ni	Join negative statements.	*Marisol ni quiere estudiar ni quiere trabajar.* (Marisol doesn't want to study or work.)
Disjunctive	Signals a choice between options, similar to English 'or', 'either . . . or'.	
o (or *u* before words starting with *o-* or *ho-*) *o . . . o* *bien . . . bien*		*O vienes conmigo a la compra o vas con tu madre; no puedes quedarte aquí.* (Either you come shopping with me or you go with your mother; you can't stay here.)
Adversative	Shows elements in opposition to each other to show restriction or contrast, similar to the English 'but' or 'however'.	
pero	Placed in the middle of the compound sentence; very much like 'but'	*Fue a vivir a la capital pero no le gustó nada.* (She went to live in the capital but she did not like it at all.)
sino (to join single elements) *sino que* (to join whole sentences)	Contradicts or corrects the negative statement in sentence A.	*No, no fue a Uruguay sino a Paraguay.* (No, she did not go to Uruguay but to Paraguay.) *No les compró un regalo sino que les pagó unas vacaciones en las Bermudas.* (She did not buy them a present but she paid for a holiday in Bermuda.)
mas	Same use as *pero*, although it sounds old-fashioned	*Deseaba con todas sus fuerzas declarar su amor a la muchacha, mas no conseguía reunir el coraje suficiente.* (He wanted to declare his love to the girl with all his might, but he could not muster enough courage to do it.)

Connector	Function and remarks	Examples
sin embargo	Must be placed in the middle of the compound sentence, separated by a comma or a full stop	*Perdió su reloj de oro, **sin embargo**, lo encontró al día siguiente en la lavadora.* (He lost his gold watch. However, he found it in the washing machine the next day.)
Consecutive	Shows consequence in relation to the previous clause or a cause-and-effect relationship. Similar to English 'so', 'therefore' or 'with the result of'.	
así, así que	Separated from the previous clause by a comma	*No apareció, **así que** nos fuimos sin ella.* (She did not turn up so we went without her.)
por tanto, por lo tanto	Separated from the previous clause by a comma	*España ha sido un país de emigrantes hasta hace bien poco, **por lo tanto** podría mostrar más solidaridad con los inmigrantes.* (Spain has been a country of emigrants until very recently, therefore it could show more solidarity with immigrants.)
luego	Separated from the previous clause by a comma	*Pienso, **luego** existo.* (I think therefore I am.)
por consiguiente	Separated from the previous clause by a comma	*No se llegó a un acuerdo sobre el desarme, **por consiguiente**, el gobierno decidió abandonar las negociaciones de paz.* (No agreement on disarmament was reached and as a consequence the government decided to abandon the peace talks.)
de manera que, de modo que, de forma que	Followed by indicative. 👁 When followed by the subjunctive, they become connectors expressing purpose. ☞ Section 26.5(g)	*Les regalé a mis hijos un juego de ajedrez **de forma que** aprendieron a pensar estratégicamente.* (I gave my children a chess set with the result that they learnt to think strategically.)
conque	Colloquial	*Tú no me invitaste a tu cumpleaños **conque** yo tampoco te invito al mío.* (You did not invite me to you birthday party so I am not inviting you to mine.)

Ejercicios

Level 1/2

1 Join the following pairs of sentences to form compound sentences.

    a Hacía un día maravilloso. Decidimos ir a la playa. (consecutive)

    b No queríamos ir al cine. No queríamos ir al parque. (copulative)

    c ¿Vas a pasar las vacaciones con tus abuelos? ¿Vas a quedarte en Irlanda? (disjunctive)

    d Ganamos poco. Hemos decidido ahorrar para comprarnos un piso más grande. (adversative)

2 Use *pero* or *sino* as appropriate in the following sentences.

  a No ganaron . . . que perdieron por mucha diferencia.
  b Llegaron tardísimo a cenar . . . esta vez tenían una buena excusa.
  c No fue a visitarlo para pedirle ayuda . . . para ofrecerle un negocio.

3 Use *sino* or *sino que* as appropriate.

  a A él realmente no le gusta mucho el teatro, . . . el cine.
  b No es que sea tímida . . . es de pocas palabras.
  c No vengo a discutir . . . quiero hacer las paces contigo.
  d No he sacado un Sobresaliente en el examen, . . . un Notable.

4 Substitute the connector in bold for another one so that the meaning of the sentence does not change.

  a Veo que no soy bien recibida, **por lo tanto** me marcho.
  b **Ni** ha pagado el vestido ni lo ha devuelto.
  c El pueblo en sí no es demasiado bonito, **sin embargo** los alrededores son preciosos.

26.2 The complex sentence

Complex sentences consist of a main clause and one or more subordinate clauses:

complex sentence = main clause + subordinate clause(s)

Si quieres,   *te llamaré*   *cuando aterrice.* (If you want, I'll call you when I land.)

subordinate   main clause   subordinate clause 2
clause 1

Subordinate clauses

Subordinate clauses – *las oraciones subordinadas* – do not express a complete thought and therefore cannot stand alone. They are always part of a bigger unit (the complex sentence) and are dependent on another clause called the **main clause** – *la oración principal*. The verb in the subordinate clause can be conjugated or be in an impersonal form (infinitive, gerund or past participle).

Te lo **daré** si me **visitas** mañana con la familia.
subordinate clause
(I'll give it to you if you come and visit me tomorrow with your family.)

In this sentence *daré* is the main verb and *si me visitas mañana con la familia* is the subordinate clause, which has a verb (*visitas*), plus information about 'whom' (*me*), 'when' (*mañana*) and 'with whom' (*con la familia*). *Si* is the connector, which has the double function of joining the subordinate clause to the main clause and providing the meaning of the subordinate clause (in this case, a condition).

Types of subordinate clauses

(a) The noun clause A subordinate clause which can stand in place of a noun	*Cuando era pequeña me encantaba **saltar a la cuerda**.* (When I was little I loved skipping with my rope.)
(b) The adjectival or relative clause A subordinate clause which modifies a noun phrase (in the way that an adjective would)	*El perro **que vimos** era el de Julián.* (The dog we saw was Julián's.)
(c) The adverbial clause A subordinate clause which modifies its main clause by adding meanings similar to those of adverbs, such as time, manner, place, instrument, circumstance, concession, purpose, result, cause or condition	*Lo haré **como me has enseñado**.* (I'll do it the way you taught me.) *Lo hizo **porque estaba enfadado**.* (He did it because he was angry.)

☞ You can find out about the noun clause, the adjectival or relative clause and the adverbial clause in Sections 26.3, 26.4 and 26.5 respectively.

26.3 The noun clause

The noun clause – *la oración sustantiva o completiva* – is a type of subordinate clause which can stand in place of a noun or noun phrase, as illustrated in the following example:

Noun phrase	Subordinate noun clause
*Quiero **una casa de campo**.* (I want a house in the country.)	*Quiero **que vengas ahora mismo**.* (I want you to come right now.)

The verb of the subordinate noun clause can be in the infinitive, the indicative or the subjunctive.

Noun clause conjunctions and other link words

Where a connector is needed, *que* is the most common one, but there are others:

que	Used in statements	*Me aconseja **que** me relaje.* (She advises me to relax.)
si	Used in indirect closed questions	*Quiero saber **si** me vas a ayudar o no.* (I want to know whether you are going to help me or not.)
(preposition +) interrogative (*qué*, *cuándo*, etc.)	Used in indirect open questions	*Mamá pregunta **cuándo** empieza la película.* (Mum is asking when the film is due to start.)

◉ The conjunction *que* is similar to the English 'that' but, in contrast to English, it cannot be omitted: 'She says (**that**) she will do it', – *Dice **que** lo hará.*

◉ Remember that the interrogatives in indirect questions (e.g. *cuándo)* must be written with an accent. ☞ You can revise them in Unit 11.

Que or de que?

De que must be used when the item that precedes *que* normally requires the use of *de,* as in the following examples:

darse cuenta **de**	*Se dio cuenta **de** <u>que le engañaban</u>.* (He realised he was being cheated.)
la posibilidad **de**	*La posibilidad **de** <u>que le llamen para una entrevista</u> es remota.* (The possibility of his being called for an interview is remote.)
antes **de**	*Llegaré a casa antes **de** <u>que los niños salgan para el colegio</u>.* (I'll get home before the children leave for school.)

All other prepositions work in the same way:

ir **a** → *Voy **al** <u>dentista</u>. Voy **a** <u>que me saquen una muela</u>.* (I'm going to the dentist's. I'm going to have a tooth taken out.)

◉ Infinitive or *que* clause?

Compare these sentences:

*Los trabajadores queríamos **elegirlo a él**.* (We workers wanted to choose him.)

*Los trabajadores queríamos **que él eligiera a otro candidato**.* (We workers wanted him to choose another candidate.)

When the subject of the main verb and the subordinate verb is the same, an infinitive is used. When the subjects of the verbs are different (as in the second example, *los trabajadores* (i.e. *nosotros)* and *él),* then the subordinate with *que* must be used, and the verb in the subordinate clause must agree with its subject.

Que followed by indicative or subjunctive

☞ You can revise the types of verbs which require a noun phrase in the subjunctive in the section 'Types of noun clauses where the subjunctive is needed', in Section 21.1.

Ejercicios

Level 2

1 Write three complex sentences with a subordinate noun clause.
   a   Se comenta que . . . (subir los precios).
   b   Te deseo que . . . (tú tener un feliz cumpleaños).
   c   No se sabe con seguridad si . . . (los terroristas firmar la tregua).

Level 2

2 Translate the following sentences into Spanish using a noun clause (with *que, si* or appropriate interrogatives).
   a   We don't know whether she will sing or not.
   b   His greatest dream is for his daughter to study architecture.
   c   I think he wants his daughter to come and live with him but he won't say so.

Level 3

3 Complete the sentences with *que* or *de que,* as appropriate.
   a   No estamos seguros . . . vaya a terminar la carrera.
   b   En estos casos se aconseja . . . el paciente descanse todo lo posible.
   c   Mis abuelos estaban encantados . . . todos hubiéramos ido a visitarles.
   d   Los médicos dudan . . . pueda volver a trabajar antes de un mes.

Level 2/3

26.4 The adjectival or relative clause

An adjectival clause is a subordinate clause that modifies or qualifies a noun or a noun phrase in the way that an adjective would (see example below). Because these clauses are headed by a 'relative', they are commonly referred to as relative clauses – *oraciones relativas o de relativo.*

Adjective or adjectival phrase	Relative clause
*El hombre **alto** era mi padre.* (The tall man was my father.)	*El hombre **que vimos** era mi padre.* (The man we saw was my father.)

Relative clause connectors

The main connectors of the relative clauses are the different types of relatives – *relativos* – and prepositional groups – *grupos preposicionales relativos o de relativo.*

Relatives (*Relativos*)

Relative pronouns *Pronombres relativos*	**que** *El libro **que** leí durante las vacaciones es muy interesante.* (The book I read during the holidays is very interesting.) **quien/quienes** *Los padres son **quienes** tienen que preocuparse por la seguridad de sus hijos.* (The parents are the ones who have to worry about their children's safety.) **el/la/lo cual los/las cuales** *El alcalde tiene un plan educativo muy ambicioso **el cual** va a costar millones de euros.* (The mayor has an ambitious educational plan which is going to cost millions of euros.)

Relative adjectives	cuyo/a/os/as
Adjetivos relativos	*El curso, **cuyo** objetivo es practicar el español hablado, requiere mucha dedicación.* (The course, whose objective is to practise spoken Spanish, requires a lot of dedication.)
	👁 This relative is not used very much in the spoken language as speakers prefer to use alternative constructions indicating possession. For instance, an alternative to the example above could be:
	El curso, que tiene como objetivo practicar el español hablado, requiere mucha dedicación.
	cuanto/a/os/as
	*Le di a mi madre **cuanto** dinero tenía.* (I gave my mother as much money as I had.)
	Note that if *dinero* were to be omitted from this example, the relative *cuanto* would become a pronoun.
Relative adverbs	cuando
Adverbios relativos	*Fue en ese momento **cuando** me di cuenta (de) que había perdido mi pasaporte.* (It was then when I realised I had lost my passport.)
	como
	*Prepara el pastel de la manera **como** te dije.* (Prepare the cake the way I told you.)
	donde
	*Voy a ir de vacaciones a un sitio **donde** no haya turistas.* (I am going on holiday to a place where there are no tourists.)

👁 Note that, although the relative can sometimes be missed out in English, it always has to be included in Spanish: *El hombre **que** vi no era mi padre* (The man (that) I saw was not my father).

Relative prepositional groups (*Grupos preposicionales relativos o de relativo*)

The relatives above can sometimes be preceded by prepositions, as in the following examples:

*Esa es la razón **por la que** se marcharon.* (That is the reason why they left.)

*Caminaremos **hasta que/hasta cuando** oscurezca.* (We'll walk until it gets dark.)

The most common relative connectors and their use are listed in the summary table on pages 207–8.

👁 Unlike in English, prepositions are not separated from the relative pronoun and always go before it: *La muchacha **con la que** vine* (The girl (whom) I came with). With the prepositions *con, en* and *de* it is sometimes possible to omit the article:

*La chica **de (la) que** me hablaste.* (The girl you talked to me about.)

👁 Some non-equivalent structures which take a relative clause in Spanish:

- 'We saw a car that was carrying too many people' can be expressed with a gerund in English (We saw a car carrying too many people) but only by a relative clause in Spanish → *Vimos un coche que llevaba demasiada gente.*
- I need a friend to talk to. → *Necesito un amigo con quien hablar.*
- I need a friend to help me with my homework. → *Necesito un amigo que me ayude con los deberes.*

The non-specific relatives (*Relativos inespecíficos*)

The non-specific relatives are the equivalents of the English 'whatever', 'whoever', 'whenever', 'wherever'. In Spanish they are mainly used in formal registers, and you may come across them in written texts. In oral and informal registers they are often simplified using the simple relatives listed above or alternative phrases. The constructions that follow them require the subjunctive.

whatever	*cualquier(a)/cualesquiera*
	*Puede hacer este curso **cualquiera que sea** su edad.* (You can do this course whatever your age.)
	comoquiera
	*Se quejarán **comoquiera que sea** el resultado.* (They will complain whatever the result.)
whoever	*quienquiera/quienesquiera*
	*No estoy aquí **quienquiera que pregunte** por mí.* (I am not here, whoever asks for me.)
wherever	*dondequiera*
	*Te recordaré **dondequiera que yo esté**.* (I will remember you wherever I am.)
whenever	*cuandoquiera*
	*Podrás visitar a la abuela **cuandoquiera que vengas**.* (You will be able to visit grandma whenever you come.)

Restrictive and non-restrictive relative clauses

As in English, there are two types of relative clauses:

(a) Restrictive relative clauses (also known as defining relative clauses) – *las oraciones de relativo especificativas* – specify particular elements of the antecedent. For example, in *Metí en el maletín los papeles **que tenía que firmar al día siguiente*** (I put the papers I had to sign the next day into my briefcase), the relative clause specifies which papers I put into my briefcase.

(b) Non-restrictive relative clauses (also known as non-defining relative clauses) – *las oraciones de relativo explicativas* – give extra information about the antecedent, without restricting its meaning in any way. For example, in *Los padres de la niña, **que estaban muy preocupados**, lloraron de emoción al verla sana y salva* (The little girl's parents, who were extremely worried, cried with emotion when they saw her safe and sound), the relative clause makes a comment about the state of the parents *(los padres de la niña* is the antecedent).

👁 In the written language, non-restrictive relative clauses must appear between commas and in the spoken language they are marked by pauses.

Nominalisation of relative clauses with *el (la, los, las) que* and *lo que*

When the antecedent of the restrictive relative clause is already understood by speaker and listener, it is common to skip it and use *el que/la que/los que/las que* instead:

–*¿Es nueva esta escultura?* ('Is this sculpture new?')
-*Sí, es **la que** compramos en la Feria de Arco el año pasado.* ('Yes, it's the one we bought at the Arco Fair last year.')

Lo que is used when referring to something undefined:

Lo que *más me gusta hacer los domingos es salir al campo a merendar.* (= *La cosa que más me gusta . . .)* is similar to the English 'what': 'What I like doing most on Sundays is going for a picnic in the country'.

Use of indicative or subjunctive in relative clauses

The **indicative** is used when the action described in the relative clause verb is factual and has possibly already taken place:

*La casa donde **vive** es antigua y está llena de plantas.* (The house he lives in is old and full of plants.)

The **subjunctive** is used in relative clauses when the action has not yet happened, but is considered possible, or when it is hypothetical:

*La casa donde yo **viva** será antigua y llena de plantas.* (The house I would live in will be old and full of plants.) (I don't have a house yet.)

As mentioned, the clauses with non-specific relatives are followed by the subjunctive:

*La escucharemos **cualquiera que sea** su opinión.* (We will listen to her whatever her opinion.)

☞ More information on the use of the subjunctive in subordinate clauses can be found in Section 21.1. See also Section 26.5 for the use of the subjunctive in adverbial clauses.

Relative link	Remarks	Examples
que	The most common, used when a simple link is needed. It can refer to people or things.	Restrictive: *Este es el abrigo **que me regaló mi tía**.* (This is the coat (that/which) my aunt gave me.) Non-restrictive: *El coche, **que ya era muy viejo**, dejó de funcionar de repente el lunes.* (The car, which was already very old, suddenly stopped working on Monday.)
quien/quienes	Only applies to people. Not used in restrictive relative clauses unless preceded by a preposition	Non-restrictive: *El abuelo, **quien había luchado en la revolución cubana**, siempre tenía historias que contar.* (Granddad, who had fought in the Cuban revolution, always had stories to tell.) *Los estudiantes, **quienes ya habían terminado sus clases**, celebraron el comienzo de las vacaciones.* (The students, who had already finished their lessons, celebrated the beginning of the holidays.)
el cual, la cual, los cuales, las cuales	Similar to *que* and *quien* but more formal. Not used in restrictive relative clauses unless preceded by a preposition	Non-restrictive: *Su muerte afectó mucho a Lola, **la cual había trabajado con él durante años**.* (His death greatly affected Lola, who had worked with him for years.)
cuyo, -a, -os, -as	Used to indicate possession	Restrictive: *Es un escritor **cuyos libros se han traducido a más de 30 idiomas**.* (He Is a writer whose books have been translated into more than 30 languages.) Non-restrictive: *El museo etnográfico, **cuya colección de barcos balleneros era una de las mayores del mundo**, ardió por un incendio.* (The ethnographic museum, whose collection of whaling boats was one of the biggest in the world, burnt down in a fire.)
donde, adonde, cuando and como	Adverbs that can take the place of a relative pronoun, adding their own specific meaning of place, time or manner *Como* is found mainly in the phrases *la manera como* and *el modo como* in restrictive clauses. *Cuando* is only found in non-restrictive relative clauses.	Restrictive: *Esta es la casa **donde nací**.* (This is the house where I was born.) *El pueblo **adonde vamos de vacaciones** está a orillas del río Magdalena.* (The village where we go on holiday is on the banks of the River Magdalena.) *Me gusta la manera **como se expresa**.* (I like the way she talks.) Non-restrictive: *Covarrubias, **donde yo nací**, es un pueblo medieval maravilloso.* (Covarrubias, where I was born, is a wonderful medieval town.) *En verano, **cuando los días son más largos**, no volvemos a casa hasta las 10 de la noche.* (In summer, when the days are longer, we don't come home till 10 at night.)

Relative link	Remarks	Examples
preposition (de, desde, en, etc.) + el que, la que, los que, las que, lo que	When a preposition is needed to give a more precise meaning, it must be followed by el que, etc. It can refer to people or things.	Restrictive: *Estos son los niños **para los que he traído los bocadillos**.* (These are the children I brought the sandwiches for.) Non-restrictive: *Mi sobrina Rosa, **en la que sus padres tenían tantas esperanzas**, ha dicho que no quiere estudiar más.* (My niece Rosa, for whom her parents had such high hopes, has said she does not want to carry on studying.)
preposition (en, con, por, etc.) + quien(-es)	Only used for people	Restrictive: *Los chicos **con quienes sale mi hijo** son muy majos*. (The boys my son goes around with are very nice.) Non-restrictive: *Juan, **para quien su mujer lo era todo**, nunca aceptó su muerte.* (Juan, for whom his wife was everything, never accepted her death.)
preposition + el cual, la cual, los cuales, las cuales	Similar to el que but more formal	Restrictive: *Tendríamos que diseñar una campaña de márketing **a través de la cual lleguemos a un público más amplio**.* (We should design a marketing campaign through which we can reach a wider audience.) Non-restrictive: *Los agricultores, **para los que la sequía suponía ruina y hambre**, empezaron a emigrar a la ciudad.* (The farmers, for whom the drought meant ruin and hunger, started emigrating to the city.)
preposition (de, desde, a, hasta, hacia, etc.) + donde	To qualify the meaning of the adverb	Restrictive: *Encontré una ventana **desde donde podía ver todo el patio**.* (I found a window from where I could see the whole yard.) Non-restrictive: *La cabaña, **desde donde se veía el mar**, estaba abandonada.* (The hut, from where the sea could be seen, was abandoned.)
(preposition +) lo que, lo cual	Used as a neuter pronoun when the antecedent is an idea or any other element with no defined gender. Only used in non-restrictive relative clauses.	*Le dijo al último momento que no iría a la fiesta, **lo que le fastidió mucho**.* (At the last minute she told him she wouldn't go to the party, which annoyed him greatly.)

Ejercicios

Level 2

1 Join these pairs to form a complex sentence consisting of a main clause and a restrictive relative clause. The antecedent of the relative clause has been marked in bold.

Ejemplo

El **proyecto** no ha sido aceptado. Presentamos el proyecto el mes pasado.

El proyecto que presentamos el mes pasado no ha sido aceptado.

a El último barco con los **niños** llegó a Buenos Aires hace dos días. Los niños habían sobrevivido al terremoto.

b Tita es un **personaje** de la obra de Laura Esquivel *Como agua para chocolate*. Este personaje representa la intransigencia y represión que sufría la mujer en épocas pasadas.

Level 2

2 This exercise is similar to the previous one but this time the relative clause needs to be preceded by a preposition.

Ejemplo

En la novela, Mariela es la **mujer**. José se casa con esa mujer.

En la novela Mariela es la mujer con la que se casa José.

a Esta es la **ciudad**. En esta ciudad nació mi padre.

b En el colegio teníamos un **profesor**. Para el profesor todos los niños éramos futuros genios.

Level 3

3 Advise the person asking the following questions, starting your answer with *el que*, *la que*, *los que*, *las que*, as appropriate.

Ejemplo

–¿Qué sombrero me sienta mejor?

–El que mejor te sienta es el rojo.

a –¿Cuáles son las manzanas que más te gustan?

–. . . más me gustan son las reinetas.

b –¿Qué actor te parece más guapo de los hispanos?

–. . . me parece más atractivo es Antonio Banderas.

c –¿Quiénes llegaron los últimos?

–. . . que llegaron los últimos fueron los Pérez.

Level 2

4 Complete the gaps with an appropriate relative clause connector.

> Aquel era, por fin, el lugar con (a) . . . había soñado tantas veces. La hiedra (b) . . . trepaba por la pared cubría parte del tejado y toda la fachada. El balcón principal, desde (c) . . . se divisaban los montes lejanos, tenía un aspecto soberbio y decadente al mismo tiempo. La familia Garrido, (d) . . . retratos adornaban la escalera principal, había perdido la mansión cuando el último señor Garrido se arruinó con el negocio del arroz. Los nuevos dueños, (e) . . . vivían en Madrid, nunca la ocuparon. Y ahora esta casa y su jardín selvático, (f) . . . había jugado tantas veces de niño, eran míos. ¡Míos para siempre!

Level 2

5 In the following paragraph, decide whether the relative clauses in bold are restrictive or non-restrictive.

> El señor Martínez, (a) **que era un caballero elegante al cien por cien**, nunca salía de casa sin su chistera, (b) **la cual le hacía parecerse a un lord inglés de los de antes**. La casa (c) **donde vivía** había sido en su tiempo una gran mansión, pero ahora se percibía con demasiada claridad un descuido (d) **que amenazaba con aniquilar su esplendor para siempre**. El señor Martínez simplemente no tenía un duro.

<table>
<tr><td>Level
2/3</td></tr>
</table>

6 Choose the appropriate mood, indicative or subjunctive, for each sentence.

    a   Deseo vivir en un mundo donde no **hay/haya** violencia.

    b   La ciudad en la que **vivo/viva** no es muy grande.

    c   Ahí va el hombre que **se parece/se parezca** al profesor de música.

    d   Me gustaría encontrar una ocupación que me **dejaba/dejara** tiempo libre para dedicarme a la pintura.

<table>
<tr><td>Level
3</td></tr>
</table>

7 Translate the following sentences into English using non-specific relatives.

Ejemplo

¡Encontraremos al criminal, quienquiera que sea! *We will find the criminal, whoever he/she is!*

    a   No lo perdonaré cualquiera que sea su excusa.

    b   Estaremos aquí para recibirlos cuandoquiera que lleguen.

    c   Pepe recordará el consejo de su padre dondequiera que esté.

    d   Comoquiera que la llame esta conducta no es aceptable.

<table>
<tr><td>Level
2/3</td></tr>
</table>

26.5 The adverbial clause

The adverbial clause – *la oración circunstancial* – is a subordinate clause which relates to its main clause in the same way as any adverb, i.e. in terms of time, manner, place, instrument, circumstance, concession, purpose, result, cause or condition, as illustrated by the following example:

	Adverb or adverbial phrase	Adverbial clause
¿Cuándo?	*Lo haré **mañana**.* (I'll do it tomorrow.)	*Lo haré **cuando quieras**.* (I'll do it when you want.)

Types of adverbial clauses

There are different types of adverbial clauses, just as there are different types of adverbs:

Adverbial clause of	Meaning
(a) Cause	Expresses cause or reason and answers the question 'why?'
(b) Concession	Expresses a difficulty or restriction without preventing the fulfilment of the action in the main clause
(c) Conditional	Expresses a condition for the fulfilment of an action

(d) Comparison	Expresses a comparison and answers the question 'how?'
(e) Manner	Expresses mode or manner and answers the question 'how?'
(f) Place	Locates an event in place and answers the question 'where?'
(g) Purpose	Expresses aims and purpose and answers the question 'what for?' or 'why?'
(h) Time	Locates an event in time and answers the question 'when?'

Each type is further explained in later sections of this unit.

Use of the indicative or subjunctive in adverbial subordinate clauses

Refer to the examples in the table on the next page to clarify the use of indicative or subjunctive in adverbial clauses. In each case the connector in bold is the *basic* connector for each type of subordinate clause. There are two scenarios:

(a) Subordinate clauses that always take the subjunctive:

- Clauses of purpose, following the connectors *para que, a fin de que,* etc., e.g. *Te llamo para que me **reserves** una entrada.* (I'm calling you so you can reserve me a ticket.)
- Types of conditional sentences where the fulfilment of the condition is not probable or is impossible, e.g. *Si me **llamara** le colgaría el teléfono.* (If he called me I would hang up on him.) ☞ See Section 26.7 for more on the conditional sentence.
- Comparative sentences of the hypothetical type, such as *como si,* etc., e.g. *Todavía trata a sus hijos como si **fueran** niños de cinco años.* (He still treats his children as if they were five-year-olds.)

(b) Subordinate clauses that can take the indicative or the subjunctive.

In these cases the indicative is used to refer to actions that have taken place or are considered to be facts, while the subjunctive is used to refer to actions that have not yet taken place or are hypothetical, typically in sentences which indicate time, concession, mode or place.

☞ For more information revise the uses of the subjunctive in Section 21.1.

Adverbial clause conjunctions and other linking words

(a)   Connectors that show cause

English connectors which express similar meanings include 'because', 'as', 'since', 'given that'.

Adverbial clauses

Type	Subordinator	Example with indicative	Example with subjunctive
(a) Cause	*porque, como, debido a que, puesto que, ya que*	*Ha mentido **porque** tiene miedo.* (She lied because she was afraid.)	*No vamos a posponer la fiesta **porque** llueva.* (We are not going to postpone the party just because it rains.)
(b) Concession	*aunque, a pesar de que, por más que*	*Aunque no me gusta el cuadro, es una buena inversión y lo compraremos.* (Although I don't like the picture, it is a good investment and we'll buy it.)	*Aunque no me gustara el cuadro, lo compraríamos por ser una buena inversión.* (Even if I didn't like the picture, we would buy it because it is a good investment.)
(c) Condition	*si, a menos que, a no ser que, en el caso de que, a condición de que*	*Si trabajas mañana, lo terminarás.* (If you work tomorrow you'll finish it.)	*Si trabajaras mañana, lo terminarías.* (If you worked tomorrow you would finish it.)
(d) Comparison	*tanto . . . como; más . . . (de lo/que lo) que; menos . . . (de lo/que lo) que*	*Esta semana comimos **mejor de lo que** comimos la semana pasada.* (This week we ate better than we did last week.)	*Comí **mejor de lo que** hubiera comido en mi propia casa.* (I ate better than I would have done in my own home.)
(e) Manner	*como, según, de la manera que, del modo que*	*Ya me lo he estudiado, y te lo puedo explicar **como** lo entiendo yo.* (I've now studied it, and I can explain it to you as I understand it.)	*Cuando me lo estudie te lo intentaré explicar **como** lo entienda yo.* (When I study it, I'll try to explain it to you the way I understand it.)
(f) Place	(preposition +) *donde*	*Donde vivimos es muy bonito.* (It's very pretty where we live.)	*Espero que **donde** vivamos sea bonito.* (I hope that it will be pretty where we live.)
(g) Purpose	*para que, a fin de que, con objeto de que*		*Os voy a dar los plazos de entrega **para que** empecéis a organizar el trabajo.* (I'll give you the deadlines so that you can start organising your work.)
(h) Time	*cuando, antes de (que), después de (que), hasta que, mientras que, en cuanto, tan pronto como, apenas, cada vez que, siempre que*	*Cuando vivíamos en Perú hacíamos montañismo regularmente.* (When we lived in Peru we went mountaineering regularly.)	*Cuando vivamos en Perú podremos hacer montañismo regularmente.* (When we live in Peru we'll be able to go mountaineering regularly.)

porque	*No ha venido a ayudarnos **porque** es demasiado perezoso.* (He has not come to help us because he's too lazy.)
como (must come at the head of the sentence and is followed by the indicative)	***Como** tú has pagado las entradas, yo pagaré la cena.* (As you have paid for the tickets, I'll pay for dinner.) ☞ *Como* + subjunctive as a conditional connector in section (c), and *como* as a connector of manner in section (e).
puesto que (can be placed at the beginning or in the middle of the sentence)	***Puesto que** tú me lo aseguras, te creo.* (Since you assure me of it, I believe you.) Also *Te creo **puesto que** tú me lo aseguras.*
ya que (usually after a comma. It can be placed at the beginning of a complex sentence)	*La isla albergaba algunas especies muy raras, **ya que** estaba remota y aislada.* (The island had some very rare species, as it was remote and isolated.)
pues (as a cause connector this is quite old-fashioned and tends to be used sparingly)	*Le regaló una flor, **pues** era un romántico.* (He gave her a flower, being as he was a romantic.)
que (do not confuse with the many other uses of *que*)	*Recoge la ropa, **que** va a llover.* (Fetch the washing in because it's going to rain.)
dado que (slightly formal)	***Dado que** usted conoce mi delicada situación, iré al grano.* (Given that you are aware of my delicate position, I'll get straight to the point.)

The expression of cause can also be found in adverbial clauses formed by a gerund, e.g. ***Llegando** tan tarde, es mejor que nos quedemos en un hotel* (As we arrive so late, it is better that we stay in a hotel.). ☞ Revise this and other uses of the gerund in Section 15.2.

(b) Connectors that introduce the idea of concession

English connectors which express the same meanings include 'although', 'despite', 'in spite of', 'even if' and 'even though'.

The verbs in the subordinate clauses that follow these connectors take the subjunctive mood if they refer to an idea that is in the future or is hypothetical. Otherwise they take the indicative mood. Notice how the meaning changes in the examples with *aunque*.

aunque (can start a complex sentence.)	***Aunque** sirve a su madre como una esclava, ella jamás tiene un detalle que muestre su gratitud.* (Although she serves her mother like a slave, she never gets any sign of gratitude from her.) ***Aunque** sirva a su madre como una esclava, ella jamás tendrá un detalle que muestre su gratitud.* (Even if she serves her mother like a slave, she will never get any sign of gratitude from her.)
a pesar de que (more emphatic than *aunque*)	***A pesar de que** me lo prometió, no lo hizo.* (He did not do it, despite the fact that he promised.)
aun cuando (more emphatic than *aunque*)	***Aun cuando** hacía calor, tenía escalofríos por la fiebre.* (Even when it was hot he shivered with fever.)

si bien (normally takes indicative. More formal than the others.)	*Si bien el coche es de época, funciona perfectamente.* (Even if the car is vintage, it works perfectly well.)
y eso que (takes indicative. Colloquial.)	*No quiso que la acompañáramos, y eso que tenía miedo.* (She did not want us to go with her even though she was scared.)

Other connectors of concession (*aun, bien que, así* and *siquiera)* are less widely used.

(c) Connectors that specify a condition

These connectors are similar to the English 'if', 'unless', 'in case', 'provided that', 'as long as' and 'on condition that'. ☞ Refer to Section 26.7 for the rules of conditional sentences.

si (the most basic, like the English 'if')	*Si no viene, me voy a enfadar con él.* (If he doesn't come I'll be very cross with him.)
como (as a conditional connector it is always followed by a subjunctive)	*Como no venga me voy a enfadar con él.* (If he doesn't come, I'll be very cross with him.) ☞ Compare with *como* + indicative to express cause in section (a), and *como* as a connector to express manner in section (e).
a menos que + subjunctive, *a no ser que* + subjunctive ('unless')	*Lo haré mañana por la mañana a menos que me digas que no.* (I'll do it tomorrow morning unless you tell me not to.)
con tal de que + subjunctive, *a condición de que* + subjunctive ('provided that', 'on condition that', 'as long as')	*Puedes venir con tal de que prometas portarte bien.* (You can come as long as you promise to behave yourself.)
siempre que (as a conditional connector, it is always followed by a subjunctive)	*Podéis celebrar la fiesta en casa siempre que no hagáis demasiado ruido.* (You can have your party at home as long as you don't make too much noise.) ☞ Compare with *siempre que* + indicative in Section 26.6(a) (ii).
en (el) caso de que ('if', 'in case')	*No podemos arriesgarnos. En el caso de que descubran a Méndez, quemen todos los documentos que puedan comprometerles.* (We can't run any risks. If Méndez is discovered, burn all documents that could compromise you.)

The expression of condition can also be found in adverbial clauses formed by a gerund, e.g. ***Viviendo*** *juntos ahorraríamos un montón de dinero* (If we lived together we would save a lot of money). ☞ Revise this and other uses of the gerund in Section 15.2.

(d) Connectors that show comparison

Similar to the English 'more/less . . . than', 'as . . . as' when used between clauses.

Note that where the antecedent is an idea or concept rather than a definite object, the neuter form *lo que* is used: *Es mucho **más** grande **de lo que** pensábamos* (It is much bigger than we thought).

más . . . que más de lo que (del que/ de la que/de los que/ de las que)	*Más vale prevenir* **que** *lamentar*. (Better safe than sorry.) *Esta casa es* **más** *grande* **que** *la que vimos ayer*. (This house is bigger than the one we saw yesterday.) *Había* **más** *gente* **de la que** *me había imaginado*. (There were more people than I had imagined.)
menos . . . que menos de lo que (del que/de la que/de los que/de las que)	*La película fue* **menos** *interesante* **que** *la que vimos la semana pasada*. (The film was less interesting than the one we saw last week.) *En su cuenta bancaria tenía* **menos** *dinero* **del que** *pensaba*. (She had less money than she thought in her bank account.)
tanto/-a/-os/-as . . . como	*En esa batalla no hubo* **tantas** *bajas* **como** *se temía*. (There were not as many casualties as feared in that battle.)

👁 In the structure *más/menos . . . que/de* the article following *que* or *de* must agree in number and gender with the antecedent, whether or not it is explicitly stated, e.g. in *Tenía menos plata de* **la** *que pensaba* (She had less money than she thought), *la* agrees with *plata.*

The structure *tan . . . que* with consecutive and expressive value

The structure *tan/tanto (-as, -os, -as)* + adjective/noun + *que* + clause is used to emphasise the adjective or noun. For this reason it is commonly used as an expressive device, often based on exaggeration: *Es* **tan** *bueno* **que** *parece tonto* (He is so nice that he borders on the stupid).

☞ You can learn more on the expression of comparison in Section 4.3. For expressions equivalent to 'the more . . . the more' and 'bigger and bigger' go to Section 4.5.

(e) Connectors that express manner

Similar to the English connectors 'as', '(in) the way (that)', 'the manner (in which)', etc.

como, followed by indicative or subjunctive	*Cada uno es* **como** *es*. (We are all as we are.)
tal y como (more emphatic than como, colloquial)	*Escribió la leyenda* **tal y como** *se la había contado el anciano mapuche*. (He wrote down the legend just as the old Mapuche man had told him it.)
según ☞ según meaning 'according to' in Unit 12. ☞ según expressing progression in Section 26.6.	*Te lo cuento* **según** *me lo contaron a mí*. (I am telling it to you as they told it to me.)
en/de la manera que, en el/del modo que	*Yo pongo la mesa* **del modo que** *me enseñó mi abuela pero veo que en Inglaterra se pone de manera distinta*. (I lay the table in the way my grandmother taught me but I notice that in England it is laid differently.)

The expression of manner can also be found in adverbial clauses formed by a gerund, e.g. *Consiguió el puesto **mintiendo** sobre su pasado* (He got his post by lying about his past), or a past participle, e.g. *Mi abuela llegó al final de la guerra **avejentada** por las privaciones y la angustia* (By the end of the war my grandmother was aged by hardship and distress).

☞ Revise these and other uses of the gerund and past participle in Sections 15.2 and 15.3 respectively.

The structure *como si* + subjunctive

This structure is used to show a comparison with hypothetical value, similar to the English 'as if' and 'as though', e.g. *Derrochaba el dinero **como si fuera** millonario y vivía **como si** no **hubiera** un mañana* (He squandered his money as though he were a millionaire and lived as if there were no tomorrow).

(f) Connectors that specify place

Subordinate clauses of place take the same form and use the same connectors as the adjectival or relative clauses expressing place that you saw in Section 26.4. They are, in essence, the same construction but note that the *donde* clause does not have an antecedent:

(preposition *en, desde, hasta, hacia*, etc. . . .) + *donde* or *adonde*	***Adonde** yo voy no puedes seguirme*. (You can't follow where I'm going.) *Sacaron el dinero **de donde** pudieron y compraron dos pasajes para América*. (They got the money from wherever they could and bought two tickets for the Americas.)

(g) Connectors that denote the idea of purpose

Similar to the English 'so', 'so that' and 'in order to'.

The following connectors are always followed by the subjunctive.

para que	*Ahorramos durante años **para que** nuestro hijo pudiera ir a la universidad*. (We saved for years so that our son could go to university.)
a que	*Venía **a que** le explicaran cómo había sido el accidente*. (He was coming so that they could explain to him how the accident had happened.)
a fin de que, con el fin de que, con (el) objeto de que, con el propósito de que, con la intención de que	*La educación preescolar se ha hecho gratis **con el fin de que** las mujeres puedan reincorporarse al trabajo antes*. (Nursery education has been made free so that women can return to work earlier.)

de manera que, de modo que, de forma que (used with the subjunctive, these connectors mean 'in order that') ☞ Also as a consecutive connector (+ indicative) in Section 26.1.	*Les regalé a mis hijos un juego de ajedrez* **de manera que** *aprendieran a pensar estratégicamente.* (I gave my children a chess set so that they would learn to think strategically.)

(h) Connectors that specify relative time

These connectors express simultaneity of actions or indicate that one action took place before or after another action. Because of the complexity of time relations that can be expressed, this type of subordinate clause is covered next, in Section 26.6.

Ejercicios

Level 2

1 Link each sentence half in the left-hand column with an ending from the right-hand column to form meaningful sentences. Then decide which type of subordinate clause each sentence is, using this list:

cause • concessive • conditional • purpose • manner

a Decidimos comprarle el equipo de música que nos pidió . . .

(i) te habría podido ayudar.

b Si me hubieras dicho la verdad desde el principio . . .

(ii) para que pudieran empezar a prepararlos en las vacaciones.

c La profesora les dio los temas del proyecto . . .

(iii) debido al bloqueo económico.

d Quiero hacerlo . . .

(iv) aunque era carísimo.

e Hay escasez de gasolina . . .

(v) de la manera que lo habéis hecho vosotros.

Level 2

2 The following three sentences have a subordinate clause expressing cause. Place the right connector in each of them.

como • porque • ya que

a . . . no dejaba de llover decidimos suspender la excursión.
b Llegamos tarde . . . se nos estropeó el coche.
c No tuvo ninguna dificultad para entrar en el club, . . . era un antiguo cliente y el portero lo reconoció.

Level 2/3

3 Complete the blanks with the proper links in the comparative clause, following the code.

```
+  more . . . than
−  less . . . than
=  as . . . as
```

a   Las ruinas de Machu Picchu son mucho (+) . . . impresionantes . . . pensaba.
b   En las pasadas elecciones los socialistas no consiguieron (=) . . . votos . . .
    esperaban.
c   Hubo un 'crack' en el mercado y compramos la casa por (−) . . . dinero . . .
    habíamos presupuestado.

Level 3

4 Substitute the connector in bold for another one that fits grammatically, without
   changing the meaning of the sentence, as in the example. The meaning of the
   connector is given in brackets.

   Ejemplo

   Te recogeré a las 8 **a menos que** me llames. (conditional) a no ser que

   a   Está bien. Vendré a trabajar el sábado **a condición de que** me pases a
       recoger. (conditional)
   b   Haremos lo que dices, **ya que** estás tan segura, pero no estamos muy
       convencidos. (cause)
   c   **A pesar de que** el fuego continuó toda la noche, los guerrilleros no se
       rindieron. (concession)
   d   Hicieron una campaña **con el fin de que** los niños comprendieran la
       importancia de proteger los bosques que rodean la ciudad. (purpose)

Level 3

5 The following pairs of sentences are almost identical. In one the subordinate
   verb is in the indicative and in the other the verb is in the subjunctive. Explain the
   difference in meaning between them.

   a   (i)   Aunque los extremistas no firmen el acuerdo, el proceso de paz seguirá
              adelante.
       (ii)   Aunque los extremistas no firman el acuerdo, el proceso de paz seguirá
              adelante.
   b   (i)   Empezamos a poner las vacunas tan pronto como llegaron.
       (ii)   Empezaremos a poner las vacunas tan pronto como lleguen.
   c   (i)   Se comportó como su madre le dijo.
       (ii)   Se comportará como su madre le diga.
   d   (i)   Tuvimos cuidado y el camino por el que subimos no tenía hielo.
       (ii)   Tened cuidado que el camino por el que subáis no tenga hielo.

Level 2/3

6 The next sentences have been taken from a conversation between two friends.
   Finish them to form correct sentences and a coherent conversation. Pay attention
   to the meaning of the connectors in bold.

       —Hola, Rosa, ¿vas a ir a la fiesta esta noche?
       —Hola, Marilu. Creo que voy a ir, **aunque** (a) . . .
       —Pues, sí, anímate. Yo no puedo. Mi jefe me ha llamado hace un rato **para
       que** (b) . . .
       –¿Otra vez? ¿Pero no estuvieron aquí la semana pasada?
       –Sí, pero había problemas y han tenido que volver. No creo que pueda ir a la
       fiesta, **a no ser que** (c) . . .

—¡Pues a ver si tienes suerte! Yo voy a hacer un esfuerzo, **ya que** (d) . . .

—Ya veo que te da pereza pero seguro que luego lo pasas **mejor de lo que** (e) . . .

<table>
<tr><td>Level
3</td></tr>
</table>

7 The following text belongs to a short story by the Cuban writer Alejo Carpentier. Complete the gaps with the appropriate connector from the box to find out what it says.

> porque • después de • pero • ya que • cuando

> (a) . . . los obreros vinieron con el día para proseguir la demolición, encontraron el trabajo acabado. Alguien se había llevado la estatua de Ceres, vendida la víspera a un anticuario. (b) . . . quejarse al Sindicato, los hombres fueron a sentarse en los bancos de un parque municipal. Uno recordó entonces la historia, muy difuminada, de una Marquesa de Capellanías, ahogada, en tarde de mayo, entre las malangas del Almendares. (c) . . . nadie prestaba atención al relato, (d) . . . el sol viajaba de oriente a occidente, y las horas que crecen a la derecha de los relojes deben alargarse por la pereza, (e) . . . son las que más seguramente llevan a la muerte.
>
> (Alejo Carpentier (1980), *Cuentos completos*, 3rd edn, Barcelona: Bruguera, p. 93)

26.6 Time relations

When talking about the sequencing of actions, we often do so in relation to other actions that happen at the same time, before or after. The expression of the relationship between actions is a complex one, since to express the idea that two actions are simultaneous or contiguous to each other calls for the right connector and the right combination of tenses; it also depends on whether we are referring to the present, the past, the future or a hypothetical situation. Also – and to add to the complexity – we often want to specify that an action has interrupted another ongoing action, or that something happened every time something else happened, or that something will take place immediately after another action. To be able to express this level of complexity of meanings, Spanish, like many other languages, relies on a substantial body of connectors which are used in conjunction with a variety of possible tense combinations.

(a) To indicate that an action is *simultaneous* with another action

al + verb A in the infinitive + verb B	***Al abrir*** *la puerta sentí un fuerte olor a humo*. (When I opened the door I smelt a strong smell of smoke. Literally: On opening . . .)

mientras/cuando + verb A in imperfect, present simple or continuous tenses + verb B	**Mientras** Pedrito iba a clase de piano Pilar hacía los deberes. (While Pedrito had his piano lesson Pilar did her homework.)
Conjugated verb + gerund ☞ Section 15.2 on the gerund.	Entró **gritando**. (She came in screaming.)

Others: *en tanto que* and *entretanto que* (used like *mientras*).

(i) To specify that action A is happening (has happened, will happen, etc.) *at exactly the same time* as action B

en el momento en que/al mismo tiempo que/a la vez que + verb A + verb B	**En el momento en que** encendió la luz todas sus pesadillas desaparecieron. (The moment he switched the light on all his nightmares disappeared.)

(ii) To indicate that action A takes place (took place, will take place, etc.) *every time* that action B does

siempre que/cada vez que/todas las veces que + verb A + verb B	¡Ya estoy harta! ¡**Siempre que** cocina él comemos huevos fritos! (I'm fed up! Every time he cooks we eat fried eggs!)

(iii) To indicate that action A is *progressive and simultaneous* to action B

a medida que/según + verb A in continuous tenses/ present/imperfect/present subjunctive + verb B	**A medida que/Según** me iba acercando, la ciudad crecía ante mis ojos. (As I got nearer, the town grew before my eyes.)

👁 Note that *según* is also a preposition meaning 'according to' and a connector of manner meaning 'as'. ☞ You can revise them in Unit 12 and Section 26.5(e) respectively.

(iv) To show that an action *interrupts* (has interrupted, will interrupt, etc.) an ongoing action

Verb A in continuous tenses + cuando (+ de repente/de pronto) + verb B	Estábamos viendo la tele **cuando de pronto** saltó la alarma de incendios. (We were watching TV when suddenly the fire alarm went off.)

(b) To indicate that an action takes place (took place, will take place, etc.)
   ***after* another action**

cuando/después de (+ infinitive)/después de que/luego que/una vez (de) que + conjugated verb or después de + infinitive	**Cuando** cenes, llámame. (Call me when you finish dinner.) **Después de** hacer la caja cerró el almacén y se fue a casa. (After doing the till he locked up the store and went home.)
Perfect gerund + conjugated verb ☞ Section 15.2 on the gerund	**Habiendo dicho** lo que tenía que decir, dio la media vuelta y se marchó. (Having said what she needed to say, she turned round and left.)
Past participle + conjugated verb ☞ Section 15.3 on the past participle	**Concluida** la reunión, se fueron juntos a comer. (Having finished the meeting, they went for dinner together.)

To show that an action takes place (took place, will take place, etc.) *immediately after* another action

en cuanto/en el momento en que/tan pronto como/apenas + conjugated verb A + conjugated verb B or: nada más + infinitive verb A + conjugated verb B	**En cuanto** el padre cogió al niño en brazos, este dejó de llorar. (As soon as the father took the child in his arms, he stopped crying.) **Apenas** había terminado de cenar cuando sonó el timbre de la puerta. (No sooner had she finished dinner than the doorbell rang.)

(c) To indicate that an action took place *before* another one

Use of the pluperfect ☞ Section 18.7 on the pluperfect.	Intentamos negociar pero ellos ya **habían tomado** su decisión. (We tried to negotiate but they had already taken their decision.)
Pluperfect + cuando + preterite	**Habían cenado** ya **cuando** llegué. (They had already had dinner when I arrived.)
antes de + infinitive/antes de que + subjunctive	Acabó el libro **antes de** irse a la cama. (She finished the book before going to bed.) Acabó de preparar la comida mucho **antes de que** llegara su invitado. (She finished preparing the meal long before her guest arrived.)

☞ Go to Section 17.4 to revise the use of the future perfect to refer to actions taking place before another action in the future.

(d) To specify that an action is *the beginning* or *the end* of another action

desde que	**Desde que** le dieron la noticia está muy triste. (Since they told him the news he has been very sad.)
hasta que	Pensamos viajar por Sudamérica **hasta que** se nos acabe el dinero. (We are planning to travel around South America until we run out of money.)

☞ Refer to Unit 12 for these and other uses of the prepositions *desde* and *hasta*.

Ejercicios

Level 2

1 Read the following sentences and underline the action that took place **first**.

a Me pidieron el dinero para el regalo de Alicia, pero yo ya había pagado.
b Cuando vi que alguien me seguía, eché a correr.
c Consultó con sus padres antes de tomar una decisión definitiva.
d En cuanto su noviazgo se hizo público la prensa no la dejó en paz.

Level 2

2 Read the following sentences and explain the differences in time sequencing.

a (i) Nos contó su problema mientras dábamos un paseo.
  (ii) Nos contó su problema después de dar un paseo.
b (i) Antes de aceptar la oferta tenemos que hablar de los detalles.
  (ii) Hablamos de los detalles después de que decidimos aceptar la oferta.
c (i) Entró en casa, se quitó el abrigo y los zapatos, y telefoneó a su madre.
  (ii) Nada más entrar en casa, telefoneó a su madre.
d (i) Desde que sale con esta chica está estudiando mucho.
  (ii) Estudiaba mucho hasta que empezó a salir con esta chica.

Level 2

3 Complete the gaps with the right connector to show that the actions in the sentence took place **simultaneously**.
a Mari Luz se encontró con Miguel . . . volver a casa.
b . . . hacía la cena mi hija me contó que se había enfadado con su amiga.

mientras • en el momento • al

c Casualmente José Luis entró por la puerta . . . en que preguntaba por él.

Level 2

4 Complete the gaps with a verb in the appropriate tense to make coherent sentences.

a Al . . . los gritos, todos los vecinos salieron a la calle a ver qué pasaba.
b Mientras Beatriz . . . por el parque vio que un grupo de muchachos destrozaba un banco.
c Tina me ha prometido que cuando . . . vacaciones me llevará a ver a mi hermana.

Level 2

5 Select the appropriate connector for each sentence, following the instructions.

a Select a connector to show that the first action happened **every time** that the second action took place.
. . . lo intentaba, fracasaba. Por fin, me di por vencido.

mientras • cada vez que • cuando

b Select a connector to show that the two actions happened **at exactly the same time**.

en el momento en que • mientras • cuando

La reconocí . . . empezó a hablar.

c Select a connector to show that one of the actions happened **immediately after** the other action.
Fuimos al hospital . . . nos enteramos del accidente.

> después de que • en cuanto • cuando

d Select a connector to show that the action happens **progressively** and **simultaneously**.
. . . la iba conociendo cambiaba mi opinión sobre ella.

> cada vez que • a medida que • mientras

Level 2

6 Complete the following text with the appropriate connectors to make it coherent.
Aquel día Isabel estaba inquieta. (a) . . . desayunar bajó al patio a esperar el correo

> cuando (used twice) • cuando de repente • al • mientras • apenas • después de • hasta que • antes de • siempre que

de la mañana. (b) . . . esperaba sentada en el banco de la entrada pensaba en lo que haría después. Estaba ensimismada en sus pensamientos (c) . . . el ruido de los cascos de un caballo la devolvió a la realidad. (d) . . . se había levantado a mirar el camino (e) . . . el caballo de su padre apareció, acercándose al galope. Esperó inmóvil (f) . . . caballo y jinete se detuvieron ante la puerta. Isabel corrió hacia su padre con alegría. (g) . . . volvía de viaje le traía regalos. (h) . . . se acercó a su padre vio que estaba cubierto de sangre y, (i) . . . que pudiera ayudarlo, se desplomó como un fardo. (j) . . . intentar incorporarlo se dio cuenta de que estaba muerto.

Level 2

26.7 The conditional sentence

A conditional sentence – *la oración condicional* – consists of two clauses, a main clause and a subordinate clause. The subordinate clause expresses the **condition** for the fulfilment of the action expressed in the main clause. The most common subordinating connector is *si,* very much like 'if' in English.

> *Si llegas antes de las 5* *te llevo en coche a casa.*
> subordinate conditional clause   main clause
> (If you arrive before 5 o'clock I will take you home by car.)

☞ You can revise the conditional connectors in Section 26.5(c).

Types of conditional sentences introduced by *si*

Types of condition	Subordinate clause	Main clause verb	Examples
Past conditional: the outcome took place every time the condition was fulfilled	*si* + indicative past tenses	indicative past tenses	*Si María quería algo, Juan se lo daba.* (If María wanted anything, Juan would give it to her.)
Open condition: the fulfilment or non-fulfilment of the condition is equally possible, with the outcome in the future	*si* + present indicative	present or future indicative, or imperative	*Si el equipo gana el domingo, subirá a Primera División.* (If the team wins on Sunday, it will go up to the First Division.)
Remote condition: the condition expresses a hypothetical situation. Two possible meanings:	*si* + imperfect subjunctive	conditional simple	
(a) Possible fulfilment, similar to the open conditionals, but slightly more hypothetical. The outcome would take place in the future if the condition were fulfilled.			(a) *Si llegaran antes de las 2 podrían quedarse a comer.* (If they arrived before 2 they could stay for lunch.)
(b) The facts expressed in the conditional clause are not true, and are presented as hypothetical. The outcome is also hypothetical.			(b) *Si la quisiera de verdad, no la trataría como la trata.* (If he really loved her he would not treat her the way he does.) (The speaker does not believe that he loves her.)
Unfulfilled conditions: a hypothetical situation in the past where the condition was not fulfilled and the outcome did not take place	*si* + pluperfect subjunctive	(a) conditional perfect or (b) conditional (if the result stretches into the present)	(a) *Si hubiera ganado, te habría invitado a cenar.* (Had I won I would have invited you to dinner.) (But I did not.) (b) *Si Marcos no hubiera cogido el coche estando borracho Marta estaría ahora viva.* (If Marcos had not driven the car while drunk Marta would be alive now.)

Level 2

How to translate 'If I were you'

If I were you,	I would talk to her.
Yo en tu lugar, *Yo que tú,* *Si yo fuera tú,*	*hablaría con ella.*

Ejercicios

1 Put the verb in the subordinate clause into the correct form. Pay attention to the meaning of the main clause. Use the rules in the box as a guide.

> *Si* + present indicative → present, future or imperative
> *Si* + imperfect indicative → imperfect indicative

a ¡No desesperes! Si nos (ver) . . . aquel barco estamos salvados.
b Si el enfermo no (conseguir) . . . superar la fiebre en las próximas 24 horas, de seguro morirá.
c Le copiaba a su hermano en todo: si Moncho (decir) . . . 'sí', era 'sí', si Moncho no (querer) . . . comer, él tampoco.
d Acércate con cuidado y si el perro (empezar) . . . a ladrarnos, echa a correr.

2 The following extracts illustrate hypothetical situations expressed with a conditional sentence. Complete the gaps with the correct verb form, following this rule.

> *Si* + imperfect subjunctive → conditional

a Extract from an interview with a Cuban during the official funeral of Che Guevara in Santa Clara, Cuba, in October 1997.

> —Si aquí estuviera el Che hoy, ¿qué le (tú, decir) . . .?
>
> —Yo le (decir) . . . tantas cosas, porque tengo que agradecerle tantas cosas, que, vaya, no (tener) . . . palabras ni (terminar) . . . nunca de decirle lo que tengo que decirle.
>
> (The Open University (2000), *L204 Viento en popa, Cuadernillo de transcripciones 7* (Walton Hall: The Open University), p. 31)

b Extract from an interview with several people on what they would do if they could live their lives again.

> —Si (tú, poder) . . . volver a vivir, ¿qué harías distinto?
>
> —De mi vida personal, nada. No creo que (cambiar). . . . No, no, nada.
>
> —¿Nada? ¿Todo igualito?
>
> —Pues, yo sí creo que lo (hacer) . . . todo igualito. Pero estoy contento, bueno, no contento, pero me parece que, el transcurso de mi vida ha sido muy normal con los problemas, con los momentos de dolor, de felicidad, de cualquier humano. Y creo que si (volver) . . . a nacer (recorrer) . . . un camino muy similar, ¿no?
>
> (The Open University (2000), *L204 Viento en popa, Cuadernillo de transcripciones 7* (Walton Hall: The Open University), p. 20)

Level 2

Level 2/3

c

> Ernest Hemingway, el gran escritor estadounidense, se (sentir) . . .
> orgulloso con toda seguridad si (saber) . . . que el bar 'Harry's' de Venecia,
> que tanto frecuentó y donde parió algunos de sus relatos, ha sido incluido
> entre los monumentos protegidos por el Ministerio de Cultura de Italia.
>
> (*El Correo Español – El Pueblo Vasco*, 09/03/01, p. 88)

Level
2/3

3 Finish the following sentences to create a statement that is true about you.

> *Si* + pluperfect subjunctive → conditional or conditional perfect

a Si . . . yo también sería rico/a ahora.
b Si hubiera nacido y crecido en un país hispano . . .
c Si hubiera podido elegir mi nombre . . .
d Si . . . no lo habría creído.

27 Indirect speech

Both direct and indirect speech are used to convey what somebody has said. **Direct speech** – *el discurso directo* or *el estilo directo* – quotes what was said literally: *Él me dijo: "Pásate por aquí mañana"* (He said to me: 'Pop in tomorrow.').

Indirect, or **reported**, **speech** – *el discurso indirecto* or *el estilo indirecto* – reports what was said but without using the exact words of the speaker. What was said becomes a subordinate clause, usually joined by the conjunction *que* – *Él me dijo que me pasara por allí al día siguiente.* (He told me to pop in the following day.)

In indirect speech a number of transformations take place in the subordinate clause. They can affect:

the references to the people involved, i.e. personal pronouns, possessive forms and the person of the verb form	*pasa (tú)* → *pasara (yo)* *-te* → *me*
time references, i.e. verb tenses, adverbs or phrases of time	*pasa* (imperative) → *pasara* (imperfect subjunctive) *mañana* → *al día siguiente*
place references, i.e. demonstratives, adverbs or phrases of place	*por aquí* → *por allí*

Changes in subordinate verb tenses to agree with the tense of the reporting verb

(a) If the main verb is **in a present tense, the perfect or a future tense** there is **no change** in the tense of the verb when it becomes a subordinate verb, unless it is an **imperative**; the imperative changes to the present subjunctive.

Direct speech	Indirect speech
*Me lo ha dicho bien claro: "No **me casaré** nunca contigo."* (He told me very clearly: 'I will never marry you.')	*Me ha dicho bien claro que no **se casará** nunca conmigo.* (He told me very clearly that he'll never marry me.)
*Juan lo confiesa: "**Pasé** un miedo terrible."* (Juan confesses: 'I was (absolutely) petrified.')	*Juan confiesa que **pasó** un miedo terrible.* (Juan confesses that he was petrified.)

El 1 de enero dirá de nuevo: "**Voy a dejar** *de fumar.*" (On 1 January he will again say: 'I'm going to give up smoking'.)	*El 1 de enero dirá de nuevo que* **va a dejar** *de fumar.* (On 1 January he will again say that he's going to give up smoking.)
Imperative **Déjame** *sola unos momentos.* (Leave me alone for a few minutes.)	**Present subjunctive** *Me ha pedido que la* **deje** *sola unos momentos.* (She has asked me to leave her alone for a few minutes.)

(b) If the main verb is **in a past tense** the following **changes are needed:**

Direct speech From . . .	Indirect speech To . . .
Present simple **Queremos** *negociar.* (We want to negotiate.)	→ **Imperfect** *El director general aseguró que* **querían** *negociar.* (The managing director gave assurances that they wanted to negotiate.)
Present continuous *En estos momentos* **estoy navegando** *por el Orinoco.* (I am sailing up the Orinoco right now.)	→ **Imperfect continuous** *Me contó que en esos momentos* **estaba navegando** *por el Orinoco.* (She told me that right then she was sailing up the Orinoco.)
Preterite *El mes pasado la inflación se* **disparó** *al 5%.* (Last month inflation shot up to 5%.)	→ **Pluperfect** *La prensa confirmó que el mes anterior la inflación se* **había disparado** *al 5%.* (The press confirmed that the month before, inflation had shot up to 5%.) → **Preterite** *La prensa confirmó ayer que el mes pasado la inflación se* **disparó** *al 5%.* (Note that the use of the preterite would mean that the statement is made in the same period of time as the facts reported: The press confirmed that last month inflation shot up to 5%.)
Perfect **Han encontrado** *a la niña desaparecida.* (The missing girl has been found.)	→ **Pluperfect** *Anunciaron que* **habían encontrado** *a la niña desaparecida.* (It was reported that the missing girl had been found.)
Future simple *Te* **llamaré** *el lunes que viene.* (I'll call you next Monday.)	→ **Conditional** *Me prometió que me* **llamaría** *el lunes siguiente.* (She promised she would call me the following Monday.) → **Imperfect of 'ir a' + infinitive** *Me prometió que me* **iba a llamar** *el lunes siguiente.*
Imperative *¡No* **saltes**! (Don't jump!)	→ **Imperfect subjunctive** *Me gritó que no* **saltara**. (He shouted at me not to jump.)
Present subjunctive *Quiero que* **vengas** *con nosotros.* (I want you to come with us.)	→ **Imperfect subjunctive** *Me dijo que quería que* **fuera** *con ellos.* (He said he wanted me to go with them.)

Direct speech From . . .	Indirect speech To . . .
Perfect subjunctive *No creo que **haya llegado**.* (I don't think he has arrived.)	→ **Pluperfect subjunctive** *Dijo que no creía que **hubiera llegado**.* (She said she did not think he had arrived.)
Conditional and conditional perfect *No me **gustaría** estar en su lugar.* (I would not like to be in her shoes.)	→ **No change** *Confesó que no le **gustaría** estar en su lugar.* (He admitted that he would not like to be in her shoes.)
Imperfect indicative and subjunctive *El país **pasaba** por uno de sus peores momentos.* (The country was going through one of its worst periods.)	→ **No change** *El primer ministro afirmó que el país **pasaba** por uno de sus peores momentos.* (The prime minister said that the country was going through one of its worst periods.)
Pluperfect indicative and subjunctive *Si se **hubiera llegado** a un acuerdo el año anterior, la guerra no habría estallado.* (If there had been an agreement the previous year, war would not have broken out.)	→ **No change** *La experta en asuntos del Oriente Medio reiteró que si se **hubiera llegado** a un acuerdo el año anterior, la guerra no habría estallado.* (The Middle East expert reiterated that had there been an agreement the previous year, war would not have broken out.)

Reporting questions

Questions follow the same rules of person, verb, place and time reference transformation as the reporting of statements, but are not linked with *que.*

(a) Open questions (i.e. with an interrogative word) → interrogative	
*¿**Cómo** lo habrá averiguado?* (How has she found out?) ☞ Interrogatives in Unit 11.	*Me preguntaba **cómo** lo habría averiguado.* (I wondered how she could have found out.)

(b) Closed questions (i.e. with no interrogative word) → *si*	
¿Te has hecho daño? (Did you hurt yourself?)	*Mi amigo me preguntó **si** me había hecho daño.* (My friend asked me if I had hurt myself.)

Some common changes in time references

• *hoy*	→	*ese (mismo) día*
*La he visto **hoy**.* (I saw her today.)	→	*Dijo que la había visto **ese día**.* (He said he had seen her that day.)
• *ayer*	→	*el día antes, el día anterior*
***Ayer** se firmó el nuevo acuerdo.* (The new agreement was signed yesterday.)	→	*Confirmaron que el nuevo acuerdo se había firmado **el día anterior**.* (They confirmed that the new agreement had been signed the day before.)

• *antes de ayer/antier* (American Spanish)	→	*dos días antes*
*El atraco fue **antes de ayer**.* (The robbery was the day before yesterday.)	→	*Declararon que el atraco había sido **dos días antes**.* (It was reported that the robbery had been two days before.)
• *hace tres meses*	→	*hacía tres meses, tres meses antes*
***Hace dos años** que no la vemos.* (We haven't seen her for two years.)	→	*Confesaron que **hacía dos años** que no la veían.* (They confessed that they hadn't seen her for two years.)
• *el año pasado*	→	*el año anterior*
***El año pasado** hubo muy buena nieve.* (Last year the snow was very good.)	→	*Recordaron que **el año anterior** había habido muy buena nieve.* (They remembered that the snow had been very good the year before.)
• *mañana*	→	*al día siguiente*
*Tengo hora con el médico **mañana** a las 10.* (I have a doctor's appointment tomorrow at 10.)	→	*Me comentó que tenía hora con el médico **al día siguiente** a las 10.* (She mentioned she had a doctor's appointment the following day at 10.)
• *pasado mañana*	→	*dos días después, dos días más tarde, al cabo de dos días*
*¡Nos veremos **pasado mañana**!* (We'll see each other the day after tomorrow!)	→	*Sus últimas palabras fueron que nos veríamos **dos días después**.* (His last words were that we would see each other two days later.)
• *dentro de tres meses*	→	*tres meses después, tres meses más tarde*
*Vamos a empezar las obras **dentro de cuatro semanas**.* (We'll start work in four weeks time.)	→	*Nos aseguró que empezarían las obras **cuatro semanas después**.* (He promised us they would start work four weeks later.)
• *el año que viene*	→	*el/al año siguiente*
*Las elecciones se celebrarán **el año que viene**.* (The elections will take place next year.)	→	*Anunciaron que las elecciones se celebrarían **al año siguiente**.* (It was announced that the elections would take place the year after.)

Ejercicios

1 Change the following sentences into indirect speech, making the necessary transformations. Note that the reporting verb is in the present or the perfect.

a "Estoy encantado de haber ganado el premio." (Isidro ha comentado . . .)

b "¡Soy inocente!" (El preso no deja de repetir . . .)

c "Vamos a luchar hasta el final este domingo en el partido contra el Athletic de Bilbao." (El capitán del Real Madrid asegura . . .)

d "Mañana te devolveré el dinero que te debo." (Felipe me ha asegurado . . .)

Level 2/3

2 Now change the sentences in exercise 1 above, this time putting all reporting verbs into the past:

    a   Isidro comentó . . .
    b   El preso no dejaba de repetir . . .
    c   El capitán del Real Madrid aseguró . . .
    d   Felipe me aseguró . . .

Level 2

3 Put the following questions into indirect speech.

    a   ¿Dónde vives? (Todos los días me pregunta . . .)
    b   ¿Te has hecho daño? (Cuando me caí un señor muy amable me preguntó . . .)
    c   ¿Qué planes tienes para este verano? (Malena quiere saber . . .)
    d   ¿Sabe conducir? (En la entrevista me preguntaron . . .)

Level 2/3

4 Complete the sentences in indirect speech. Do not forget to change the time references as well as the verb forms and the person references.

    a   "Adiós, María, vendré a buscarte a las 9 mañana", se despidió Perico.
        Perico se despidió de María prometiendo . . .
    b   "¡Pide perdón a la abuela ahora mismo!", gritó Serena al niño.
        Serena gritó al niño . . .
    c   "¡Fui a visitarlo hace dos días y estaba perfectamente bien!"
        Josechu exclamó sorprendido . . .
    d   "No creo que el paquete llegue hasta la semana que viene."
        Para calmarnos, Beatriz dijo . . .

Appendix: verb tables

Regular conjugation

First conjugation -ar

	Present indicative	Present subjunctive*	Imperative	Preterite	Imperfect subjunctive	Imperfect indicative	Future indicative	Conditional	Impersonal
A	ato	ate		até	atara/atase	ataba	ataré	ataría	**Gerund** atando
T	atas	ates	ata	ataste	ataras/atases	atabas	atarás	atarías	**Participle** atado
A	ata	ate	ate	ató	atara/atase	ataba	atará	ataría	
R	atamos	atemos	atemos	atamos	atáramos/atásemos	atábamos	ataremos	ataríamos	
	atáis	atéis	atad	atasteis	atarais/ataseis	atabais	ataréis	ataríais	
	atan	aten	aten	ataron	ataran/atasen	ataban	atarán	atarían	

	Perfect indicative	Perfect subjunctive			Pluperfect subjunctive	Pluperfect indicative	Future perfect	Conditional perfect	Impersonal
A	he	haya			hubiera/hubiese	había	habré	habría	**Perfect infinitive** haber atado
T	has	hayas			hubieras/hubieses	habías	habrás	habrías	
A	ha	haya			hubiera/hubiese	había	habrá	habría	**Perfect gerund** habiendo atado
R	hemos	hayamos			hubiéramos/hubiésemos	habíamos	habremos	habríamos	
	habéis	hayáis			hubierais/hubieseis	habíais	habréis	habríais	
	han	hayan			hubieran/hubiesen	habían	habrán	habrían	
	+ atado	+ atado			+ atado	+ atado	+ atado	+ atado	

Second conjugation -er

	Present indicative	Present subjunctive	Imperative	Preterite	Imperfect subjunctive	Imperfect indicative	Future indicative	Conditional	Impersonal
C	como	coma		comí	comiera/comiese	comía	comeré	comería	**Gerund** comiendo
O	comes	comas	come	comiste	comieras/comieses	comías	comerás	comerías	**Participle** comido
M	come	coma	coma	comió	comiera/comiese	comía	comerá	comería	
E	comemos	comamos	comamos	comimos	comiéramos/comiésemos	comíamos	comeremos	comeríamos	
R	coméis	comáis	comed	comisteis	comierais/comieseis	comíais	comeréis	comeríais	
	comen	coman	coman	comieron	comieran/comiesen	comían	comerán	comerían	

COMER (continued)

	Perfect indicative	Perfect subjunctive			Pluperfect subjunctive	Pluperfect indicative	Future perfect	Conditional perfect	Impersonal
C	he	haya			hubiera/hubiese	había	habré	habría	**Perfect infinitive**
O	has	hayas			hubieras/hubieses	habías	habrás	habrías	haber comido
M	ha	haya			hubiera/hubiese	había	habrá	habría	**Perfect gerund**
E	hemos	hayamos			hubiéramos/hubiésemos	habíamos	habremos	habríamos	habiendo comido
R	habéis	hayáis			hubierais/hubieseis	habíais	habréis	habríais	
	han	hayan			hubieran/hubiesen	habían	habrán	habrían	
	+ comido	+ comido			+ comido	+ comido	+ comido	+ comido	

Third conjugation -ir

	Present indicative	Present subjunctive	Imperative	Preterite	Imperfect subjunctive	Imperfect indicative	Future indicative	Conditional	Impersonal
S	subo	suba		subí	subiera/subiese	subía	subiré	subiría	**Gerund** subiendo
U	subes	subas	sube	subiste	subieras/subieses	subías	subirás	subirías	**Participle** subido
B	sube	suba	suba	subió	subiera/subiese	subía	subirá	subiría	
I	subimos	subamos	subamos	subimos	subiéramos/subiésemos	subíamos	subiremos	subiríamos	
R	subís	subáis	subid	subisteis	subierais/subieseis	subíais	subiréis	subiríais	
	suben	suban	suban	subieron	subieran/subiesen	subían	subirán	subirían	

	Perfect indicative	Perfect subjunctive			Pluperfect subjunctive	Pluperfect indicative	Future perfect	Conditional perfect	Impersonal
S	he	haya			hubiera/hubiese	había	habré	habría	**Perfect infinitive**
U	has	hayas			hubieras/hubieses	habías	habrás	habrías	haber subido
B	ha	haya			hubiera/hubiese	había	habrá	habría	**Perfect gerund**
I	hemos	hayamos			hubiéramos/hubiésemos	habíamos	habremos	habríamos	habiendo subido
R	habéis	hayáis			hubierais/hubieseis	habíais	habréis	habríais	
	han	hayan			hubieran/hubiesen	habían	habrán	habrían	
	+ subido	+ subido			+ subido	+ subido	+ subido	+ subido	

Irregularities affecting the vowels in the stem of the verb (irregularities are shaded)

Present indicative	Present subjunctive	Imperative	Preterite	Imperfect subjunctive	Gerund

e → ie, but not in the 1st and 2nd person plural in the present indicative and subjunctive and the imperative, e.g. *cerrar*

Present indicative	Present subjunctive	Imperative	Preterite	Imperfect subjunctive	Gerund
cierro	cierre		cerré	cerrara/cerrase	cerrando
cierras	cierres	cierra	cerraste	cerraras/cerrases	
cierra	cierre	cierre	cerró	cerrara/cerrase	
cerramos	cerremos	cerremos	cerramos	cerráramos/cerrásemos	
cerráis	cerréis	cerrad	cerrasteis	cerrarais/cerraseis	
cierran	cierren	cierren	cerraron	cerraran/cerrasen	

Other verbs: *acertar, apretar, ascender, atender, atravesar, calentar, comenzar, confesar, defender, despertar, discernir, empezar, entender, enterrar, fregar, gobernar, helar, merendar, negar, nevar, pensar, perder, recomendar, regar, sembrar, sentar, temblar, tropezar*, etc.

o → ue, but not in the 1st and 2nd person plural in the present indicative and subjunctive and the imperative, e.g. *contar*

Present indicative	Present subjunctive	Imperative	Preterite	Imperfect subjunctive	Gerund
cuento	cuente		conté	contara/contase	
cuentas	cuentes	cuenta	contaste	contaras/contases	
cuenta	cuente	cuente	contó	contara/contase	
contamos	contemos	contemos	contamos	contáramos/contásemos	
contáis	contéis	contad	contasteis	contarais/contaseis	
cuentan	cuenten	cuenten	contaron	contaran/contasen	

Other verbs: *acostar, acordar, aprobar, cocer, colgar, comprobar, consolar, contar, costar, demostrar, devolver, doler, encontrar, esforzarse, llover, mostrar, mover, probar, recordar, renovar, soler, soltar, sonar, soñar, tronar, volar, volver*, etc.
Oler follows this pattern but its spelling is slightly unusual in the present indicative (*huelo, hueles, huele, olemos, oléis, huelen*), in the present subjunctive (*huela, huelas, huela, olamos, oláis, huelan*) and in the imperative (*huele, huela, olamos, oled, huelan*).

e → ie and **e → i**, e.g. *mentir*

Present indicative	Present subjunctive	Imperative	Preterite	Imperfect subjunctive	Gerund
miento	mienta		mentí	mintiera/mintiese	mintiendo
mientes	mientas	miente	mentiste	mintieras/mintieses	
miente	mienta	mienta	mintió	mintiera/mintiese	
mentimos	mintamos	mintamos	mentimos	mintiéramos/mintiésemos	
mentís	mintáis	mentid	mentisteis	mintierais/mintieseis	
mienten	mientan	mientan	mintieron	mintieran/mintiesen	

Other verbs: *arrepentirse, consentir, convertir, digerir, divertir, herir, hervir, invertir, preferir, referir, sentir, sugerir*, etc.

o → ue and **o → u**, *dormir* and *morir* (participle: *muerto*) are the only verbs to follow this pattern

Present indicative	Present subjunctive	Imperative	Preterite	Imperfect subjunctive	Gerund
duermo	duerma		dormí	durmiera/durmiese	durmiendo
duermes	duermas	duerme	dormiste	durmieras/durmieses	
duerme	duerma	duerma	durmió	durmiera/durmiese	
dormimos	durmamos	durmamos	dormimos	durmiéramos/durmiésemos	
dormís	durmáis	dormid	dormisteis	durmierais/durmieseis	
duermen	duerman	duerman	durmieron	durmieran/durmiesen	

e → i, e.g. *competir*

Present indicative	Present subjunctive	Imperative	Preterite	Imperfect subjunctive	Gerund
compito	compita		competí	compitiera/compitiese	compitiendo
compites	compitas	compite	competiste	compitieras/compitieses	
compite	compita	compita	compitió	compitiera/compitiese	
competimos	compitamos	compitamos	competimos	compitiéramos/compitiésemos	
competís	compitáis	competid	competisteis	compitierais/compitieseis	
compiten	compitan	compitan	compitieron	compitieran/compitiesen	

Other verbs: *conseguir, corregir, despedir, freír, elegir, impedir, medir, pedir, perseguir, reír, reñir, repetir, seguir, servir, vestir,* etc.

i → ie, *adquirir* and *inquirir* are the only verbs to follow this pattern in the present indicative, the present subjunctive and the imperative

Present indicative	Present subjunctive	Imperative	Preterite	Imperfect subjunctive	Gerund
adquiero	adquiera		adquirí	adquiriera/adquiriese	adquiriendo
adquieres	adquieras	adquiere	adquiriste	adquirieras/adquirieses	
adquiere	adquiera	adquiera	adquirió	adquiriera/adquiriese	
adquirimos	adquiramos	adquiramos	adquirimos	adquiriéramos/adquiriésemos	
adquirís	adquiráis	adquirid	adquiristeis	adquirierais/adquirieseis	
adquieren	adquieran	adquieran	adquirieron	adquirieran/adquiriesen	

u → ue, *jugar* is the only verb with this pattern in the present indicative, the present subjunctive and the imperative

Present indicative	Present subjunctive	Imperative	Preterite	Imperfect subjunctive	Gerund
juego	juegue		jugué	jugara/jugase	jugando
juegas	juegues	juega	jugaste	jugaras/jugases	
juega	juegue	juegue	jugó	jugara/jugase	
jugamos	juguemos	juguemos	jugamos	jugáramos/jugásemos	
jugáis	juguéis	jugad	jugasteis	jugarais/jugaseis	
juegan	jueguen	jueguen	jugaron	jugaran/jugasen	

Irregularities affecting consonants in the verb (irregularities are shaded)

Present indicative	Present subjunctive	Imperative	Preterite	Imperfect subjunctive	Gerund
z → zc before o, a in verbs ending in -ecer and -ocer in the present indicative and the imperative, e.g. *agradecer*					
agradezco	agradezca		agredecí	agradeciera/agradeciese	agradeciendo
agradeces	agradezcas	agradece	agradeciste	agradecieras/agradecieses	
agradece	agradezca	agradezca	agradeció	agradeciera/agradeciese	
agradecemos	agradezcamos	agradezcamos	agradecimos	agradeciéramos/agradeciésemos	
agradecéis	agradezcáis	agradeced	agradecisteis	agradecierais/agradecieseis	
agradecen	agradezcan	agradezcan	agradecieron	agradecieran/agradeciesen	

Other verbs in –ecer: *aparecer, apetecer, compadecer, conocer, crecer, desobedecer, empobrecer, enriquecer, enrojecer, entristecer, envejecer, establecer, favorecer, merecer, obedecer, ofrecer, parecer, permanecer, pertenecer, restablecer*, etc. and a few others: *complacer, lucir, nacer*

Present indicative	Present subjunctive	Imperative	Preterite	Imperfect subjunctive	Gerund
z → zc before o, a + preterite and imperfect subjunctive with **-duj-** in verbs ending in **-ducir**, e.g. *conducir*					
conduzco	conduzca		conduje	condujera/condujese	conduciendo
conduces	conduzcas	conduce	condujiste	condujeras/condujeses	
conduce	conduzca	conduzca	condujo	condujera/condujese	
conducimos	conduzcamos	conduzcamos	condujimos	condujéramos/condujésemos	
conducís	conduzcáis	conducid	condujisteis	condujerais/condujeseis	
conducen	conduzcan	conduzcan	condujeron	condujeran/condujesen	

Other verbs: *deducir, introducir, producir, reducir, reproducir, traducir, seducir*, etc.

Present indicative	Present subjunctive	Imperative	Preterite	Imperfect subjunctive	Gerund
i → y before a, e, o in verbs ending in **-uir**, e.g. *incluir*					
incluyo	incluya		incluí	incluyera/incluyese	incluyendo
incluyes	incluyas	incluye	incluiste	incluyeras/incluyeses	
incluye	incluya	incluya	incluyó	incluyera/incluyese	
incluimos	incluyamos	incluyamos	incluimos	incluyéramos/incluyésemos	
incluís	incluyáis	incluid	incluisteis	incluyerais/incluyeseis	
incluyen	incluyan	incluyan	incluyeron	incluyeran/incluyesen	

Other verbs: *concluir, constituir, contribuir, construir, destruir, disminuir, distribuir, excluir, huir, influir, instruir, obstruir, reconstruir, sustituir*, etc.

The Spanish verb conjugation: especially complex irregular verbs (shaded boxes show irregular forms)

	Present indicative	Present subjunctive	Imperative	Preterite	Imperfect subjunctive	Imperfect indicative	Future indicative	Conditional	Other
A	ando	ande		anduve	anduviera/anduviese	andaba	andaré	andaría	**Gerund** andando
N	andas	andes	anda	anduviste	anduvieras/anduvieses	andabas	andarás	andarías	**Participle** andado
D	anda	ande	ande	anduvo	anduviera/anduviese	andaba	andará	andaría	
A	andamos	andemos	andemos	anduvimos	anduviéramos/anduviésemos	andábamos	andaremos	andaríamos	
R	andáis	andéis	andad	anduvisteis	anduvierais/anduvieseis	andabais	andaréis	andaríais	
	andan	anden	anden	anduvieron	anduvieran/anduviesen	andaban	andarán	andarían	

But also regular conjugation: *andé*, etc. and *andara/andase*, etc. in some regions

	Present indicative	Present subjunctive	Imperative	Preterite	Imperfect subjunctive	Imperfect indicative	Future indicative	Conditional	Other
C	quepo	quepa		cupe	cupiera/cupiese	cabía	cabré	cabría	**Gerund** cabiendo
A	cabes	quepas	cabe	cupiste	cupieras/cupieses	cabías	cabrás	cabrías	**Participle** cabido
B	cabe	quepa	quepa	cupo	cupiera/cupiese	cabía	cabrá	cabría	
E	cabemos	quepamos	quepamos	cupimos	cupiéramos/cupiésemos	cabíamos	cabremos	cabríamos	
R	cabéis	quepáis	cabed	cupisteis	cupierais/cupieseis	cabíais	cabréis	cabríais	
	caben	quepan	quepan	cupieron	cupieran/cupiesen	cabían	cabrán	cabrían	
C	caigo	caiga		caí	cayera/cayese	caía	caeré	caería	**Gerund** cayendo
A	caes	caigas	cae	caíste	cayeras/cayeses	caías	caerás	caerías	**Participle** caído
E	cae	caiga	caiga	cayó	cayera/cayese	caía	caerá	caería	
R	caemos	caigamos	caigamos	caímos	cayéramos/cayésemos	caíamos	caeremos	caeríamos	
	caéis	caigáis	caed	caísteis	cayerais/cayeseis	caíais	caeréis	caeríais	
	caen	caigan	caigan	cayeron	cayeran/cayesen	caían	caerán	caerían	
D	doy	dé		di	diera/diese	daba	daré	daría	**Gerund** dando
A	das	des	da	diste	dieras/dieses	dabas	darás	darías	**Participle** dado
R	da	dé	dé	dio	diera/diese	daba	dará	daría	
	damos	demos	demos	dimos	diéramos/diésemos	dábamos	daremos	daríamos	
	dais	deis	dad	disteis	dierais/dieseis	dabais	daréis	daríais	
	dan	den	den	dieron	dieran/diesen	daban	darán	darían	
D	digo	diga		dije	dijera/dijese	decía	diré	diría	**Gerund** diciendo
E	dices	digas	di	dijiste	dijeras/dijeses	decías	dirás	dirías	**Participle** dicho
C	dice	diga	diga	dijo	dijera/dijese	decía	dirá	diría	
I	decimos	digamos	digamos	dijimos	dijéramos/dijésemos	decíamos	diremos	diríamos	
R	decís	digáis	decid	dijisteis	dijerais/dijeseis	decíais	diréis	diríais	
	dicen	digan	digan	dijeron	dijeran/dijesen	decían	dirán	dirían	

	Present indicative	Present subjunctive	Imperative	Preterite	Imperfect subjunctive	Imperfect indicative	Future indicative	Conditional	Other
ESTAR	estoy	esté		estuve	estuviera/estuviese	estaba	estaré	estaría	**Gerund** estando
	estás	estés	está	estuviste	estuvieras/estuvieses	estabas	estarás	estarías	**Participle** estado
	está	esté	esté	estuvo	estuviera/estuviese	estaba	estará	estaría	
	estamos	estemos	estemos	estuvimos	estuviéramos/estuviésemos	estábamos	estaremos	estaríamos	
	estáis	estéis	estad	estuvisteis	estuvierais/estuvieseis	estabais	estaréis	estaríais	
	están	estén	estén	estuvieron	estuvieran/estuviesen	estaban	estarán	estarían	
HABER	he	haya		hube	hubiera/hubiese	había	habré	habría	**Gerund** habiendo
	has	hayas	he	hubiste	hubieras/hubieses	habías	habrás	habrías	**Participle** habido
	ha/hay	haya	haya	hubo	hubiera/hubiese	había	habrá	habría	
	hemos	hayamos	hayamos	hubimos	hubiéramos/hubiésemos	habíamos	habremos	habríamos	
	habéis	hayáis	habed	hubisteis	hubierais/hubieseis	habíais	habréis	habríais	
	han	hayan	hayan	hubieron	hubieran/hubiesen	habían	habrán	habrían	
HACER	hago	haga		hice	hiciera/hiciese	hacía	haré	haría	**Gerund** haciendo
	haces	hagas	haz	hiciste	hicieras/hicieses	hacías	harás	harías	**Participle** hecho
	hace	haga	haga	hizo	hiciera/hiciese	hacía	hará	haría	
	hacemos	hagamos	hagamos	hicimos	hiciéramos/hiciésemos	hacíamos	haremos	haríamos	
	hacéis	hagáis	haced	hicisteis	hicierais/hicieseis	hacíais	haréis	haríais	
	hacen	hagan	hagan	hicieron	hicieran/hiciesen	hacían	harán	harían	
IR	voy	vaya		fui	fuera/fuese	iba	iré	iría	**Gerund** yendo
	vas	vayas	ve	fuiste	fueras/fueses	ibas	irás	irías	**Participle** ido
	va	vaya	vaya	fue	fuera/fuese	iba	irá	iría	
	vamos	vayamos	vayamos	fuimos	fuéramos/fuésemos	íbamos	iremos	iríamos	
	vais	vayáis	id	fuisteis	fuerais/fueseis	ibais	iréis	iríais	
	van	vayan	vayan	fueron	fueran/fuesen	iban	irán	irían	
OÍR	oigo	oiga		oí	oyera/oyese	oía	oiré	oiría	**Gerund** oyendo
	oyes	oigas	oye	oíste	oyeras/oyeses	oías	oirás	oirías	**Participle** oído
	oye	oiga	oiga	oyó	oyera/oyese	oía	oirá	oiría	
	oímos	oigamos	oigamos	oímos	oyéramos/oyésemos	oíamos	oiremos	oiríamos	
	oís	oigáis	oíd	oísteis	oyerais/oyeseis	oíais	oiréis	oiríais	
	oyen	oigan	oigan	oyeron	oyeran/oyesen	oían	oirán	oirían	

PODER

	Present	Pres. Subj.	Imperative	Preterite	Imperf. Subj.	Imperfect	Future	Conditional
P	puedo	pueda		pude	pudiera/pudiese	podía	podré	podría
O	puedes	puedas	puede	pudiste	pudieras/pudieses	podías	podrás	podrías
D	puede	pueda	pueda	pudo	pudiera/pudiese	podía	podrá	podría
E	podemos	podamos	podamos	pudimos	pudiéramos/pudiésemos	podíamos	podremos	podríamos
R	podéis	podáis	poded	pudisteis	pudierais/pudieseis	podíais	podréis	podríais
	pueden	puedan	puedan	pudieron	pudieran/pudiesen	podían	podrán	podrían

Gerund pudiendo **Participle** podido

PONER

	Present	Pres. Subj.	Imperative	Preterite	Imperf. Subj.	Imperfect	Future	Conditional
P	pongo	ponga		puse	pusiera/pusiese	ponía	pondré	pondría
O	pones	pongas	pon	pusiste	pusieras/pusieses	ponías	pondrás	pondrías
N	pone	ponga	ponga	puso	pusiera/pusiese	ponía	pondrá	pondría
E	ponemos	pongamos	pongamos	pusimos	pusiéramos/pusiésemos	poníamos	pondremos	pondríamos
R	ponéis	pongáis	poned	pusisteis	pusierais/pusieseis	poníais	pondréis	pondríais
	ponen	pongan	pongan	pusieron	pusieran/pusiesen	ponían	pondrán	pondrían

Gerund poniendo **Participle** puesto

QUERER

	Present	Pres. Subj.	Imperative	Preterite	Imperf. Subj.	Imperfect	Future	Conditional
Q	quiero	quiera		quise	quisiera/quisiese	quería	querré	querría
U	quieres	quieras	quiere	quisiste	quisieras/quisieses	querías	querrás	querrías
E	quiere	quiera	quiera	quiso	quisiera/quisiese	quería	querrá	querría
R	queremos	queramos	queramos	quisimos	quisiéramos/quisiésemos	queríamos	querremos	querríamos
E	queréis	queráis	quered	quisisteis	quisierais/quisieseis	queríais	querréis	querríais
R	quieren	quieran	quieran	quisieron	quisieran/quisiesen	querían	querrán	querrían

Gerund queriendo **Participle** querido

SABER

	Present	Pres. Subj.	Imperative	Preterite	Imperf. Subj.	Imperfect	Future	Conditional
S	sé	sepa		supe	supiera/supiese	sabía	sabré	sabría
A	sabes	sepas	sé	supiste	supieras/supieses	sabías	sabrás	sabrías
B	sabe	sepa	sepa	supo	supiera/supiese	sabía	sabrá	sabría
E	sabemos	sepamos	sepamos	supimos	supiéramos/supiésemos	sabíamos	sabremos	sabríamos
R	sabéis	sepáis	sabed	supisteis	supierais/supieseis	sabíais	sabréis	sabríais
	saben	sepan	sepan	supieron	supieran/supiesen	sabían	sabrán	sabrían

Gerund sabiendo **Participle** sabido

SALIR

	Present	Pres. Subj.	Imperative	Preterite	Imperf. Subj.	Imperfect	Future	Conditional
S	salgo	salga		salí	saliera/saliese	salía	saldré	saldría
A	sales	salgas	sal	saliste	salieras/salieses	salías	saldrás	saldrías
L	sale	salga	salga	salió	saliera/saliese	salía	saldrá	saldría
I	salimos	salgamos	salgamos	salimos	saliéramos/saliésemos	salíamos	saldremos	saldríamos
R	salís	salgáis	salid	salisteis	salierais/salieseis	salíais	saldréis	saldríais
	salen	salgan	salgan	salieron	salieran/saliesen	salían	saldrán	saldrían

Gerund saliendo **Participle** salido

SER

	Present	Pres. Subj.	Imperative	Preterite	Imperf. Subj.	Imperfect	Future	Conditional
S	soy	sea		fui	fuera/fuese	era	seré	sería
E	eres	seas	sé	fuiste	fueras/fueses	eras	serás	serías
R	es	sea	sea	fue	fuera/fuese	era	será	sería
	somos	seamos	seamos	fuimos	fuéramos/fuésemos	éramos	seremos	seríamos
	sois	seáis	sed	fuisteis	fuerais/fueseis	erais	seréis	seríais
	son	sean	sean	fueron	fueran/fuesen	eran	serán	serían

Gerund siendo **Participle** sido

TENER

	Present indicative	Present subjunctive	Imperative	Preterite	Imperfect subjunctive	Imperfect indicative	Future indicative	Conditional	Other
	tengo	tenga		tuve	tuviera/tuviese	tenía	tendré	tendría	**Gerund** teniendo
	tienes	tengas	ten	tuviste	tuvieras/tuvieses	tenías	tendrás	tendrías	**Participle** tenido
	tiene	tenga	tenga	tuvo	tuviera/tuviese	tenía	tendrá	tendría	
	tenemos	tengamos	tengamos	tuvimos	tuviéramos/tuviésemos	teníamos	tendremos	tendríamos	
	tenéis	tengáis	tened	tuvisteis	tuvierais/tuvieseis	teníais	tendréis	tendríais	
	tienen	tengan	tengan	tuvieron	tuvieran/tuviesen	tenían	tendrán	tendrían	

TRAER

	Present indicative	Present subjunctive	Imperative	Preterite	Imperfect subjunctive	Imperfect indicative	Future indicative	Conditional	Other
	traigo	traiga		traje	trajera/trajese	traía	traeré	traería	**Gerund** trayendo
	traes	traigas	trae	trajiste	trajeras/trajeses	traías	traerás	traerías	**Participle** traído
	trae	traiga	traiga	trajo	trajera/trajese	traía	traerá	traería	
	traemos	traigamos	traigamos	trajimos	trajéramos/trajésemos	traíamos	traeremos	traeríamos	
	traéis	traigáis	traed	trajisteis	trajerais/trajeseis	traíais	traeréis	traeríais	
	traen	traigan	traigan	trajeron	trajeran/trajesen	traían	traerán	traerían	

VALER

	Present indicative	Present subjunctive	Imperative	Preterite	Imperfect subjunctive	Imperfect indicative	Future indicative	Conditional	Other
	valgo	valga		valí	valiera/valiese	valía	valdré	valdría	**Gerund** valiendo
	vales	valgas	vale	valiste	valieras/valieses	valías	valdrás	valdrías	**Participle** valido
	vale	valga	valga	valió	valiera/valiese	valía	valdrá	valdría	
	valemos	valgamos	valgamos	valimos	valiéramos/valiésemos	valíamos	valdremos	valdríamos	
	valéis	valgáis	valed	valisteis	valierais/valieseis	valíais	valdréis	valdríais	
	valen	valgan	valgan	valieron	valieran/valiesen	valían	valdrán	valdrían	

VENIR

	Present indicative	Present subjunctive	Imperative	Preterite	Imperfect subjunctive	Imperfect indicative	Future indicative	Conditional	Other
	vengo	venga		vine	viniera/viniese	venía	vendré	vendría	**Gerund** viniendo
	vienes	vengas	ven	viniste	vinieras/vinieses	venías	vendrás	vendrías	**Participle** venido
	viene	venga	venga	vino	viniera/viniese	venía	vendrá	vendría	
	venimos	vengamos	vengamos	vinimos	viniéramos/viniésemos	veníamos	vendremos	vendríamos	
	venís	vengáis	venid	vinisteis	vinierais/vinieseis	veníais	vendréis	vendríais	
	vienen	vengan	vengan	vinieron	vinieran/viniesen	venían	vendrán	vendrían	

VER

	Present indicative	Present subjunctive	Imperative	Preterite	Imperfect subjunctive	Imperfect indicative	Future indicative	Conditional	Other
	veo	vea		vi	viera/viese	veía	veré	vería	**Gerund** viendo
	ves	veas	ve	viste	vieras/vieses	veías	verás	verías	**Participle** visto
	ve	vea	vea	vio	viera/viese	veía	verá	vería	
	vemos	veamos	veamos	vimos	viéramos/viésemos	veíamos	veremos	veríamos	
	veis	veáis	ved	visteis	vierais/vieseis	veíais	veréis	veríais	
	ven	vean	vean	vieron	vieran/viesen	veían	verán	verían	

Key to exercises

Unit 1 Accentuation

1 man<u>za</u>na, <u>lám</u>para, <u>co</u>rren, <u>di</u>ces, flo<u>re</u>ros, pa<u>red</u>, gene<u>ral</u>, efi<u>caz</u>, al<u>bón</u>digas, <u>cár</u>cel

2 **(a)** *Mamá* has a written accent because it ends in a vowel and it is not stressed on the penultimate syllable but the last. It doesn't follow the accentuation rule.

(b) *Delantal* doesn't have a written accent because it ends in a consonant different from -n or -s and it is stressed on the last syllable. It follows the accentuation rule.

(c) *Corazón* has a written accent because it ends in the consonant -n and it is not stressed on the penultimate syllable but the last. It doesn't follow the accentuation rule.

(d) *Respirar* doesn't have a written accent because it ends in a consonant different from -n or -s and it is stressed on the last syllable. It follows the accentuation rule.

(e) *Áspero* has a written accent because it finishes in a vowel and is not stressed on the penultimate but on the antepenultimate syllable. It doesn't follow the accentuation rule.

3 **(a)** hablo; **(b)** habló; **(c)** continuo; **(d)** continúo; **(e)** continuó

4

Cobardía (Amado Nervo)
Pasó con su madre. ¡Qué rara belleza!
¡Qué rubios cabellos de trigo garzul!
¡Qué ritmo en el paso! ¡Qué innata realeza
de porte! ¡Qué formas bajo el fino tul . . . !
Pasó con su madre. Volvió la cabeza:
¡me clavó muy hondo su mirar azul!
Quedé como en éxtasis.
Con febril premura,
«¡Síguela!», gritaron cuerpo y alma al par.
. . . Pero tuve miedo de amar con locura,
de abrir mis heridas, que suelen sangrar,
¡y no obstante toda mi sed de ternura,
cerrando los ojos, la dejé pasar!

Unit 2 Nouns

2.1   Natural gender

1 **(a)** – **(iv)** la profesora; **(b)** – **(ii)** la campeona; **(c)** – **(v)** la abogada; **(d)** – **(i)** la iraquí; **(e)** – **(iii)** la atleta

2 **(a)** el doctor; **(b)** el presidente; **(c)** el ciclista; **(d)** el bailarín; **(e)** el policía; **(f)** el estudiante

3 **(a)** el genio; **(b)** el personaje; **(c)** el bebé; **(d)** la modelo; **(e)** la testigo

2.2   Grammatical gender

1 **(a)** la multitud; **(b)** el enigma; **(c)** el/la capital (with change of meaning); **(d)** la bronquitis; **(e)** la fraternidad; **(f)** la reunión

2 **(a)** el/la dentista; **(b)** la apendicitis; **(c)** la suposición; **(d)** la mano; **(e)** el síntoma; **(f)** la juventud

3 **(a)** el capital; **(b)** la guía; **(c)** el margen; **(d)** el guía or la guía

2.3   Number

1 **(a)** las estaciones; **(b)** las mesas; **(c)** los lunes; **(d)** los actores; **(e)** los virus; **(f)** los cafés; **(g)** los tabús; **(h)** las estudiantes; **(i)** los atlas

2 **(a)**   **En España los niños y las niñas** empiezan el colegio a las nueve.
   (b)   **El abuelo y la abuela** de Mariana viven en Orense.
   (c)   **Los profesores y las profesoras** trabajan mucho.

3

	Masculino	Femenino	Singular	Plural
(a) Mediterráneo	✔		✔	
(b) gas	✔		✔	
(c) problemas	✔			✔
(d) crisis		✔	✔	or ✔
(e) ciclistas	✔	or ✔		✔

2.4   Collective nouns

1 The following are collective nouns:

la mayoría; la minoría; el público; el grupo. Although they refer to a group of things or people, they are grammatically singular.

2 **(a)** La policía **encontró** . . . (collective); **(b)** Los policías **llevan** . . . (not collective); **(c)** El comité **tomó** . . . (collective); **(d)** El ejército **realiza** . . . (collective).

2.5   Diminutive, augmentative and pejorative suffixes

1 **(a)** la islita; **(b)** el abuelito; **(c)** el cafecito (note that no accent is needed); **(d)** el relojito; **(e)** el pajarito (note that no accent is needed); **(f)** el piquito (note the spelling change); **(g)** el cuenquito (note the spelling change); **(h)** el bastoncito (note that no accent is needed); **(i)** la manita (in some parts of Latin America the diminutive is *la manito*)

2 **(a)**   Me compré un monedero **pequeñito** muy mono.
  (b)   El Real Deportivo marcó un **golazo** en el último minuto.
  (c)   Después giras a la izquierda y verás una **callecita** estrecha. Mi casa está al fondo.
  (d)   Tienen un **perrote** enorme para que no les entre nadie en el jardín.

3 **(a)**   Little Red Riding Hood and the Big Bad Wolf
  (b)   The Three Little Pigs
  (c)   The Ugly Duckling
  (d)   Snow White and the Seven Dwarfs
  (e)   Goldilocks

4 Menú diminutivo

Ya sé que te gusta comer poco* y sano, pero rico*, y estoy preparada para complacerte *también* en la mesa.

En la mañana iré al mercado y compraré la leche más fresca*, el pan recién horneado, y la naranja más chaposa. Y te despertaré con la bandeja del desayuno, una flor fragante y un beso. "Aquí está su jugo sin pepas**, sus tostadas con mermelada de fresa y su café*** con leche sin azúcar*, señor."

* Note change in the spelling qu → c

** *Pepas* is used in Latin America for 'pips', whereas in Spain one would say *pepitas*.

*** Notice that you need an accent.

Unit 3 Articles
3.1   The definite article

1 Remember that you need to add the correct article:

Me gusta/No me gusta el vino; el agua; el té; la cerveza; la sangría; la sal; la pimienta; la ensalada; el pollo; la carne; la verdura; el melón; el flan; la fruta; el yogur

2 **(a) Los** lunes; **(b) el** Reino Unido; **(c) la** Avenida de la Paz, **la** calle Cuervo; **(d) La** semana que viene

3 **(a)** On Mondays; **(b)** the United Kingdom; **(c)** Paz Avenue, Cuervo Street; **(d)** Next week

4 **(a)** **El** desayuno se sirve de 9 a 10.30, y **la** cena de 8.30 a 11. (Names of meals take an article.)
   (b) Mi color favorito es **el** azul.
   (c) Tengo una chaqueta azul. (No article needed, as *azul* is an adjective.)
   (d) Hablo francés, italiano y español. (No article with languages with the verb *hablar*.)

3.2 The indefinite article

1 Teresa es abogada. Es mujer. Es colombiana.

2 Remember that you do not need the article for any of these categories. Suggestions: Soy mecánico. Soy escocés. Soy conservador.

3 Remember that, unlike in English, you do not need to use the article for any of the words in the box, so your sentences should look like these: tengo coche, no tengo moto, etc.

4 **(b)** Tiene la boca grande. **(c)** Tiene el rabo largo. **(d)** Tiene la nariz rota. **(e)** Tiene la cabeza pequeña.

Unit 4 Qualifying adjectives

4.1 Agreement in gender and number

1 **(a)** españoles; **(b)** argentinos; **(c)** guatemalteca; **(d)** chilenas; **(e)** mexicana; **(f)** mexicanos; **(g)** chileno

2 Suggestions:
   (a) Estoy aprendiendo alemán. Es una **lengua difícil**.
   (b) Abre la ventana. Necesitamos un poco de **aire fresco**.
   (c) En algunas playas mexicanas hay **hoteles excelentes**.
   (d) Mi padre se ha comprado un Mercedes. Es un **coche caro**.
   (e) He encontrado una **foto preciosa** de mi abuela cuando era pequeña.

4.2 Shortened forms and change of meaning

1 **(a)** gran; **(b)** gran; **(c)** buena; **(d)** mal; **(e)** primer

2 **(a)** una casa grande; **(b)** un gran hombre; **(c)** un antiguo colega/una antigua colega; **(d)** una universidad antigua; **(e)** media naranja

4.3 Comparison of adjectives

1 **(a)** Tu coche es muy pequeño. El mío es **más grande que** el tuyo.
   (b) Este queso es caro. Es **más caro que** el jamón.
   (c) Esta chaqueta roja es muy bonita. Es **más bonita que** el jersey.

2 **(a)** Mi idea no es buena. La tuya es **mejor**.
   (b) El colesterol es malo, pero el tabaco es **peor**.

3 Suggestions:

Cristina es tan rubia como su madre.
Cristina es tan alta como su padre.
Cristina es tan delgada como su madre.
Cristina es tan pecosa como su madre.
Cristina es tan aventurera como su madre.

4.4   The superlative

1 **(a)** – **(v)**: La edad del licenciado universitario más joven del mundo: 10 años y 4 meses (el estadounidense Michael Kenearney, que se licenció en Antropología en 1994)
(b) – **(ii)**: La nación con mayor número de aparatos telefónicos por cabeza: Mónaco (con 1994 teléfonos por cada mil habitantes)
(c) – **(i)**: La altura de la montaña más alta del sistema solar: 25 km (el monte Olimpo, en Marte)
(d) – **(iii)**: La longitud del tendedero de ropa más largo del mundo: 24.160 km. El récord se batió en México en 1999
(e) – **(vi)**: La edad de la persona más vieja del mundo: 122 años (la francesa Jeanne Louise Calment (1875–1997))
(f) – **(vii)**: La estatura de la persona más alta del mundo: 2,72 metros (Robert Wadlow, (1918–40))
(g) – **(iv)**: La temperatura más fría jamás registrada en el mundo: 89,2 grados bajo cero (registrados en Vostok, Antártica, en 1983).

2 The irregular superlatives are: *pésimo*, *mínima*, *mínimo* and *máxima*.

4.5   Comparison of adverbs, nouns and verbs

1 **(a)** —Yo hablo rápido, pero mi hermana habla **más rápido que yo**.
        —No, no es verdad, no habla **tan deprisa como tú**.
  (b) —Yo como despacio, pero mi hijo come **más despacio que yo**.
        —No, no es verdad, nadie come **tan despacio como tú**.
  (c) —Mi marido habla bien italiano, pero yo hablo **mejor que él**.
        —No, no es verdad. No hablas tan bien como él.

2 Suggestions:

En mi ciudad hay menos museos que en Madrid.
En Madrid hay menos pubs, y hay menos parques y jardines que en mi ciudad.
En Madrid hay más tráfico que en mi ciudad.
En mi ciudad no hay tanta contaminación como en Madrid.
En Madrid hace más sol que en mi ciudad, y no hace tanto frío.

3 Suggestions:

Mi hermana gana más dinero que yo.
Mi hermano tiene menos vacaciones que yo.
Mi padre tiene muchísimo más tiempo libre que yo, porque está jubilado.
Mi madre trabaja más que los demás, pero gana menos.
Mis sobrinos hablan inglés mejor que yo.

4 Cuanto más aprendo, más olvido.
Cuanto más olvido, menos sé.

Cuanto menos sé, más tengo que estudiar.
Pero cuanto más estudio, más olvido . . .

Unit 5 Personal pronouns

5.1 Subject pronouns

1 **(a)** *Nosotros* or *nosotras*
(b) *Ustedes*, *ellos* or *ellas*
(c) *Tú*, *vos* (but not in River Plate area, as the verb would be *sós*)
(d) *Yo*

2 Yo tengo un gato pero ella tiene un perro.
Yo vivo en Madrid pero ella vive en Miami.
Yo estoy casado/casada pero ella está divorciada.
Yo soy rubio/rubia pero ella es morena.

3 **(a)** ¿Hablas italiano?
(b) La mayoría de la gente tiene ordenador. ¿Tú tienes uno?
(c) Yo trabajo de 9 a 5, pero él trabaja sólo por la mañana.
(d) Salgo de casa a las 8 y llego a la oficina a las 9.
(e) ¿Ella te dijo eso? ¡Está loca!

5.2 Forms of address

1 **(a)** Spanish norm
(b) Latin American norm, *América voseante*
(c) Latin American norm, *América tuteante* and *América voseante*
(d) Spanish norm or *America tuteante* norm
(e) Spanish norm (polite use) or Latin American norm, *América tuteante* and *América voseante* (either familiar or polite use)

2 The instances of *vos* and its verb form are:

[. . .] "Quiero hablar con <u>vos</u>." [. . .]
—Yo a <u>vos</u> . . . ¿te conozco?
—Sí, me <u>conocés</u> . . .
—Porque, <u>vos</u> acá <u>aparecés</u> . . . —sobrevoló la información del Sordo— . . . me <u>venís</u> a buscar a la mesa, me <u>presionás</u> para que venga a hablar con <u>vos</u> . . . Me <u>hacés</u> levantar de la mesa donde . . .
—Sí me <u>conocés</u> . . .

3 The text in the 'tú' form would read:

[. . .] "Quiero hablar **contigo**". [. . .]
—Yo a **ti** . . . ¿te conozco?
—Sí, me **conoces** . . .
—Porque, **tú** acá **apareces** . . . —sobrevoló la información del Sordo— . . . me **vienes** a buscar a la mesa, me **presionas** para que venga a hablar **contigo** . . . Me **haces** levantar de la mesa donde . . .
—Sí me **conoces** . . .

5.3 Direct object pronouns

1 **(a)** ¡Hazlos ahora mismo!; **(b)** ¡Recógela ahora mismo!; **(c)** ¡Apágala ahora mismo!

2 **(a)** La estamos viendo nosotros./Estamos viéndola nosotros.
(b) Los está preparando Miguel./Está preparándolos Miguel.
(c) Las está ordenando Cristina./Está ordenándolas Cristina.
(d) Lo estoy haciendo yo./Estoy haciéndolo yo.
(e) Lo está cortando Raquel./Está cortándolo Raquel.

3 **(a)** No, todavía tengo que llamarlo (llamarle)./No, todavía lo (le) tengo que llamar.
(b) No, todavía tengo que recogerlo./No, todavía lo tengo que recoger.
(c) No, todavía tengo que fregarlos./No, todavía los tengo que fregar.
(d) No, todavía tengo que mandarlo./No, todavía lo tengo que mandar.
(e) No, todavía tengo que verla./No, todavía la tengo que ver.
(f) No, todavía tengo que terminarla./No, todavía la tengo que terminar.
(g) No, todavía tengo que escribirlas./No, todavía las tengo que escribir.
(h) No, todavía tengo que pagarlos./No, todavía los tengo que pagar.

5.4 Indirect object pronouns

1 **(a)** Me contó un secreto. **(b)** Te quiero pedir un favor/Quiero pedirte un favor.
(c) Les mandaron un paquete. **(d)** Le regalaste unas flores.

2 **(a)** Recuérdame que tengo que ir al dentista. **(b)** Dale el libro. **(c)** Explícales cómo se llega a la estación. **(d)** Enséñanos las fotos.

5.5 Object pronouns with prepositions

1 **(a)** Quiere escribir un libro sobre mí.
(b) No me esperaba eso de ti.
(c) Nadie me escucha salvo tú.
(d) Dicen que piensan mucho en mí.
(e) Estas flores son para ti/vos/usted/vosotros/vosotras/ustedes.
(f) Decoramos el salón entre mi hermana y yo.

2 **(a)** Quiere hablar con ellos/ellas. **(b)** ¿Quieres casarte conmigo? **(c)** Estamos muy contentos con ella. **(d)** ¿Señorita, puedo bailar con usted?

3 **(a)** Alicia está muy contenta consigo misma. **(b)** Estoy enfadada conmigo misma. **(c)** Están furiosos consigo mismos. **(d)** Veo que estáis furiosos con vosotros mismos.

5.6 Order of object pronouns

1 **(a)** Ya se lo he dado. **(b)** Ya se las he prestado. **(c)** Ya se lo he explicado. **(d)** Ya se lo he entregado.

2 **(a)** —¡Cómpramelo!
—No, no voy a comprártelo./No, no te lo voy a comprar.
(b) —¡Cómpramelas!
—¡No, no voy a comprártelas./No, no te las voy a comprar.
(c) —¡Cómpranosla!
—No, no voy a comprárosla./No, no os la voy a comprar.
(d) —¡Cómpranoslos!
—No, no voy a comprároslos./No, no os los voy a comprar.

Unit 6 Demonstratives

1 **(a)** Esos niños están en clase de Inés. **(b)** Estas son mis primas. **(c)** Pruébate esas faldas. **(d)** Aquellas chicas que vienen por ahí son mis vecinas.

2 Alicia: ¿Qué te parece **este** vestido?
Clara: Es mono, pruébatelo. ¿Pero por qué no te pruebas también **esa/aquella** falda?
Alicia: ¿Cuál?, ¿**esta** de rayas?
Clara: No, **esa/aquella** de flores que está detrás.
Alicia: Ah sí, es bonita. Mira, y me voy a probar también **este** otro vestido rojo.

Unit 7 Possessives

7.1 Possessive adjectives

1 **(a)** ¿Te gusta **mi** piso? **(b)** Elisa ha perdido **sus** maletas. **(c)** Lo más importante es la salud de **nuestras** hijas. **(d)** No entiendo a **su** madre.

2 **(a)** Vienen unos/algunos amigos míos. **(b)** Este bolso es tuyo. **(c)** No tengo nada suyo. **(d)** Tienes muchos libros míos.

7.2 Possessive pronouns

1 **(a)** Este es tu periódico. **El mío** está en la cocina.
    (b) Estas son tus gafas. **Las mías** no las encuentro.
    (c) Me prestas tu diccionario. **El mío** me lo dejé en casa.
    (d) Tus hijas son buenas estudiantes, pero **las mías** no.

2 **(a)** —La mía es más grande que la tuya.
    (b) —El mío tiene más flores que el tuyo.
    (c) —La mía es más agradable que la tuya.
    (d) —Los nuestros son más simpáticos que los vuestros.

Unit 8 Numerals

8.1 Cardinal numbers

1 Un kilo de naranjas; una bolsa de patatas; cien gramos de paté; un paquete de té; una botella de vino; doscientos gramos de queso; una docena de huevos; una barra de pan

2 ochenta y uno, sesenta y dos, diecisiete
dos cincuenta y siete, cuarenta y seis, catorce
noventa y cuatro, ocho ochenta y seis, ochenta y tres, veinticuatro
cero cero, treinta y cuatro, noventa y uno, dos cincuenta, setenta y siete, veintiocho

4 **(a)** – **(iv)** el doce de octubre de mil cuatrocientos noventa y dos; **(b)** – **(iii)** el veintitrés de abril de mil seiscientos dieciséis; **(c)** – **(i)** el once de noviembre de mil novecientos dieciocho; **(d)** – **(ii)** el seis de agosto de mil novecientos cuarenta y cinco

8.2   Ordinal numbers

1 (a) segunda, tercera; (b) primero; (c) tercero; (d) primera; (e) segundo; (f) primer

2 The popes are: (a) León X (diez or décimo); (d) Pío XII (doce); (e) Julio II (segundo);
(f) Juan Pablo I (primero); and (h) Juan XXIII (veintitrés).
(b) Enrique VIII (octavo) es un rey inglés, y (c) Luis XVI (dieciséis) y (g) Luis XIV
(catorce) son reyes franceses.

8.3   Collective numbers and fractions

1 (a) una docena de huevos; (b) media docena de niños; (c) una decena de personas;
(d) cuatro pares de zapatos; (e) un par de calcetines

2 (a)   Hay **una veintena de niños** en la clase.
(b)   **Un centenar de personas** vinieron a la boda.
(c)   Había **una treintena de cuadros** del museo en la exposición.
(d)   Tengo **un par de libros** nuevos muy buenos.
(e)   Tiene **veinte pares de zapatos** en el armario.
(f)   Para esta receta se necesitan **dos docenas de huevos**.

Unit 9 Indefinites

1 (a) misma; (b) mismo; (c) uno; (d) mucho; (e) poca; (f) todos; (g) todo

2 (a) Cualquiera; (b) Cada vez; (c) Cada uno; (d) Cada cual

3 (a)   Each to his own. (lit. Each little owl to its olive tree.)
(b)   Much ado about nothing. (lit. A lot of noise and few nuts.)
(c)   Chip off the old block. (lit. From such a stick comes such a chip.)
(d)   Life is not a bowl of cherries. (lit. The whole mountain is not covered in oregano.)

Unit 10 Adverbs

1 elegantemente; especialmente; silenciosamente; tranquilamente; sinceramente;
profundamente

2 Suggestions:

La actriz iba elegantemente vestida.
El examen fue especialmente difícil.
El ladrón se acercó silenciosamente a la casa.
Estaba sentado tomándose una copa tranquilamente.
Te digo sinceramente que no sé dónde está.
El bebé estaba profundamente dormido.

3 Martina **siempre** conducía **demasiado** deprisa. Aquella mañana, salió de casa más
tarde que de costumbre. Dio un portazo al salir de casa, y se metió **rápidamente**
en el coche. **Nunca** le gustaba llegar tarde, y menos aún cuando tenía que ir a
ver a algún cliente importante. Unos metros antes del cruce vio un camión que
señalaba con el indicador para pararse **delante** del supermercado. Lo adelantó sin
mirar y ¡zas!, se dio con un coche que venía en sentido contrario. Afortunadamente,
no le pasó nada. Menos mal que el otro iba bastante **despacio**. Si no, podía haber
sido más grave.

4 —¿**Ya** has puesto la mesa?
—No, **todavía** no he terminado.
—Pero la cena **ya** está preparada, ¿verdad?
—Sí, **ya** está todo listo.
—Acaba de llamar a Elena y dice que **todavía** no han salido de casa.
—Menos mal, pensé que **ya** estarían casi aquí.
—Bueno, pues entonces, déjame que te ayude a poner la mesa.
—Vale.
—Bueno, **ya** está.
—**Ya** no hay nada más que hacer hasta que lleguen los demás.

Unit 11 Interrogatives

1 You may have written sentences like these.

Los mismos físicos no comprenden cómo funciona la luz.
El pirata no recordaba dónde había escondido la plata.
El director explicó por qué había decidido dimitir.
No hemos oído ninguna noticia sobre quiénes ganaron los Premios Nóbel.
El gobierno no sabe cuánto costó el proyecto.

2 **(a)** qué (Spain)/cuál (Spanish America); **(b)** cuál/cuáles; **(c)** qué (Spain)/cuál (Spanish America); **(d)** qué; **(e)** cuáles

3 You may have written questions like these.

(a) ¿Adónde fuisteis/fueron de vacaciones?
(b) ¿Qué (Spain)/Cuál (Spanish America) casa decidisteis/decidieron comprar?
(c) ¿Cómo es la nieve?
(d) ¿Quién escribió *Cien años de soledad*?
(e) ¿Para qué/por qué compraste ese libro de italiano?

4 The following is a model answer.

Character: Che Guevara
¿Cuál es su verdadero nombre?
¿En qué país nació?
¿Cuándo y por qué decidió hacerse revolucionario?
¿Cómo conoció a Fidel Castro?
¿Por qué fue a luchar a Bolivia después de la Revolución Cubana?

Unit 12 Prepositions

1 **(a)** – ; **(b)** a; **(c)** a; **(d)** a; **(e)** –

2 **(a)** a, por, en; **(b)** de, para, para, de, de, de, de; **(c)** con/por, con; **(d)** en (Spain)/a (Spanish America), a, a; **(e)** de, a

3 **(a)** por, por delante de; **(b)** por debajo de/bajo (with a slightly different meaning); **(c)** tras/detrás de; **(d)** por encima de/sobre; **(e)** sobre/por encima de

4 **(a)** para (Spain)/por (Spanish America); **(b)** por; **(c)** por; **(d)** para; **(e)** por, por

5 You may have answered like this.

    (a)   Next week my parents are going to Menorca for a fortnight. (for = adverb of time)

    (b)   I would never vote for the Conservatives again. (for = on behalf of, in support of)

    (c)   A new prison has been built because of the greater number of criminals.

    (d)   Shah Jahan had the Taj Mahal built as a tomb for his beloved wife. (for = destined for)

    (e)   My colleague couldn't come to the conference owing to unforeseen circumstances, but she has asked me to present the paper in her place.

6 **(a)** a; **(b)** en; **(c)** para/a; **(d)** por/en; **(e)** en; **(f)** de; **(g)** a través de; **(h)** en

Unit 13 Interjections

1 **(a)** dismissive reaction; **(b)** annoyance/surprise; **(c)** encouragement; **(d)** annoyance; **(e)** surprise

2 You may have translated them as follows:

    (a) Well!/Huh! **(b)** Oh, no!/What! **(c)** Go for it!/Come on! **(d)** Damn it!/Blast! **(e)** Wow!/Great!

Unit 14 The Spanish verb

1 **(a)** Continúan (simple); **(b)** ha descubierto (perfect); **(c)** está entrando (continuous); **(d)** sufren (simple); **(e)** salimos (simple), había oscurecido (perfect)

2 **(a)** *Continúan*: transitive, direct object: *las negociaciones*; **(b)** *ha descubierto*: transitive, direct object: *una nueva vacuna*; **(c)** *está entrando*: intransitive; **(d)** *sufren*: transitive, direct object: *la irresponsabilidad*; **(e)** *salimos*: intransitive, *había oscurecido*: intransitive

3 There are four sentences in the paragraph:

    (a)   La casa se levanta en la cima del cerro.
            Subject: **la casa**; verb: **se levanta**

    (b)   Los abuelos pintaron la chocita de blanco.
            Subject: **los abuelos**; verb: **pintaron**; direct object: **la chocita**

    (c)   Tiene el techo de tejas rojizas.
            Subject: **la chocita**; verb: **tiene**; direct object: **el techo**

    (d)   La familia saborea la sopa casera y las arepas de maíz.
            Subject: **la familia**; verb: **saborea**; direct object: **la sopa casera y las arepas de maíz**

Unit 15 Impersonal forms of the verb

15.1 The infinitive

1 **(a)** cerrar; **(b)** venir; **(c)** reír; **(d)** impedir; **(e)** nadar

2 **(a)** imperative; **(b)** complement to the verb *poder*; **(c)** noun, subject of *es*; **(d)** following a preposition; **(e)** complement to the verb *saber*

3

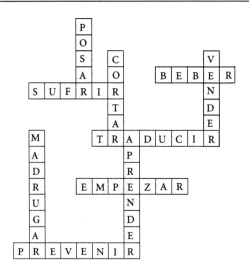

15.2 The gerund

1 (a) jugando; (b) leyendo; (b) yendo; (d) estudiando; (e) cayendo; (f) escribiendo

2 (a) bailar; (b) presentando; (c) ver; (d) viviendo; (e) sacando

3 (a) lleva; (b) continúan/siguen; (c) empiezan/acaban/terminan/siguen;
(d) está/anda/sigue/continúa; (e) van/continúan/siguen

15.3 The past participle

1 (a) vivido; (b) descubierto; (c) desayunado; (d) soltado; (e) escrito

2 (a) salido; (b) atrapados; (c) importado; (d) herido; (e) bloqueado

3 (a) comido; (b) dejado; (c) llegado; (d) puesto; (e) muerto; (f) asustado;
(g) encendida; (h) entrecerrada; (i) emocionado; (j) abiertos

Unit 16 Present tenses of the indicative

16.1 The present simple

1

	cantar	beber	subir
(yo)	canto	bebo	subo
(tú)	cantas	bebes	subes
(él, ella/Ud.)	canta	bebe	sube
(nosotros, -as)	cantamos	bebemos	subimos
(vosotros, -as)	cantáis	bebéis	subís
(ellos, -as/Uds.)	cantan	beben	suben

2 **(a)** comienzas; **(b)** despierto; **(c)** duermen; **(d)** acostamos; **(e)** seguimos; **(f)** consigo; **(g)** puedo; **(h)** dices; **(i)** confieso

3 **(b)** *oyen*, adds a *y* to the stem; **(c)** *gobierna*, stem changes *e → ie*; **(d)** *salgo*, adds a *g* to the stem in the first person singular; **(e)** *encuentras*, stem changes *o → ue*; **(f)** *repiten*, stem changes *e → i*

4 **(a)** llueve; **(b)** brilla; **(c)** vemos; **(d)** tiene; **(e)** es; **(f)** preparan

16.2   The present continuous

1 **(a)** está cambiando; **(b)** están viajando; **(c)** están corriendo; **(d)** estamos leyendo; **(e)** estáis/están vendiendo

2 A la izquierda: **(b)** está sonriendo; **(c)** está durmiendo; **(d)** están consultando
A la derecha: **(i)** está bebiendo; **(ii)** está llorando; **(iii)** está corriendo; **(iv)** están comiendo

Unit 17 Future tenses of the indicative

17.1   The future with *ir a*

1 **(a)**   Voy a hablar con el gerente.
(b)   Carlos va a confirmar el viaje.
(c)   Luis y Mariela van a visitar el museo de arte.
(d)   No vais a encontrar las llaves.

2 **(a)** vamos a visitar; **(b)** van a jugar; **(c)** voy a conocer; **(d)** va a subir; **(e)** vas a hacer

17.2   The future simple

1 **(a)**   Hablaré con el gerente.
(b)   Carlos confirmará el viaje.
(c)   Luis y Mariela visitarán el museo de arte.
(d)   No encontraréis las llaves.

2 **(a)** vendrán; **(b)** daré; **(c)** pondrá; **(d)** sabremos

3 **(a)** se sentirá; **(b)** mantendrá; **(c)** ayudarán; **(d)** dará; **(e)** podrán; **(f)** avisarán; **(g)** irá; **(h)** será

4 **(a)** buscará; **(b)** podrá; **(c)** será; **(d)** presentarán; **(e)** estará

17.3   The future continuous

1 **(a)** estará terminando; **(b)** se estará despertando; **(c)** estarán acabando; **(d)** estará saliendo

17.4   The future perfect

1 **(a)**   Habrá estado enferma.
(b)   Habrá tenido mucho trabajo.
(c)   Habrán terminado.
(d)   Habrá tomado el tren antes que ellos.

2 **(a)** ¿Cuándo se habrán ido?
(b) ¿A quién habrá llamado?
(c) ¿Dónde lo habrá encontrado?
(d) ¿Cuál habrá ganado?

3 **(a)** habremos terminado
(b) habrá subido
(c) habrán desaparecido
(d) habrá contaminado
(e) habrán perdido

Unit 18 Past tenses of the indicative

18.1 The imperfect

1

jugábamos	estudiaba	aprendías	leíais
crecía	trabajaban	bebían	escribía
ayudaba	vivían	caminaba	construía

3 Suggestions: ¿Dónde vivías cuando eras pequeño/a? ¿A qué hora te levantabas para ir al colegio? ¿Cuál era tu comida favorita? ¿Tocabas algún instrumento?

4 Mi madre tenía gafas y el pelo negro. Cantaba muy bien.
Mi profesora de matemáticas era una mujer joven y que enseñaba muy bien.
Mi primer novio era guapísimo. Estudiaba mucho pero sacaba malas notas.

5 Modelo:

Mi habitación **era** un auténtico desastre. Yo jamás **hacía** la cama y la almohada siempre **estaba** en el suelo. Casi nunca **cerraba** la puerta del armario y dentro se **veían** las camisas y pantalones desordenados y arrugados. Siempre **había** alguna ropa y zapatos por el suelo. A mí me **gustaba** el desorden pero algunas veces **resultaba** muy incómodo porque no **podía** encontrar nada. Mi madre **odiaba** el desorden y siempre **discutíamos** por esta razón.

6 **(a)** quedaba/había; **(b)** entraba; **(c)** estaba; **(d)** defendía; **(e)** crecía/estaba; **(f)** estaban; **(g)** era; **(h)** Había; **(i)** parecía

18.2 The imperfect continuous

1 **(a)** Estábamos paseando por el parque cuando . . . ; **(b)** Los niños estaban haciendo tanto ruido que . . . ; **(c)** Estábamos viendo la televisión y de repente . . . ; **(d)** El viento estaba soplando tan fuerte que . . .

18.3 The preterite

1

saltamos	estudié	aprendiste	leisteis
creció	trabajaron	bebieron	escribió
ayudó	vivieron	caminó	volé

2

pude	dijeron	viniste	estuvisteis
puse	hicieron	dijiste	tuvisteis
supe	quisieron	quisiste	hicisteis

4 **(a)** se vistió (vestirse); rieron (reír); **(b)** murió (morir); durmieron (dormir); **(c)** introduje (introducir); deduje (deducir); **(d)** oyeron (oír); huyó (huir); concluyó (concluir); **(e)** ronqué (roncar); **(f)** pegué (pegar); **(g)** abracé (abrazar); empecé (empezar)

5 **(a)** Pedro contó un chiste y todos **se rieron. (b)** Mi padre **murió** cuando yo tenía cuatro años. **(c) Introduje** la llave en la cerradura y la puerta se abrió. **(d) Oyeron** ruidos y se asustaron mucho. **(e)** Dice mi marido que anoche **ronqué. (f) Pegué** los bordes del sobre con pegamento. **(g) Empecé** a jugar al fútbol a los diez años.

6 **(a)** nació; **(b)** vendieron; **(c)** llegó; **(d)** Fue; **(e)** tuvo; **(f)** Permaneció; **(g)** casó; **(h)** Murió; **(i)** contribuyó; **(j)** se convirtió

18.4   Choosing between the preterite and the imperfect

1 Into the imperfect: was (*era*); had (*tenía*); appeared (*parecía*); pretended (*fingía*); labelled (*describía*)

Into the preterite: took (*tomó*); spoke (*habló*); said (*dijo*); were spotted (*se vio a otros . . . /fueron vistos*)

2 **(a)**   Pedro no **vino** a comer ayer. (preterite)
  (b)   Todos los días **daba** un paseo de media hora. (imperfect)
  (c)   La vista desde la cima **era** magnífica. (imperfect)
  (d)   Le **fastidió** mucho la actitud de sus compañeros. (preterite)
  (e)   **Era** una chica muy equilibrada pero ese día **se enfadó** muchísimo. (imperfect, preterite)

3 **(a)** Había (Do you know the expression *Había una vez* (Once upon a time)?); **(b)** era; **(c)** Iba; **(d)** encontraba; **(e)** vio; **(f)** preguntó; **(g)** replicó; **(h)** sacó; **(i)** puso

4 **Background**: from *Había una vez . . .* to *todo a precio justo.* (in the imperfect)
Setting the scene for what is to happen: from *Un mediodía de agosto . . .* to *una plaza.* (in the imperfect)
The narration of events: from *vio avanzar hacia ella* to the end. (in the preterite)

5 **(a)** comía; **(b)** pensaba; **(c)** producía; **(d)** podía; **(e)** detuvo; **(f)** Tenía; **(g)** podía; **(h)** pensó

18.5   The perfect

1 **(a)** hemos estado; **(b)** has oído; **(c)** ha llegado; **(d)** has tenido, ha vuelto

2 **(a)** he podido; **(b)** he estado; **(c)** estoy; **(d)** he ido; **(e)** me he quedado; **(f)** escribo; **(g)** he levantado; **(h)** he hecho (irregular past participle)

3 **(a)** The use of the preterite in sentence **(i)** indicates that Juana no longer likes going for long journeys. This sentence would be used in the case that Juana had died, for instance. Sentence **(ii)**, on the other hand, indicates that Juana has always liked this and still does.
(b) Sentence **(i)** indicates that the person saying it still wants to be a journalist and that this dream is long-felt; sentence **(ii)** simply talks about a dream that the speaker had in the past. **(c)** Sentence **(i)** means 'Have you ever read the book?' Sentence **(ii)** relates to a specific time in the past: 'Did you read it when I lent it to you?'

18.6   The perfect continuous

1 **(a)** Porque he estado saliendo con otra chica.
   (b) No, ¡y he estado pensando en ello toda la noche!
   (c) No, he estado trabajando allí ayer y hoy.
   (d) He estado preguntando pero nadie sabe nada.

18.7 The pluperfect

1 había pasado; **(b)** había abierto; **(c)** habíamos reñido; **(d)** había quebrado

2 You may have written sentences like these:

   (a) Corrí con todas mis fuerzas hasta llegar a casa. Los bomberos habían llegado unos minutos antes.
   (b) Luis dio su primer concierto de violín cuando tenía 13 años. Había empezado a tocar con su padre cuando tenía seis años.
   (c) La guerra había terminado el año anterior y el país estaba totalmente destrozado.
   (d) Cuando fueron a detenerlo a su casa, él se había escapado y ya había cruzado la frontera.

3 **(a)** siguieron; **(b)** habían hecho; **(c)** giraron; **(d)** Habían empezado; **(e)** rebasó; **(f)** cerró; **(g)** tuvo

18.8 The pluperfect continuous

1 **(a)** Habíamos estado caminando; **(b)** había estado tomando; **(c)** Habían estado trabajando

Unit 19 Imperatives

1

(tú)	(Ud.)	(vosotros, -as)	(Uds.)	(nosotros)
Compra el pan.	Compre el pan.	Comprad el pan.	Compren el pan.	Compremos el pan.
Lee la nota.	Lea la nota.	Leed la nota.	Lean la nota.	Leamos la nota.
Acuéstate pronto.	Acuéstese pronto.	Acostaos pronto.	Acuéstense pronto.	Acostémonos pronto.
Apaga la luz.	Apague la luz.	Apagad la luz.	Apaguen la luz.	Apaguemos la luz.
Empieza ya.	Empiece ya.	Empezad ya.	Empiecen ya.	Empecemos ya.

2 No leas la nota; No lea la nota; No leáis la nota; No lean la nota; No leamos la nota.

3 **(a)** Tenga; **(b)** Escuchen; **(c)** Di; **(d)** habléis

4 **(a)** pierda, aplíquese/use; **(b)** Use, Vaya; **(c)** piense; **(d)** olvide

Unit 20 Conditional tenses

20.1 The conditional

1 (a) tendríamos; (b) volverían; (c) debería; (d) cerrarían; (e) podrías

2 (a) Yo (la) reservaría en una pensión.
(b) Yo dibujaría un paisaje.
(c) Yo llevaría unos chocolates.
(d) Yo abriría una cafetería.

3 (a) Irene dijo que (ella) haría la tortilla.
(b) Manolo dijo que (él) llevaría tres botellas de vino.
(c) Elena dijo que (ella) podría comprar los platos y las servilletas de papel.
(d) Santiago dijo que (él y Juana) prepararían una ensaladilla rusa.

20.2 The conditional perfect

1 (a) habría regresado; (b) habría concluido; (c) habríamos podido; (d) habría publicado; (e) habría dado

2 (a) Lo habría puesto en el garaje.
(b) Habrían perdido la llave.
(c) Habría vuelto muy tarde de la fiesta anoche.
(d) Habrían venido por la mañana.
(e) Habría estudiado mucho.

3 The following are examples of possible answers:
(a) . . . habrían trabajado durante el fin de semana.
(b) . . . no habría tenido que quedarse en el apartamento del vecino.
(c) . . . ella nunca se lo habría perdonado.
(d) . . . ya se habría recuperado.
(e) . . . su madre los habría llevado al parque.

Unit 21 Subjunctive tenses

21.1 The present subjunctive

1 (a) escuche; (b) se diviertan; (c) sea; (d) haga; (e) caiga

2 exista; hayan; tengan; sean (note that *pensemos* here is strictly speaking an imperative, although it takes the form of a present subjunctive)

3 (a) ¡Ojalá haya! (b) ¡Ojalá salgan! (c) ¡Ojalá acabemos! (d) ¡Ojalá nos oigan!

21.2 The perfect subjunctive

1 (a) hayan cumplido; (b) hayamos obtenido; (c) haya sufrido; (d) haya pasado

2 (a) - (iv); (b) - (ii); (c) - (i); (d) - (iii)

3   Here are some suggestions:
Quizá lo hayan publicado; **(b)** Tal vez haya salido; **(c)** Ojalá hayamos terminado para entonces; **(d)** Posiblemente se lo hayan dado.

21.3   The imperfect subjunctive

1   **(a)** viviera/viviese; **(b)** salieran/saliesen; **(c)** firmaran/firmasen; **(d)** respondiera/respondiese; **(e)** supiera/supiese

2   **(a)** Sugirió, avisaran/avisasen; **(b)** Nos extrañó/extrañaba, tuviera/tuviese; **(c)** Te prohibí, hablaras/hablases; **(d)** Nos temíamos/temimos, viniera/viniese

3   **(a)** hubiera(n)/hubiese(n); **(b)** fuera/fuese; **(c)** costaran/costasen; **(d)** supiéramos/supiésemos

21.4   The pluperfect subjunctive

1   **(a)** se hubiera/hubiese aparecido; **(b)** hubiéramos/hubiésemos sabido; **(c)** hubieras/hubieses pasado; **(d)** hubieran/hubiesen oído

2   **(a)**   Estaba orgulloso de que le hubieran/hubiesen dado un buen trabajo.
  (b)   Estábamos muy contentos de que nos hubieran/hubiesen dado el premio.
  (c)   Me enfureció que me hubiera/hubiese gritado.
  (d)   Le afectó mucho que sus padres se hubieran/hubiesen divorciado.

3   **(a)**   Si hubiéramos/hubiésemos terminado el trabajo, . . .
  (b)   Si no hubiera/hubiese perdido las llaves, . . .
  (c)   Si hubiéramos/hubiésemos llegado temprano, . . .
  (d)   Si no hubieran/hubiesen hablado con el profesor, . . .

Unit 22 Special verbs

22.1   To be: *ser* and *estar*

1   **(a)**   Este **es** Enrique (to identify someone). **Es** el marido de Laura (to indicate family relationship). **Es** ingeniero (to indicate profession).
  (b)   Esta caja **es** de plata (to talk about the material it is made of). **Era** de mi abuela (to indicate possession). **Es** para guardar las sortijas (followed by *para*, to indicate purpose).
  (c)   La conferencia **es** a las dos (to say when something is taking place). **Será** en el salón de actos (to say where something is taking place).

2   **(a)**   Mar **está** en Londres (to indicate the place where she is). **Está** de *au pair* con una familia inglesa (to indicate that it is a temporary occupation).
  (b)   Después de las vacaciones Violeta **está** muy morena (to express the result of a change). La verdad es que **está** muy guapa (to indicate a subjective opinion).
  (c)   Su habitación **estaba** muy desordenada (to express that it is a temporary state), así que la **está** ordenando (to form the present continuous).

3   **(a)**   Necesito ir a comprar leche, pero creo que la tienda **está** cerrada.
  (b)   Aunque sólo lo tengo desde hace cuatro años el coche ya **está** bastante viejo.
  (c)   Ya **está** todo listo para la fiesta.
  (d)   Carlitos ya está en la cama pero todavía **está** despierto.
  (e)   Como persona, Carlos **es** bastante cerrado.
  (f)   **Es** evidente que la niña **es** muy lista porque a los tres años ya sabe leer.

(g) La abuela de María tiene 92 años y **está** bastante delicada.

(h) Mi hija ha sacado muy buenas notas y **estoy** muy orgullosa de ella.

4 (a) Tengo 46 años.

(b) El bebé tiene hambre.

(c) ¿Tienes sueño, Laura?

(d) Hoy hace calor, pero ayer hacía bastante frío.

22.2 The verb *haber*

(a) Hay naranjas en la nevera.

(b) ¿Hay un banco por aquí?

(c) No hay azúcar. ¿Hay miel?

(d) Había mucha gente en el concierto, ¿verdad?

(e) Aquí no hay nada.

(f) En el jardín de la abuela había muchísimas flores.

22.3 *Gustar* and other similar verbs

1 (a) les; (b) os; (c) te; (d) nos; (e) le

2 (a) gusta; (b) gusta; (c) gustan; (d) gustan; (e) gusta

3 You may have written something like this.
Me gusta estudiar lenguas.
A mis padres les gusta pasar el invierno en un clima soleado.
A mi hermana María no le gustaban los tomates cuando era joven.
A toda la familia nos gusta mucho buscar portales interesantes en Internet.
A mi mejor amigo le gusta la ornitología.

22.4 *Soler* and *acostumbrar*

1 You may have rewritten the passage like this.

Rodolfo Suárez era prisionero. Para él todos los días **solían ser/acostumbraban (a) ser** iguales. El despertador **solía sonar/acostumbraba (a) sonar** a las seis de la mañana. **Solía levantarse/acostumbraba (a) levantarse** en seguida y **solía ir/acostumbraba (a) ir** al comedor a desayunar. A las siete **solía empezar/ acostumbraba (a) empezar** a trabajar en el taller de hamacas. **Solía terminar/ acostumbraba (a) terminar** a la una y, después de almorzar, **solía pasar/ acostumbraba (a) pasar** una hora haciendo ejercicio en el corral de la cárcel. Luego **solía tener/acostumbraba (a) tener** dos horas de tiempo libre: **solía jugar/ acostumbraba (a) jugar** a las damas o al ajedrez. **Solía volver/acostumbraba (a) volver** a su celda a las siete y las luces **solían apagarse/acostumbraban (a) apagarse** a las nueve.

2 You may have written something like this:

Suelo levantarme a las 7.
Acostumbro ducharme antes de desayunar.
Suelo llegar al trabajo a las 9.
Acostumbro a volver a casa a eso de las 6.
Suelo acostarme a medianoche.

22.5   Pronominal verbs

1 (a) nos; (b) te; (c) se; (d) os; (e) me

2 (a) se está lavando las manos; (b) se están peinando; (c) se están comunicando a señas; (d) se están riendo; (e) se están gritando

3 se quita (quitarse) (2); se sienta (sentarse); se sumerge (sumergirse); te creías (creerse); bañándote (bañarse); te niegas (negarse) (3)

Unit 23 Special verb constructions

23.1   Impersonal sentences

1 Suggestions: (a) hablan/se habla; (b) han llamado/llamaron; (c) anunciarán/se anunciará/se va a anunciar; (d) intentas/uno intenta/una intenta

2 Suggestions:

(a) Para hacer este pastel se necesita harina. (b) En España se para de trabajar a la hora de comer. (c) Se avisará por teléfono a los ganadores del concurso. (d) En Argentina se habla mucho de fútbol.

23.2 The passive

1 (a) – (iii); (b) – (i); (c) – (iv); (d) – (ii)

2 (a) Frank Ghery diseñó el Museo Guggenheim-Bilbao. (b) Han descubierto/ La policía ha descubierto a los autores del fraude de Tabacos Serguiya. (c) Los grandes modistos europeos presentarán la nueva colección primavera-verano en Mónaco.

3 (a)   Mil puestos de trabajo han sido creados en Veracruz.
   (b)   El presunto ladrón fue arrestado y (fue) puesto a disposición judicial.
   (c)   Las cartas son clasificadas en la Oficina Central de Correos; a continuación son repartidas a sus destinatarios.

4 (a) se puede(n); (b) se puede añadir/se añade; (c) se siguen; (d) se debe nivelar/se deberá nivelar/se nivelará; (e) se espolvorean; (f) se entierran; (g) se riega

5 (a) ha sido probada; (b) Fue elaborada; (c) fue administrada; (d) fueron arrancados; (e) ha sido denegada

23.3   Uses of *se*

1 (a) reciprocal, reciprocal; (b) impersonal or passive; (c) *se* instead of *le;* (d) pronominal verb; (e) pronominal verb; (f) *se* instead of *le;* (g) impersonal or passive; (h) reflexive; (i) reciprocal, reciprocal

2 (a) Se dirá/Se va a decir que fue un accidente. (b) Se entraba al palacio por una magnífica puerta. (c) La polka se baila así. (d) En mi opinión, la mejor poesía española del siglo XX se escribió en el periodo anterior a la guerra civil. (e) Se sospechaba que era un espía.

Unit 24 Sentence organisation: the simple sentence

1 Exclamative: **(a)** (The marks are the exclamation marks '¡/!'.)
Negative: **(b)** (The mark is the negative adverb *nunca*.)
Interrogative: **(c)** (The marks are the question marks '¿/?'.)
Declarative-affirmative: **(d)** (Because it is not marked as interrogative, exclamative or negative.)

2 **(a)** ¿Te llamas Rosa Mari Bermúdez?/Te llamas Rosa Mari Bermúdez, ¿verdad?
(closed)
    (b) Several possibilities: ¿Cómo te llamas?, ¿Quién llamó?, etc. (open)
    (c) ¿Cuándo/En qué año nació Neruda? (open)

3 **(a)** Estás invitado a la boda, ¿no?/¿verdad?/¿cierto?
    (b) No has visto a Juani en todo el día, ¿verdad?/¿cierto?
    (c) El año pasado fuisteis de vacaciones a Miami, ¿cierto?/¿no?/¿verdad?

Unit 25 Negatives

1 **(a)** No, él no descubrió nada. Ya había gente allí (en el continente).
    (b) No, apenas se puede decir eso. Los vikingos llegaron antes.
    (c) No, ni siquiera lo reconoció como tal. Creía que había llegado al Extremo Oriente.
    (d) No, creo que no. Nunca se dio cuenta de su error.
    (e) No, ni siquiera eso. Murió en la miseria.

2 No había nadie en la fábrica. Ninguna de las máquinas funcionaba, no se oía nada, y tampoco había ninguna actividad fuera en el área de carga-descarga.

3 You may have written something like this:

Todavía no he logrado hacerme millonario, ni he escrito ninguna novela, ni he pintado ningún cuadro que sea digno de colgarse en la galería nacional. Ni siquiera he visitado Machu Picchu. ¡Y tampoco he conseguido dominar por completo el español! Sin embargo, aún me gustaría hacer estas cosas.

Unit 26 Sentence organisation: compound and complex sentences

26.1 The compound sentence

1 Suggestions (a number of links could have been used):

    (a) Hacía un día maravilloso, así que decidimos ir a la playa.
    (b) No/Ni queríamos ir al cine ni ir al parque.
    (c) ¿Vas a pasar las vacaciones con tus abuelos o vas a quedarte en Irlanda?
    (d) Ganamos poco pero hemos decidido ahorrar para comprarnos un piso más grande.

2 **(a)** sino; **(b)** pero; **(c)** sino

3 **(a)** sino; **(b)** sino que; **(c)** sino que; **(d)** sino

4 **(a)** así que/conque/de modo que/por consiguiente, etc. **(b)** No; **(c)** pero

26.3   The noun clause

1   Suggestions:

   (a)   Se comenta que dentro de unas semanas subirán los precios.
   (b)   Te deseo que tengas un feliz cumpleaños.
   (c)   No se sabe con seguridad si los terroristas firmarán/van a firmar la tregua.

2   Suggestions:

   (a)   No sabemos si va a cantar o no.
   (b)   Su mayor sueño es que su hija estudie arquitectura.
   (c)   Creo que quiere que su hija venga a vivir con él, pero no lo dice.

3   **(a)** de que; **(b)** que; **(c)** de que; **(d)** que

26.4   The adjectival or relative clause

1   **(a)**   El último barco con los niños que habían sobrevivido al terremoto llegó a Buenos Aires hace dos días.
   (b)   Tita es un personaje de la obra de Laura Esquivel *Como agua para chocolate* que representa la intransigencia y represión que sufría la mujer en épocas pasadas.

2   **(a)**   Esta es la ciudad en la que/en la cual/donde nació mi padre.

   (b)   En el colegio teníamos un profesor para quien todos los niños éramos futuros genios.

3   **(a)** las que; **(b)** el que; **(c)** los que

4   **(a)** el que/el cual; **(b)** que; **(c)** donde/el cual/el que; **(d)** cuyos; **(e)** que/los cuales/quienes; **(f)** donde/en el que

5   **(a)** non-restrictive; **(b)** non-restrictive; **(c)** restrictive; **(d)** restrictive

6   **(a)** haya; **(b)** vivo; **(c)** se parece; **(d)** dejara

7   **(a)**   I won't forgive him whatever his excuse.
   (b)   We will be here to greet them whenever they arrive.
   (c)   Pepe will remember his father's advice wherever he is.
   (d)   Whatever you call it, this conduct is not acceptable.

26.5   The adverbial clause

1   **(a)** – **(iv)** concessive; **(b)** – **(i)** conditional; **(c)** – **(ii)** purpose; **(d)** – **(v)** manner; **(e)** – **(iii)** cause

2   **(a)** *como* is the most natural choice because it can only appear at the beginning of a sentence, although *ya que* is possible; **(b)** *porque* is best, *ya que* does not fit the context and *como* is not possible in mid-position; **(c)** *ya que/porque*, although the comma makes *ya que* a better choice and *como* is again not possible.

3   **(a) más** impresionantes **de lo que** pensaba; **(b) tantos** votos **como** esperaban; **(c) menos** dinero **del que** habíamos presupuestado

4   **(a)** con tal de que; **(b)** puesto que/pues (sounds old-fashioned); **(c)** aunque/aun cuando/si bien; **(d)** para que/con objeto de que/con el propósito de que/con la intención de que/de manera que/de modo que/de forma que

5 **(a)** In **(i)** it is not known whether the terrorists are to sign the agreement or not; in **(ii)** it is a fact that they are not signing it. In both cases the peace process is going ahead.

(b) Sentence **(i)** takes place in the past and **(ii)** in the future. Time subordinates referring to the future take the verb in the subjunctive, while those referring to the past take the indicative, since the action has already happened and is a fact.

(c) Similar argument as above: sentence **(ii)** indicates how she will behave in the future (the way her mother tells her), while **(i)** refers to a past action, and therefore the indicative is needed.

(d) In **(ii)** the path they will take is not known and the advice is that whichever path they take, to take one that does not have ice. Sentence **(i)**, told in the past, tells about the path that was taken, one which did not have ice.

6 You may have written something like this:

(a) estoy muy cansada/no me encuentro muy bien; **(b)** me quede a esperar a los clientes alemanes/vaya a cenar con unos clientes que vienen de Alemania; **(c)** terminemos pronto/ellos estén cansados y se retiren pronto; **(d)** me han invitado/es la despedida de Juana; **(e)** crees/esperas

7 **(a)** Cuando; **(b)** Después de; **(c)** Pero; **(d)** porque; **(e)** ya que

26.6   Time relations

1 **(a)** pagar; **(b)** ver que alguien me seguía; **(c)** consultar con sus padres; **(d)** hacerse el noviazgo público

2 **(a)** In **(i)** the problem was discussed at the same time as they had their walk; in **(ii)** it was discussed after the walk. **(b)** In **(i)** the discussion of the details goes before the acceptance of the offer; in **(ii)** it goes after. **(c)** **(i)** specifies that the action of phoning mother happens after a delay, whereas in **(ii)** it happens immediately after arriving home. **(d)** In **(i)** worthwhile study happens after going out with the girl; in **(ii)** it stops then.

3 **(a)** al; **(b)** mientras; **(c)** en el momento

4 **(a)** oír/escuchar, etc.; **(b)** paseaba/andaba, etc.; **(c)** tenga/coja, etc.

5 **(a)** cada vez que; **(b)** en el momento en que (note that *cuando* gives the same broad meaning but does not specify the nuance of meaning requested here); **(c)** en cuanto (same comment as for **(b)**); **(d)** a medida que

6 **(a)** Después de; **(b)** Mientras; **(c)** cuando de repente; **(d)** Apenas; **(e)** cuando; **(f)** hasta que; **(g)** Siempre que; **(h)** Cuando; **(i)** antes de; **(j)** al

26.7   The conditional sentence

1 **(a)** ve; **(b)** consigue; **(c)** decía, quería; **(d)** empieza

2 **(a)** dirías, diría, tendría, terminaría; **(b)** pudieras, cambiaría, haría, volviese (*or* volviera), recorrería; **(c)** sentiría, supiera (*or* supiese)

3 You may have written something like this:

(a) Si mis padres hubieran sido millonarios . . . ; **(b)** . . . no habría tenido/tendría que aprender español; **(c)** . . . me habría llamado Inés; **(d)** Si me hubieran dicho hace unos años que mi amigo Martín iba a ser famoso . . .

Unit 27 Indirect speech

1 **(a)** Isidro ha comentado que está encantado de haber ganado el premio.
  (b) El preso no deja de repetir que es inocente.
  (c) El capitán del Real Madrid asegura que este domingo van a luchar hasta el final en el partido contra el Athletic de Bilbao.
  (d) Felipe me ha asegurado que mañana me devolverá el dinero que me debe.

2 **(a)** Isidro comentó que estaba encantado de haber ganado ese premio.
  (b) El preso no dejaba de repetir que era inocente.
  (c) El capitán del Real Madrid aseguró que al domingo siguiente lucharían hasta el final en el partido contra el Atlético de Bilbao.
  (d) Felipe me aseguró que me devolvería al día siguiente el dinero que me debía (if the money was paid after this comment)/el dinero que me debe (if the money has not been paid yet, at the moment this comment is made).

3 **(a)** Todos los días me pregunta dónde vivo.
  (b) Cuando me caí un señor muy amable me preguntó si me había hecho daño.
  (c) Malena quiere saber qué planes tengo para este verano.
  (d) En la entrevista me preguntaron si sabía conducir.

4 **(a)** Perico se despidió de María prometiendo que iría a buscarla al día siguiente, a las 9 de la mañana.
  (b) Serena gritó al niño que pidiera perdón a su abuela en ese mismo momento.
  (c) Josechu exclamó sorprendido que había ido a visitarlo dos días antes y que estaba perfectamente bien.
  (d) Para calmarnos, Beatriz dijo que no creía que el paquete llegara hasta la semana siguiente.

Bibliography

Alarcos Llorach, E. (1994) *Gramática de la lengua española,* Madrid: Espasa Calpe.

Alonso, A. and Henríquez Ureña, P. (1964) *Gramática castellana* (20th edn), Buenos Aires: Losada.

Asociación de academias de la lengua española (2010) *Nueva gramática de la lengua española*, Madrid: Espasa Calpe.

Batchelor, R. E. and Pountain, C. J. (1992) *Using Spanish: A Guide to Contemporary Usage,* Cambridge: Cambridge University Press.

Bello, A. and Cuervo Rufino, J. (1964) *Gramática de la lengua castellana* (7th edn), Buenos Aires: Sopena.

Benito Mozas, A. (1992) *Gramática práctica* (4th edn), Madrid: EDAF.

Butt, J. and Benjamin, C. (2004) *A New Reference Grammar of Modern Spanish* (4th edn), London: Hodder Education.

Carrasco Gutiérrez, A. (2000) *La concordancia de tiempos,* Madrid: Arco.

Diccionario Salamanca de la lengua española (1996), Madrid: Santillana / Universidad de Salamanca.

Fernández Cinto, J. (1991) *Actos de habla de la lengua española: Repertorio*, Madrid: Edelsa.

Garcés, M. P. (1997) *Las formas verbales en español: Valores y usos,* Madrid: Verbum.

Gili Gaya, S. (1976) *Curso superior de sintaxis española* (11th edn), Barcelona: Bibliograf.

Gómez Torrego, L. (1998) *La impersonalidad gramatical: Descripción y norma,* Madrid: Arco.

Gómez Torrego, L. (1998) *Valores gramaticales de "se"*, Madrid: Arco.

González Araña, C. and Herrero Aísa, C. (1997) *Manual de gramática española: Gramática de la palabra, de la oración y del texto,* Madrid: Castalia.

González Hermoso, A., Cuenot, J. R. and Sánchez Alfaro, M. (1996) *Gramática de español lengua extranjera*, Madrid: Edelsa.

Gutiérrez Araus, M. L. (1995) *Formas temporales del pasado en indicativo*, Madrid: Arco.

Gutiérrez Araus, M. L. (2001) *Caracterización de las funciones del pretérito perfecto en el español de América*, Congreso Internacional de la lengua española, Centro Virtual Cervantes. Available at: http://www.congresosdelalengua.es/valladolid/ponencias/unidad_diversidad_del_espanol/2_el_espanol_de_america/gutierrez_m.htm.

Hernández Alonso, C. (1996) *Gramática funcional del español* (3rd edn), Madrid: Gredos.

Hurtado González, S. M. (1998) 'El perfecto simple y el perfecto compuesto en el español actual: estado de la cuestión' in *Epos: Revista de Filología*, XIV, pp. 51–67.

Kattán-Ibarra, J. (1991) *Spanish Grammar: A Functional Guide,* London: Teach Yourself Books.

Kattán-Ibarra, J. (1997) *Modern Spanish Grammar Workbook*, London and New York: Routledge.

Kattán-Ibarra, J. and Pountain, C. J. (1997) *Modern Spanish Grammar: A Practical Guide*, London: Routledge.

Llorente Vigil, C. (1999) *Las perífrasis verbales*, Salamanca: Colegio de España.

Marcos Marín, F. (1980) *Curso de gramática española*, Madrid: Cincel-Kapelusz.

Marcos Marín, F. (1974) *Aproximación a la gramática española*, Madrid: Cincel.

Martín Zorraquino, M. A. (1988) 'Los marcadores del discurso desde el punto de vista gramatical' in Martín Zorraquino and Montolío Durán (Coords.), pp. 19–53.

Martín Zorraquino, M. A. and Montolío Durán, E. (Coords.) (1988) *Los marcadores del discurso: Teoría y análisis*, Madrid: Arco.

Martínez, R. (1997) *Conectando texto*, Barcelona: Octaedro.

Matte Bon, F. (1995) *Gramática comunicativa del español. Tomo I: De la lengua a la idea*, Madrid: Edelsa.

Matte Bon, F. (1995) *Gramática comunicativa del español. Tomo II: De la idea a la lengua*, Madrid: Edelsa.

Montolío Durán, E. (2001) *Conectores de la lengua escrita*, Barcelona: Ariel.

Portolés, J. (1998) *Marcadores del discurso*, Barcelona: Ariel.

Pountain, C. J. and de Carlos, T. (2006) *Practising Spanish Grammar: A Workbook* (2nd edn), London: Hodder Education.

Puebla Ortega, J. (1995) *Cómo conjugar todos los verbos del español*, Madrid: Playor.

Real Academia Española (1989) *Esbozo de una nueva gramática de la lengua española*, Madrid: Espasa-Calpe.

Richards, J. C., Platt, J. and Patt, H. (1992) *Diccionario de lingüística aplicada y enseñanza de lenguas*, traducido y adaptado al español por Carmen Muñoz Lahoz and Carmen Pérez Vidal, Barcelona: Ariel.

Ruiz Gurillo, L. (2001) *Las locuciones en español actual*, Madrid: Arco.

Sagües Subijana, M. (1983) *Manual de gramática española*, San Sebastián: Txertoa.

Sánchez, A., Martín, E. and Matilla, J. A. (1980) *Gramática práctica de español para extranjeros*, Madrid: SGEL.

Seco, R. (1982) *Manual de gramática española*, Madrid: Aguilar.

Seco, R. (1980) *Gramática esencial del español*, Madrid: Aguilar.

Spinelli, E. (1998) *English Grammar for Students of Spanish*, London: Arnold.

Zarzalejos, A. (1999) *¿Ser o estar?*, Madrid: Edinumen.

Grammatical index